GÖRAN ROSENBERG is one of Sweden's best-known writers and journalists.

More praise for *A Brief Stop on the Road from Auschwitz*:

'Not often can prosaic prose embed such piteous sorrow, and human tragedy so starkly revealed' Sari Nusseibeh, author of *Once Upon A Country: A Palestinian Life*.

'Gripping and poetic . . . From its lyrical opening pages to its shocking conclusion, *A Brief Stop on the Road from Auschwitz* is an unforgettable book about memory, grief, and fate' Adam Kirsch, poet and literary critic.

'Beautifully wrought . . . Written with tender precision, *A Brief Stop on the Road from Auschwitz* is the most powerful account I have read of the other death – the death after the camps' Roger Cohen, *New York Times*

'By drawing a bright line between facts and imagination, and by holding himself to the highest burden of proof, [Rosenberg] has given us an intimate family chronicle that is also a document of the Holocaust, a conversation with a ghost that can also serve as testimonial evidence in the court of history' *Los Angeles Review of Books*

'Devastating and emotive . . . not only a brilliantly researched and measured exploration of the past, but also a tender examination of a child's relationship with his father' *Irish Examiner*

'His story will stay with you long after you've closed the book' *Manchester Evening News*

'A moving account [which] masterfully blends the poetic and allegorical with journalistic rigour' *Jewish Renaissance*

'Books like *A Brief Stop on the Road from Auschwitz* are vital if we are to prevent a collective slide towards oblivion' *Jewish Quarterly*

'By dint of assiduous research and even more by virtue of penetrating human insight, Göran Rosenberg achieves a level of understanding that brings to the reader, perhaps also to the writer, a sense of catharsis' Bernard Wasserstein, *The Tablet, UK*

A BRIEF STOP

ON THE ROAD FROM AUSCHWITZ

by Göran Rosenberg

Translated from the Swedish by
SARAH DEATH

Edited by
JOHN CULLEN

GRANTA

Granta Publications, 12 Addison Avenue, London W11 4QR

First published in Great Britain by Granta Books, 2014
This paperback edition published by Granta Books, 2015
Published by arrangement with Other Press LLC, New York, NY 10016

Originally published in Swedish as *Ett kort uppehåll på vägen från Auschwitz* by Albert Bonniers Förlag, Stockholm, in 2012

Translation copyright © Sarah Death, 2014

1 3 5 7 9 10 8 6 4 2

ISBN 978 1 78378 130 0 (paperback)
ISBN 978 1 784708 779 9 (ebook)

Text design by Julie Fry

Offset by Avon DataSet Ltd, Bidford on Avon, Warwickshire

Printed and bound by CPI Group (UK) Ltd, Croydon, CR0 4YY

www.grantabooks.com

MIX
Paper from
responsible sources
FSC® C020471

THE PLACE

For a long time I imagined him coming over the Bridge, since the Bridge is the gateway to the Place, and the key to it as well, but of course he can't have come over the Bridge because he must have arrived from the south. You come over the Bridge only when you arrive with the train from the north. Only then does the vertiginous precipice over the Canal open up, and only then do you cross the perilous boundary between home and away. Perhaps the peril is not so much the Canal as the Bridge. The Canal's only water, after all, whereas the Bridge is a truly ominous passage, a cold skeleton of riveted steel girders, welded and screwed together in angular arcs that form a pair of bony shoulders rising from four massive stone columns on either side of the drawbridge across the waterway.

Anyone coming by train sees none of this, of course, and may not even be aware that the entire structure is vibrating and shaking beneath the engine and the coaches, or hear the screech of the rails and the echo of the steel girders answering the wheels' metallic hammering and scraping, or catch the burnt smell of sparking contacts and cables. Nor can anyone crossing the Bridge by train ever share the terror of crossing it on foot. To cross the Bridge on foot, you first have to make your way through a little copse between the Place and the Canal, then negotiate a narrow, winding set of steps up to a height of twenty-six meters, and after that step out onto a narrow catwalk for pedestrians that runs on one side of the double railroad track, all the way across the water. You can stare straight down into the abyss through the gaps in the catwalk's wooden planks, and you can all too easily swing yourself over its all too low metal railing. In the Place, horror stories are constantly circulating about people who did just that, and about how their broken and bloated bodies were fished out afterward, and about what God has to say on the subject. I always keep a tight hold on the inner railing, the one nearest the tracks, to counteract the black, vertiginous pull. Except when a train comes thundering along the track nearest the catwalk and the metallic wind tugs at your clothes and the shuddering wooden planks jolt your feet and you're left balancing between one hell and another. In my nightmares, I'm incessantly falling from the Bridge. In my nightmares, I also reach the other side. For on the other side of the Bridge, down an equally narrow and winding set of steps, beyond an equally dark copse, death is waiting, or at least the nameless local gangs against which the gangs on my side of the Bridge fight an endless and lawless war. Making it over the Bridge is no guarantee of survival. The nightmare of getting ambushed and beaten up in enemy territory isn't wholly divorced from reality. The Bridge marks the Place's natural boundary, and there's rarely any reason to cross it on your own.

If you come by train from the south, you traverse no such border, just a nondescript panorama of forests and fields that makes it harder to know where the Place begins. Also harder to understand why it is where it is, and why the station where the express trains make their brief stops on their way to and from the world was built just here and not in the town of the same name. All this is best explained by the Bridge, since the station is located here because of the Bridge, and the Place sprang up because of the station, and maybe that's why I like to imagine him coming over the Bridge before he gets off the train at seven in the evening on August 2, 1947, seeking to start his life over again in this particular place, below this particular station.

Is it chance that makes him get off precisely here? No, not more of a chance than anything else on his journey. And presum ably less, since the most chanceful aspect of his life is the fact that he's alive. Naturally it's only by chance that any of us are alive, but along his road death has been more of a strictly sched- uled and predictable stop than it is for most of us, making the fact that he's still alive a bit more unexpected. Besides, he knows very well why he's getting off precisely here and not somewhere else. He's got the name of the station carefully written down on the piece of paper he's shown the conductor, who has promised to alert him when they're getting close. And besides all that, A. and S. are waiting for him on the platform as agreed, and in fact a third person, too, whom he at first mistakes for a fellow student from the grammar school in Łódź. It's not him, of course, and it's highly improbable that it could be, but since he has passed so many improbabilities along his road, it's not that far-fetched to imagine another one or two. At any event, there they are, standing on the platform waiting for him, and they embrace him and help him down the steps with his suitcases and come along to show him the way to the room where he'll be lodging, and on that still, light, August evening they tell him everything they know about the Place, where they've all just arrived and which

5

none of them knows very much about, and they in turn want to know everything about people and events in the place where the man boarded the train, which is where they last met. They're all still on a journey, and every place is just a brief halt on the road to somewhere else, and those who are here for the time being do their best to keep themselves posted about those who are somewhere else, because this restless, mobile community is the only community they have. Little by little, each of them will try to make one of these many places his own, and one place after another will gradually separate them, usually for good, and this particular place will eventually do the same. Only one of the men will try to make this particular place his own, and that's the man who's just stepped down from the train.

I'm still unaware of all this, for I don't yet know the man who just got off the train and who is not yet my father and who doesn't yet know that this will be his final stop. I don't think he can even imagine a final stop, because I don't believe he can imagine any place as his own. Nevertheless, I visualize him continually and curiously looking around, inspecting it all to see if this could be such a place, because the need for at least a slightly more extended stop is starting to become pressing. And I think that's why he notes with interest and commits to memory the brand-new rows of attractive three-story apartment blocks along the newly built road, lined with rowan trees, that runs through the new housing area just below the train station. I think that's also why he immediately wants to know what kind of town this is and what sort of people live here and what the working conditions are like in the big factory where he hopes to get a job and what opportunities there might be for a woman not quite twenty-two years old with no vocational training and only the briefest exposure to the language they speak here, briefer

6

than his own. I think he's already inquired about such a job and just needs to look into it a bit more closely, and above all to see if he can exchange his rented room for an apartment before he asks her to take the train from the place he's just left to the place where he's barely arrived.

But what he thinks about his future on that August evening in 1947 is mere speculation on my part, and I'd rather not speculate, and most of all I don't want to run ahead of his life. He's lived for only twenty-four years, yet he's already lived through so much, and he has the right to carry on with his life without my prematurely burdening him with what's going to happen to the rest of it. I shall take his days as they come, and where I can't see how they come to him, I'll let them come to me.

So on this day, in the lingering brightness of early evening, he finds himself lugging two battered and rather heavy suitcases in the company of three not very close friends. After all, he means to take up residence here for an unspecified length of time, and even the possessions of a newly begun life soon start to weigh a good deal. Naturally he's wearing one of the suits, perhaps the elegant, pale-gray check, and a white shirt and matching tie, and a hat even though it's still summer. It's been the hottest summer for a hundred years and the evening is warm, and it would have been nicer to walk bareheaded, but there hadn't been any room in his luggage for the hat anyway, and taking the train to an unfamiliar place in a new country is something he wouldn't dream of doing in his shirtsleeves. The four men have set off from the station on foot, taking turns carrying the cases, and A., who has been here the longest, says they'll have to take the bus from the next stop because there's still quite a way to go and otherwise they won't have enough time to find a place to eat, and besides it's Saturday evening and there's a good movie showing in town and they might just catch it if they hurry. So they hurry for all they're worth, and the man who just got off the train scarcely has time to settle into his lodgings in the recently built detached house or to introduce himself to his landlady, whose husband has recently died, and so instead of turning the place into a home for herself she's obliged to rent out rooms to single men working at the factory, but she's nonetheless friendly and welcoming. Then they briskly move on to celebrate the fact that they're all, at least for now, in the same place and in one another's company. The movie, for which they arrive just in time, is being shown at the Castor cinema, located in the middle of the town, by the idyllic harbor where the little lift-net boats are moored for their Saturday rest and the townsfolk are taking their evening stroll along the quaysides. The film is set on a slave ship whose captain intends to get married and become respectable and wants to give up slave trading. He orders his first mate to change both the cargo and the crew, but when he goes on board with his young bride for what's meant to be their honeymoon, he discovers that both the cargo and the crew are still the same. It's a thrilling story with a script by William Faulkner, starring Mickey Rooney and Wallace Beery, and although it's set in the nineteenth century, I imagine they're able to identify with it a little, having all just experienced the way apparently ordinary ships, or in their case apparently ordinary trains, can prove to be something else entirely. And none of them is yet quite sure what kind of ship or train it is that they've just boarded, or rather, what kind of place it is where they've just disembarked. Perhaps they all go back to one of the rented rooms afterward, have a glass or two of lukewarm vodka, envelop the place in a haze of cigarette smoke, tell each other stories, and play cards, forgetting for a moment that they're in a place they don't know, a place that doesn't know them; they're still young, and it's Saturday evening and the night is as silver as the full moon and they want to make as much as they possibly can of this brief stop on the long journey that has accidentally and probably only for a short time brought them all together precisely here.

I know nothing further about the three men waiting on the platform beyond the fact that they, like most of the others on this journey, will soon be moving on. What I do know is that the following day, the man who will be my father writes a letter to the woman who will be my mother and who's been his wife for six months, informing her that the town, which is called Södertälje, seems bigger than the one he just left, which is called Alingsås. He notes that like all towns in this new country it seems sparsely populated, that it's a long walk from one part of the town to another, and that there are large areas of newly built houses and blocks of flats, laid out with generous amounts of light, air, and greenery extending around a small but not particularly dense town center. There also seem to be big trees everywhere, whole forests of them, in fact, growing almost up to the doorsteps, and more importantly there's a large pharmaceutical factory, where there are plenty of jobs for young women who can pack medicinal drugs deftly in cartons and bottles, and the defter they are, the more they can earn. "I didn't get home all that late last night, eleven at the latest," he assures her, "because I wanted to unpack my cases and inspect my room, but my roommate was already in bed asleep and so I had to wait." The following day is Sunday, when everyone's off and a breakfast of coffee, bread, and cheese is served in the lodging-house dining room—you aren't allowed even to heat water for tea in your rooms—and so that

9

morning his roommate, a "young and quiet snail," has had time to tell him that work at the big truck factory starts at seven and ends at four, with a half-hour lunch break at 12:30. You can come to work in your ordinary clothes and change there, because you can take a shower and wash up properly after your shift. They have modern toilets as well, but if you need to go during working hours you have to ask permission, and the doors don't shut properly, let alone lock, so nobody can loiter in there for a rest or a nap. But he doesn't really consider any of this important enough to write about. The letter is short, the tone rather dutiful, and the handwriting too rushed, because he wants to get the letter posted right away. The only thing that matters, he writes, is for me to find a place where we can live, or at least a room we can have to ourselves, where we can heat water and make a home, so that you can get on the train and come here.

He's worried about her too, you can tell; even a bit too much, you might think. Be careful on your bike and when you go swimming, he writes, as if she were a child. They've been continuously together for almost a year now, following nearly two years of being continuously separated, if you can say such a thing. Yes, "separated" may not be the right expression when the place where you're forced to separate is the selection ramp at Auschwitz-Birkenau. And "worried about each other" may not adequately express their state of mind, when everything a human being could possibly fear might happen to him or her has already happened to them both, as has everything that no one was able to imagine could happen and yet happened all the same, everything except for that one final thing that could still happen but absolutely must not, and for which the word "worry" no longer seems satisfactory. Not when a weight of worry big enough to poison a world has been concentrated into a single black drop

10

of corrosive anxiety that's forever poised above what is at present the weakest point in this still improbable, and therefore not yet quite real, connection between two young people who last parted on the selection ramp in Auschwitz-Birkenau. No, wrong. Who last parted on a railroad platform in Alingsås.

But it's no longer easy to distinguish one parting from another. No, she mustn't have a fatal accident on her bike or drown in a lake or trip on the stairs or suffer any eventuality, conceivable or inconceivable, that might sever the last, fragile thread connecting them to what could, after all, turn out to be a new life. "There's absolutely no need to worry about me at all," he adds cockily. "And tomorrow morning I'll apply for the truck factory job M. thinks I'm bound to get with all my first-rate 'qualifications,' and this very day I'll ask the poor landlady who lost her husband if a room will become available anytime soon, and as I say I'm terribly worried about you, and you're never out of my thoughts for a second, and maybe it really would have been best if you had traveled here with me, because then we wouldn't have had to worry so much and no doubt everything would have worked out all right, even so. Everything's sure to work out before long, and soon you'll be here with me."

As the sender's address he gives B 639 B, Södertälje. What kind of address is that? No street, no name, just a code. The address of yet another barrack in yet another camp? Can a letter of reply really be delivered to an address like that? How long can such an address be allowed to keep them apart?

Two days later, he starts work at the truck factory. His job is to weld fuel pipes on truck chassis. He has no problem getting hired. "Conscientious and hardworking," says the type-written notepaper from the personnel manager at the textile factory, Alingsås Bomullsväfveri, and that's presumably all the

11

personnel manager at Scania-Vabis needs to know, though he's also informed that the man in front of him has some experience in truck building. "Worked as a welder of truck axles at Firma Büssingwerke in Braunschweig/Vechelde from September 1944 to March 1945" is duly noted on the new-employee form under the heading "Qualifications and Experience." Not that this makes any difference, as previously noted. Europe is currently demanding more trucks than Scania-Vabis can produce, and Scania-Vabis is seeking more workers than it can currently lay hands on. Many of Europe's truck factories are still in ruins, incapable of making the trucks needed to rebuild them, not to mention everything else in Europe that needs trucks for rebuilding, a situation that presently gives Scania-Vabis in Södertälje a competitive advantage over, say, Büssingwerke in Braunschweig, which has not been able to turn any truck axles at all in the past two years.

Two weeks later, a new possibility becomes available at R 639 B in Södertälje, and the worry that can't be dispelled in any other way is dispelled when the woman who is to be my mother takes the train to join the man who is to be my father, to share with him a rented room that has no kitchen. In those early, steadily darker autumn mornings, they surreptitiously heat their water on an upturned iron before he goes off to the truck factory and she to the pharmaceutical factory, and after a while to the family-owned clothing factory where she sews coat linings at piecework rates to musical accompaniment. "The girls don't like marches, but apart from that we play everything from classical music to popular hits," the manager tells the local paper. She's young and deft, with a year's experience of sewing work at Sveriges Förenade Linnefabrikers AB in Alingsås. On a good eight-hour working day she can get up to seventy-five öre an hour, which along with the meager but slightly higher wage from the truck factory soon puts them on a sounder footing. By the first of October 1947 they're able to move into a sublet, one-room apartment with a kitchenette and a proper address: 22 Villagatan. One year later at that address, in a house I have no memory of, the young man becomes my father and the young woman my mother.

We move to the house I actually remember a year or two later. The documents say one thing and the aging memory another, but it doesn't matter; this is where it all begins, in the building below the railroad station where the young man who will be my father alighted from the train on an early August evening in 1947, and which you can see right beneath the window on the left-hand side of the coach if you arrive by train from the north, across the Bridge.

This is it; this is the Place. This is where my world assumes its first colors, lights, smells, sounds, voices, gestures, names, and words. I'm not sure how far back a human being can remember; some people say they have memories going back to their second year, but my first memories are of snow and cold and therefore probably date from somewhat later, since I was born in October. But one thing I'm certain of is that even before the point where my memories of that first world of mine begin, it had already set its stamp on so much that even things I can no longer remember aren't forgotten either. This is the Place that will continue to form me even when I'm convinced that I've formed myself.

That's the difference between them and me. They have encountered the world for the first time in an entirely different place, and carry with them an entirely different world, and for them so much has already started and already ended, and it's still unclear whether anything can start afresh here, since a great deal of what they can't remember, or don't want to remember, they cannot forget. For them, the colors and the shifting light and the smells and sounds and voices of this place will often remind them of something else, though they might not always know what it is. For them to be able somehow to make this place their own, they'll have to get to know it well enough, and let it stamp them deeply enough, so that sometimes it will be this place they're reminded of when they hear a freight train rattle past at night, or inhale the smell of fried herring in the stairwell, or walk under tall pines, or catch a whiff of tar and sea, or see rowanberries glowing in the fall, or look at their children.

What quickly binds them to the Place is the Child, who happens to be me. I don't want to exaggerate my own importance in this context, and I could be wrong, but on a purely practical level, a child makes it harder to move on. Moving on with only a hat on your head and a suitcase in your hand is one thing. Moving on with a newborn child is another proposition entirely. For the sake of the Child, a brief stop must be extended indefinitely, and big plans associated with their journey onward must be reduced to little plans associated with the place where they happen to be, a happpenstance that the Place confirms with a miracle.

"Housing Shortage" is one of the first expressions the language of the Place forces upon them. Housing Shortage and Housing Emergency. The local newspaper, *Stockholms Läns & Södertälje Tidning*, popularly known as the *Länstidningen* (the

County News), publishes reports about a family living in a tent on the beach. About five hundred applicants for sixty flats. About the truck factory's barracks for its single male workers. "Catastrophic Housing Shortage in Vivid Focus," shouts the front page on July 19, 1948.

Not that they need to read the local paper to know. Anyone in the Place can tell you that an apartment of your own is a miracle.

And yet it happens. An almost new apartment with a small, all-purpose living room and a little kitchen, a bathroom with a WC and hot running water, a wood-fired laundry in the basement of the neighboring house and a rubbish chute in the stairwell, a letterbox and a nameplate on the front door. In the small living room, a sofa that turns into a bed, a height-adjustable round table made of varnished wood, walnut-brown with an extension leaf, and four matching chairs with upholstered fabric seats. A child's bed in a sleeping alcove. In one corner, on a little table covered with a white, lace-edged cloth, a Philips radio set. Somewhere there's also a linen cupboard, with drawers for sheets, towels, and children's clothes. In the kitchen, a couch in pale wood, a refrigerator and a sink unit, a wall cupboard with sliding Masonite doors painted pale gray, a crockery set with a blue pattern, six of everything. On the wall above the radio, an oil painting of a vase with red and yellow flowers. In the basement, two secondhand bikes, one with a child's seat, hung on hooks from the ceiling. I'm also looking for a stroller, but I'm not sure where to place it. All I know is that there must have been a place for it somewhere, just as there will eventually have to be a place for a wooden toy train and a shelf of children's books borrowed from the town library and a box with a basic Meccano set sorted in compartments and a few of those expensive, cast-metal

15

model cars, a Volvo PV444 definitely among them. In an apartment with just one room, it's easy to see what a lot of space a single child takes up.

In this flat, the Child takes up more space than the naked eye can see. Around the Child, an expanding web of ambitions and plans. The little cardboard box of alphabet blocks, made and decorated by hand, is not just a Toy but also a Project, and the perpetually changing letter combinations that the Child and the young man who is now his father lay out on the living room floor on those long Sunday afternoons form not only the words of a new language but also the building blocks of a new world. *The Child shall make the Place his own so that a new world will become possible for them as well* is the Project that rapidly fills the small apartment with its invisible inventories of dreams and expectations. After all, what the two new arrivals need is not a roof over their heads but firm ground beneath their feet, and if the child can take root somewhere, perhaps they too, in time, will find a foothold.

The Child, then, is me. And the Place I will make theirs by making it mine has its geographic center in a yellow three-story apartment block with two entrances and eighteen rental units just below Platform 1 of the railroad station, where the big passenger trains make a brief stop on their way south, even the expresses, even the night trains, even the trains to Copenhagen and Hamburg. From the kitchen and living room windows in the small first-floor apartment in the block nearest the forest, you can see people moving about in the railroad cars. And people being moved along by the railroad cars. And with every train, behind the reflections in the railroad car windows, a new world, mutely oblivious of its brief stop in the world that is to be mine.

Foreign kings are also said to have made a brief stop here, to be greeted by flag-waving people on the platform or to have their royal railroad cars routed into a siding for a royal breakfast and then coupled to the Swedish royal train in order to arrive in full state at Stockholm Central and the Royal Palace, but I have no memory of such a world outside our kitchen window. Presumably it was before the war, before our block was built, and before I existed, when the only things to be seen if one happened to look out of the railroad car window in our direction were sandy heath and sparse pine forest.

What's certain is that a few months after the end of the war, General Patton, who first won fame as an armored division commander, made a brief stop on Platform 1 before boarding the 21:53 train to Malmö. Earlier that day he'd visited the Södermanland tank regiment at Strängnäs and studied the twenty-two-ton Swedish tank model 42 and the Swedish armored troop carrier SKP, built by Scania-Vabis, and he'd declared the Swedish carrier to be superior to the corresponding American model. Though perhaps he was just being polite. And perhaps not at the

17

moment seeing entirely eye to eye with the American military leadership, which had just relieved him of his command of the Third Army. It was the evening of December 3, 1945, and a large crowd had gathered at the station to pay tribute to "the popular general." As Patton's train pulled away from the platform on the southbound track, loud cheers were heard. That too was before I existed, but by then our apartment block was already in its ringside seat, newly built and filled with tenants, and perhaps some of those who had just moved in had been tempted on that late December evening into opening one of their windows facing the platform to see if they could catch a glimpse of the man who only a year before had crushed German resistance in northern France with a sensational combination of genius and brutality. George S. Patton was his full name. I remember him only as George C. Scott in *Patton* and might therefore have been inclined to cheer less lustily, but those who with no reservations whatsoever shouted hurrahs for the real Patton on the platform outside our future kitchen window and saw him in the flesh as he climbed aboard the train to Malmö, and who maybe still felt the anxiety of wartime in their bodies, would surely never forget what they had seen, since they turned out to be among the last people to see General George S. Patton alive. Just a few days later, he was fatally injured in a car crash outside Mannheim in defeated, occupied Germany.

My first proper memory of the station outside the kitchen window is of trains that never stop as they clatter endlessly through the nights—caravans of freight cars, open or covered, screeching and whining like an overburdened chain gang on a punishment march. I remember them because they're the first things to wake me as the windowpanes rattle and the rail joints hammer against the wheels and the crackling flashes from the double locomotives cut through the curtains and a putrid smell of chemicals and decay rolls down from the platforms and into our beds and our dreams.

On the narrow strip of ground between the apartment blocks and the steep slope up to the fence and the platforms, the architects of the Place have left some of the original pines standing and encouraged grass and white clover to spread beneath them. It's my first playground. I hunt for four-leafed clover in the grass, play hide-and-seek among the trees, and float bits of bark in the puddles on the footpath below the embankment. A four-leafed clover is an early sign of luck, a double four-leafed clover an early mystery. Gradually the games grow bolder and more absorbing and go on later and later into the afternoon and can't be immediately interrupted just because somebody opens the kitchen window and shouts that it's time to come home: *Chodź do domu*, calls the voice from my kitchen window. The person calling is the young woman who's now my mother, and she's calling in the first language I learn and the first language I forget. In winter the largest stretch of grass between the pines is hosed with water, and the bigger boys come down with their ice hockey sticks and the games grow rougher and it gets dark earlier and the voice at the window takes on a more anxious tone. And soon, another language.

They want to leave nothing to chance. Nothing is to come between the Child and the Place. No foreign words. No foreign names. Nothing that might make the Child lose the foothold for all of them. So when they hear that the Child's first words are in a foreign language, they force themselves to speak to him in a language still alien to them, and they're quick to put books in the new language into his hands and to spell out the words of the new language for him in alphabet blocks on the living room floor.

On the advice of new friends, they've already fixed on a name for the Child. It's the most common boy's name in the new language. The name is important, their friends have told them. A foreign name stands out and becomes a handicap. The name they initially chose, Gershon, after the Child's paternal grandfather, is therefore superseded by Göran, a name that seems devised to distinguish between foreigners and natives. The complicated intonation of the long ö is what does it. They could also call him Jakob, after his maternal grandfather, which would be easier to pronounce and wouldn't really stand out because it's a name that belongs here too, but I imagine they want to play it safe in the name game. They give him the name Jakob as well, but a middle name isn't something you shout out of a kitchen window.

In the matter of the Language, they've calculated correctly. Perhaps in the matter of the Name too, but that's harder to know for sure. It's safe to say that the Language is what first binds the Child to the Place, since it's here that the Child sees everything for the first time, absolutely *everything*, without the weary discernment that comes with knowledge of what everything in the world is supposed to be called and experience of how everything in the world is supposed to look.

The first bird is a house sparrow in the barberry hedge outside the dairy shop. The first squirrel climbs up the first bark of the first pine outside the kitchen window. The edge of the first forest extends along the first route to school. The first woodland path is carpeted with the first warm pine needles and bordered by the first bilberries. The first pungent reek of *surströmming*, fermented herring, comes from the Hedmans' apartment on the ground floor. The first street is called Hertig Carls väg and is bordered by the first pavement (play only on the pavement!), the first cycle path (watch out for the cyclists!), and the first rowanberries. It's also paved with stones that resound with the rubbery bumping and thudding of the first automobile tires. The first automobile belongs to Anders's dad in the next-door apartment and sometimes needs a starting crank to get it going and has a windshield I can't reach when we're allowed to play in the driver's seat and turn the steering wheel. The first garbagemen in my first garbage truck hook the first garbage dumpsters onto a lift mechanism at the back of the truck and press a button to raise the dumpster into the air, fit it to a circular opening, and tip it forward so that the trash catapults down into the belly of the truck, the last bits shaken out with a few sharp tugs of a lever before the dumpster is lowered, unhooked, and carried on strong backs into the secret room behind the locked door in the concrete chill of the basement in the newly built apartment blocks where we live. My first garbage truck is a Norba, and three of them have been purchased at great expense by the Södertälje public sanitation department; they are described as a step forward in providing cleaner and more convenient refuse collection, having "a hood for spill-free emptying, a hydraulic dumpster-emptying device, and a scraper to distribute material in the refuse unit, plus a tipping mechanism." My first garbage chute is presumably a backward step, since the shaft that carries the garbage down to the refuse storage room hasn't been built correctly and there's a kink at the bottom that sometimes makes the garbage get stuck, so the chute blocks up. This is in spite of the fact that the local housing committee directive for garbage chute construction, dated November 5, 1940, clearly states that "the shaft must run straight and vertically for its entire length, and the whole of its lower end must be entirely aligned with a

21

refuse container, such that a vertical line drawn along the inside wall of the shaft will run 5 cm inside the edge of the container." The regulations also say that "the refuse storage room shall be provided with sufficient electric lighting so that the entire room is well lit." My first refuse storage room is not well lit. It's dark and cold and gives off the sweet-sour odor of kitchen waste and a raw breath of damp concrete.

Early one morning I get a ride from my first garbageman in my first garbage truck while the two new arrivals who have become my father and mother are still asleep on the sofa bed in the living room with the blinds drawn and the street outside lies silent, apart from the chatter of the sparrows in the barberry hedge and the screech of brakes from the first morning train on its way south. My first mornings are always early and always bright, and on one of those mornings I slip out of the front door and down the stairs to the entrance hall and out onto the sunlit pavement, because I don't have the patience to go on lying there on the pull-out settle in the kitchen and don't want to wake the two sleepers until the alarm clock rings and the street is filled with the cries and sounds of the growing caravan of bicycles making their way down the rowanberry avenue with rattling chains and creaking saddles and a daily load of filled lunchboxes and drowsy riders.

So I take early possession of the Place without their really noticing; sometimes, in fact, while they're still asleep. I've been told not to go off with strangers or accept anything from strangers, but the garbagemen aren't strangers. They're part of the Place, in the same way as the dockers and sailors at the port where I go fishing for my first roach, and the bakers and assistants all dressed in white at the bakery on the other side of the road where I buy my first crusty bread roll and my first milk is ladled out with a long-handled liter measure from a hole in the counter. The speciality there is a bread loaf known as the SS loaf, named after the shop, which is called the SS Bakery, named after the Place itself, Södertälje Södra; but that's a loaf we never buy. Just to the right as you enter the dairy, my first bottles of fizzy pop are ranged in dark green crates stacked on end against the wall. The very first is called Pomril and tastes of apples.

Seated in the driver's cab, I'm allowed to ride in the garbage truck from one end of the rowanberry avenue to the other, from the end where we live, in the last building before you reach the edge of the forest and the road to the Beach, all the way to the other end, where the row of buildings comes to an end and the street makes a sharp left turn and disappears under a railroad viaduct. The forest and the road to the Beach are part of my territory, but not the road beyond the viaduct. Beyond the viaduct is the big factory that swallows the caravans of bikes and spits out trucks, sheltering behind its front gates a world I can neither reach nor name. Dad's a pipe fitter, but what a pipe fitter is I have no idea. He could just as well be a founder, borer, tracer, clerk, plater, punch-card operator, balancer, manager, smith, foreman, filer, capstan lathe operator, or designer. The words of the world beyond the factory gates can't be seen or touched or smelled, so it's impossible for them to lend their names to anything in my world. Thus an early distinction is drawn between the world I can make into my own and the world Dad must try to make into his, because at seven every morning he and his bike disappear through something called the Chassis Gate and I don't see him again until Mom calls out of the kitchen window to say that dinner's ready.

The boundaries of my world are sharp and forbidding, and the two garbagemen who have given me a seat with a view in

23

their cab know very well where those limits are: the busy main-line railroad tracks, the railroad viaduct that spans the street, the railroad bridge over the canal, the canal itself, the steep-sided quays of the port area, the sharp fences around the factories and coal depots along the bay at Hallfjärden.

Steel and water. Fences and cul-de-sacs. Barriers and precipices.

The only road that doesn't end at something hard and impenetrable is the road that continues where the paved street ends and the forest begins, the road that in spring is edged with cowslips and lilies of the valley and in summer is crowded with bikes and eventually with cars, and which on my long Sunday walks with Dad seems never-ending. This is the road to the Beach, Havsbadet, and it ends in a sandy shoreline. Havsbadet is the most open and inviting of the boundaries in my world, but a boundary it is nonetheless; the road comes only this far, and this is how large my world is allowed to be.

The area of predominantly new housing where the garbage truck stops at every block, empties every refuse storage room, and carefully shakes the last scraps out of every dumpster is no larger than can be explored by a young child on foot and is in fact a strictly encircled enclave comprising, roughly speaking, a railroad station with auxiliary red-brick accommodations for its employees; sixteen new, three-story housing blocks in yellow or gray plaster lining both sides of a stone-paved avenue; some smaller side streets with two-story detached houses; an open square; two playgrounds; a day nursery and a post office; two grocery shops, Kling's with cooling water running in the window, and the Co-op with the first frozen-food counter; a tobacconist's; a haberdasher's; a bakery and a cafe. In front of the train station, there's a newspaper kiosk and a telephone booth with a removable floor of wooden laths through which escaped ten-öre coins lie glinting. It's a perfectly enclosed, idyllic world, which you can enter or exit only by passing under dark railroad viaducts, balancing across vertiginous railroad bridges, climbing over prohibited embankments, jumping on treacherous ice floes, or making holes in skull-marked factory fences.

On the other hand, it's a place that can easily be explored and taken possession of. Not only because it's so small and so circumscribed, but also because it's so new. In fact, it's practically without a history. Not long ago, there were no people here at all, just pine forest and sandy heath. Not long ago, there was no railroad passing through here and there were no plans for one to do so. Not long ago, the intention was to put something else here, something grander and more visionary. Not long ago, the idea was for these unchartered backwoods to be the site of an ideal society, meticulously planned in every detail. "The forested area of Näset to the south of the city" was to become a workers' paradise of self-owned homes, adjoining one-family houses, each with its own patch of garden, an esplanade punctuated with parks and hills, a square with a covered market, public baths, a church on a slight rise, a public park and sports area down by the factories, and a bathing beach, Havsbadet, by the sea.

Only much later did I learn that the place where I applied my first words to the world is a wrecked planners' dream.

The name of the architect behind the dream was Per Olof Hallman, and the dream was inspired by a social movement that sought to replace the rectilinear, antinature urban ideal of the industrial age with something more organic, more in tune with the natural world. The town plan was to be adapted to the landscape, and not the other way around. Streets were to be built around or over rises and hills, not blasted through them. Existing natural conditions were to be exploited, not obliterated. "A town planner unfamiliar with the terrain can all but ruin a place with a few strokes of the pen," Hallman wrote in 1901. Two years later, he put forward his plan "for the disused land to the south of, and belonging to, the town of Södertelge."

Hallman's ambitions, and indeed those of the whole movement, were far-reaching. The people involved wanted to plan away the disadvantages of industrialization, the dirt, the overcrowding, the ravaging of the countryside, the social injustices, and to plan forth its hidden potential: a freer and more equal society, closer to nature. One of the movement's leading proponents was Camillo Sitte, an Austrian who wanted to re-create the human community of the medieval town, with its winding alleys and irregular squares. Another was the Englishman Ebenezer Howard, who wanted to forge a new connection between country and town, between agriculture and industry, gardens and backyards. Bulging metropolises would be decentralized and green, and airy garden cities would be built in surrounding rural areas. A bit of forward-thinking town planning would enable the tenement blocks of industrialization to be peacefully torn down and a new and better society to be peacefully built. Ebenezer Howard was the author of *Tomorrow: A Peaceful Path to Real Reform*, a book which Per Olof Hallman had undoubtedly read before he brought his draftsman's pen to bear on the southern lands and forests. Here there were no tenements to be torn down, no streets to be reconfigured, no memories to be dug up, no traditions to be broken.

Nor were there yet any plans for the railroad embankment that would cut the place in two, nor for the deep furrow of the canal that would cut it off to the north, nor—obviously—for the railroad bridge or the viaduct or the factory fences or the oil terminals that would very soon turn Per Olof Hallman's dream into wastepaper.

Much later I'd understand that this in a way was a speciality of the Place: nothing there ever turned out as planned. Not the development of the disused land to the south. Not the route of the railroad. Not the course of the canal. Not Havsbadet. Not the population. Not the town.

It was as if chance had developed a special affection for this particular place. And as if that same chance, like a magnet, had attracted the most fortuitous of human destinies, making the fact that he got off the train at this very Place to start his life anew perhaps the least arbitrary element in the story. A place perfectly chosen for doing exactly that, in fact, or so it sometimes, much later, seemed to me: no strong ties to the past, no fixed plans for the future, no readymade scenario to step into— or be ejected from.

Oh, that "much later"! How insidiously it creeps in, that all-narrowing perspective of hindsight wisdom and rationalization. How easy it is, with only a few strokes of the pen, to inscribe people into a narrative which to them must still be unwritten, burdening them with a knowledge they can't possibly have yet, closing horizons which to them must still remain open.

■

So let me be honest about the hindsight, since it's pervasive, inescapable, and treacherous. When I diverge from the story of myself as General Patton in a tank disguised as a garbage truck,

27

busily inspecting my newly won territory, and slip into a digression on Per Olof Hallman and his abandoned plan for the southern fringes, I'm five years old and will in a few months' time be caught hopping on ice floes in the canal. I will be seduced into doing this by Tommy Hedman, who's two years older and lives in the right-hand apartment on the ground floor and comes from Falun and has parents who eat fermented herring once a year, though my parents think it's a bag of rotting garbage caught in the unfortunate kink near the bottom of the garbage chute. I'm not allowed to visit the Hedmans, and I'm not allowed to play with Tommy.

Actually, to be perfectly honest, what I can remember of these events is fragmentary at best. The early mornings with the garbagemen are fragments of the sleeping apartment, the sun-warmed pavement, the pungent yet sweet smell of the garbage, the clatter of the dumpsters, the dirty, oily overalls, and the vinyl seat sticking to my bare legs. I'm not even sure if the fragments are real, still less whether I've put them together correctly. I'm not sure I remember the fragments either, if remembering means actively recalling something. How can you recall something you haven't yet named and therefore don't yet have a word for?

Reflections then, rather than fragments: diffuse reflections of physical perceptions, of sensory experiences without words or order. Jumping on the ice floes: the rasp of frozen trousers on skin blue with cold, the glare of chalk-white faces in a black door opening, the pressure of hard hands, the sound of sharp voices, the feel of a thrashing. In my world, thrashing is a word linked to the sensation of ice floes.

Other words come only much later, words like dread and desperation, and, later still, words for the nightmares wallpapering the small apartment facing the railroad tracks, and even finally the words for what the man who is my father and the woman who is my mother might think and feel when their united night-mares suddenly stand before them in the winter darkness of the hall, dripping deep-black water on their threshold, the thin ice crunching beneath their feet, the lethal cold burning against their skin.

Only much later can sensations turn into stories. Only much later can mute expanses of wordlessness be strewn with scattered fragments of language. Only much later do I slither behind Tommy down the steep slope to the canal bank by the railroad bridge and slide out onto the creaking ice and see dark cracks of water open beneath our feet and feel my feet slipping and the water getting into my boots and the cold and stiff trousers chafing against my body on the heavy way home and the sensations of dread and thrashing.

Only much later can I become the child who tells a tale. Only much later can I dig in the mute expanses for fragments, sieve them out of the layered deposits of time, and put them together into a story. It's not the child who's remembering. It's me, trying much later to recall the child's sensations.

"Memory is not an instrument for exploring the past but its theater," writes Walter Benjamin in an essay about the Berlin of his childhood.

It is the medium of past experience, as the ground is the medium in which dead cities lie buried. He who seeks to approach his own buried past must conduct himself like a man digging. He must not be afraid to return again and again to the same matter; to scatter it as one scatters earth, to turn it over as one turns over soil. For the "matter itself" is only a deposit, a stratum, which yields only to the most meticulous investigation what constitutes the real treasure hidden within the earth: the images, severed from all earlier associations, that stand—like precious fragments or torsos in a collector's gallery—in the prosaic rooms of our later understanding.

The image: a shiny yellow disk of metal, sharp and uneven around the edges, a bit like thinly rolled-out gingerbread dough, and the size of a five-öre coin. It's burning hot in my hand.

The later understanding: we're romping noisily along the sleepers of the railroad track that runs along the path to my first school and leads to the factory where they make milk separators. It also leads to the factory where they prefabricate building blocks of aerated concrete and to the black mountains of coal and coke beneath the tall cranes on the docks and to the gigantic grain silo whose purpose we don't yet understand. But the separator factory is what we're running toward, because our school is just beside it, and because the separator factory's renowned canteen ("Every housewife's dream: appliances, appliances, and more appliances of every conceivable kind") is where we walk to in a column every day and consume the free school meal to which we have just become entitled but about which we've already taken the liberty of developing cautious opinions.

But no, it must have been on our way home from school. On our way to school in the mornings, when we were always late and racing against the clock, the idea wouldn't have occurred to anybody. So it's in the afternoon, and we're running along the sleepers leading away from the factory, and it must be from behind, from the factory, that the train is coming. Well, no, not a train really, just a shunting locomotive, and it's making quite a racket because it's a diesel. No danger, we can all see and hear it coming, and it's coming only very slowly. But some danger still, because now somebody's got the idea that we're in a competition to see who's last off the track. It's not Tommy this time, he's too old to be in my class. So who is it? The picture won't come into focus.

The engine's getting closer, nobody budges, I get an idea.

Am I the one who puts the two-öre coin on the rail? Is it really my idea?

We hide in the waste-filled and weed-covered ditch and watch the engine grow against the sky. The ground trembles. The rails screech. The coin vibrates.

I imagine myself in the place of the two-öre piece.

A shiny disk of yellow metal larger than a five-öre piece is lying thinly flattened against the rail. It's burning hot in my hand.

The image: Anders and I on the pavement outside our house. I test out a word I've heard someone say, maybe Tommy. "If you say that word again, you can't come to God's party in Heaven," says Anders.

I ask who God is. And where Heaven is. And who's allowed to come to God's party.

The later understanding: that's how God and Heaven are added to my world. I've passed my fourth birthday and learned to read the words that Dad puts together on the floor with the letter blocks, but God and Heaven are not among them. Nor is Hell. These are words that Anders has learned before me, and he's the one who teaches me them for the first time, and it's on the pavement at the front entrance to our house on the rowan avenue that God and Heaven and Hell forever assume a sense of someone else's party.

These are the sensations I dig for much later, when I want to tell the story of how my world came into being: the sensation of the images and the sounds and the smells of those moments when I put names to the world for the first time. And at best, the sensation of a small dark-haired boy who for some reason bears my name and somehow is me and who on a small plot of earth between the railroad bridge and Havsbadet, the port and the embankment, is busy making the world into his own.

There are times when I feel a bit ashamed for him. Not because his mother dresses him in home-knitted jerseys and plus-fours, and on special occasions, if I'm not mistaken, in a mottled brown woolen cap, all of which are quite possibly a source of shame for the little boy since no one else in his world wears such things, but not for me. Not for the person who much later is me. What that person much later is a bit ashamed of is his behavior. Of the fact that he so often rings the doorbell at Rickard and Bosse's in the house next door and silently buries himself in their piles of comic books even when Rickard and Bosse aren't home. I'll wait for them, the boy tells their mother, and he vanishes into the adventures of Captain Miki in the twenty-five-öre *Wild West* comic that comes out weekly in a kind of checkbook format and always ends with the baddies in hot pursuit of Captain Miki, forcing the boy to read on through comic after comic, pile after pile.

It shames me to think of him reading so many comics when I know how hard his dad is trying to stop him from reading comics at all and to steer him toward the books carefully selected and brought home for him from the town library every two weeks in a brown leather briefcase.

He reads the books too, of course, sometimes with a flashlight under the covers when the reading light has been switched off for the night. Or if it's summer and still light outside, with the book held up to the slightly wider chink of light at the edge of the blind. After a late night with Sherlock Holmes and the

Mystery of the Speckled Band, he dares not sleep with his back to the wall, for fear that a deadly poisonous snake will come crawling down it. After a late night with Poe and the Case of M. Valdemar, he dares not sleep at all, for fear of dissolving into a rotting mass.

So the boy is to be preserved from comics. As from so much else that the two new arrivals fear could bring down the world the boy is busy making into his own, and which for them is the only world they can pin their hopes on.

Actually, they're not the only people having fears. Per Olof's mom in number 43 gives the little boy who somehow is me a book entitled *Young People Astray* or *Big City Dangers* or *Godless Inferno* or something in that vein, which she thinks the boy ought to take home to his mom and dad. I must be about seven or eight and there's a little sister now and we've moved across the road from our one-room apartment at number 42 to a two-room apartment at number 45, and like a one-man plague of locusts, I consume any reading matter that crosses my path, be it the shop signs along the main city street or the cereal box on the kitchen table. The book has a pulp-fiction-style cover, a black hand grabbing the naked arm of a woman against a background of flickering flames or something to that effect, and it's easy to mistake it for that kind of a book. But that isn't why Dad takes it away from me and insists that I return it right away with thanks for the loan, which is something I can't do because the book is a gift and not a loan. No, it has something to do with Per Olof's parents, and with something Dad calls propaganda. The book with the seductive cover is propaganda for Per Olof's parents' religion, which is not the same as my parents' religion. Per Olof's parents are Pentecostalists or Baptists or something like that. Part of their religion seems to be that children drink coffee with their parents. Per Olof always drinks coffee with his parents. My parents' religion seems to stipulate that children under no circumstances shall drink coffee. At any rate, I'm never allowed to taste even a drop when they have it. I'm given my first coffee by Auntie Ilonka in her tobacco shop at Strängnäsvägen when I'm ten. I'm also entrusted by her with taking payments and counting change and putting money in the till, but not in the till for lottery tickets, which we must be very careful about. The coffee has been simmering all day and tastes bitter, and I feel no urge whatsoever to join the Pentecostalists.

But it's true that Per Olof's parents are anxious, too. They're anxious about what will become of the world when young people are going astray and families are breaking up and the film matinees and the comics and the swearwords and the rock music and the immorality and the general godlessness are spreading. And about what will become of Per Olof's dark-haired classmate in the house next door if there's no one to show him the way and the truth.

On the other hand, it could be that the little boy doesn't have the book with the inviting cover foisted on him at all, but in fact asks politely if he can borrow it, and that Per Olof's mother kindly gives it to him as a present and says that maybe his mom and dad might enjoy it too, and that the whole episode is not a sign that Per Olof's parents are anxious but that they're kind.

Much later, I have only the fragment to work on. Dad takes a book away from me with surprising severity, not a comic (God forbid), and it has something to do with the smell of coffee in Per Olof's mom's kitchen. And with a sense of anxiety.

Much later, I fill out the mute areas with sensation and memory, and add some belated finds from the local paper.

At the Roxy cinema, Easter Day 1952 is celebrated with a film about the sexual morass of the big city, with an introductory talk by Pastor K.-E. Kejne.

At a housewives' meeting, the editor Sture Olsson issues a warning about the serious problems arising from children going to the cinema: "The maladjusted young idolize shady characters, and bad detective films spark criminal acts. The hooliganism of the children, who are generally the sole occupants of the auditorium at cinema matinees, can have a disastrous impact on the youngsters' development."

"No more Laurel and Hardy," declares a Mother Against Matinees.

The boy loves going to matinees. He devours the films as indiscriminately as he does books. It's true that there's always a rumpus at the matinees. Maybe even hooliganism. When the film starts, everybody folds their tickets down the middle and blows into them. It takes a particular technique to generate the right sound. You hold the folded ticket between your thumbs, cup your hands behind, and blow carefully so that the two sides of the ticket start to vibrate. If you're lucky, it makes a terrible racket. The boy's very good at making a noise with his ticket. He learns a lot at the matinees, like siding with the Red Indians against the Palefaces. He learns this from the western *White Feather*, which he sees three times. When the children play cowboys and Indians, which they often do in the forest that takes over where the rowanberry avenue ends, the boy with the dark hair is always an Indian.

So yes, there may well be good reason to be anxious.

Don't I see that little darkhead among the minithugs making a terrible screech with rosined wires against the S. family's windowsill on the ground floor of number 38? What on earth is he doing there, he who'll soon be toting around a violin case to jeers of "catgut scraper"?

And isn't that him with that gang of older boys, shouting "Old hag" at Miss Bergerman one early spring morning as she cycles past them on the way to the school by the factories in Baltic? I can't see who's making him do it, and I don't understand it, because I know that he loves Miss Bergerman and would give his life for her, and that he'll forever remember the way her flowery dress flutters in the factory-tainted breeze from the port, and the way her red hair caresses her fair, freckled face as she turns her head in surprise to look at them, and the way she will forever stand there in front of him in the creaking classroom in the yellow wooden schoolhouse, explaining with an otherworldly smile that the word hurled at her, in Swedish *kärring*, is derived from the word *kär*, meaning "beloved."

And the way the shame burns in his stomach.

The thing that much later fills me with shame, or perhaps not shame, that's too strong, the boy is only a child, but what makes me feel very uncomfortable all the same, is how hard he's trying to please, to fit in, to do as the others do even though he isn't like them. How easily, in fact, the Place takes hold of him and draws him in and makes him its own. How unresistingly he lets the Place come between him and his parents. How unthinkingly he puts their world behind him and his world beyond them.

How badly he performs his part of the Project.

The boy is certainly no Patton, taking possession of the Place for them. He's a deserter, all too ready to let himself be captured by it and all too often turning it against them. All too often he feigns deafness when they address him in the language that's still theirs, and all too often he pretends to be someone else when their accents distort the language that's already his. He nags

36

them into letting him attend Scripture classes, even though he's excused from them. And into having a Christmas tree like everybody else, even though he knows he isn't like everybody else.

He's different and he knows it, and he doesn't want to be.

I can explain him to some extent, and to some extent this is what the Project's all about: the Child shall make the Place his, so that a new world will be possible for them.

What the Project is not about is the Place turning the Child away from them. And what I much later find hard to explain is why he so readily lets it do so.

Summer 1956. The boy has just finished his first year at school and can reasonably be expected to have learned a thing or two. But when the pitiful remnant of his almost extinguished family comes from the other side of the globe on a visit to the paradise on the rowanberry avenue and fits itself surprisingly well into the small apartment on the ground floor of number 45, he hastily pulls up the drawbridge and barricades himself behind comics and excuses.

Aunt Bluma is plump and loud and makes breakfasts the way they do in Israel, with salads of finely chopped vegetables. Cousins Isaac and Jacob are his age and ginger-haired and wild and immediately do their best to lure him into doing all kinds of things.

It could have been a great summer. Havsbadet. The forest. The playground. The port. The Sunday outings in the brand-new car with room for two children folded up in the little space between the back seat and the engine.

And everything's there. Not least the forest. His cousins can't get enough of it. They've never seen a forest like this before. The paths so thick with layers of pine needles, the huts, the warm trunks of the pines in the clearing. They pick lots of bilberries this summer. One day Isaac, or maybe it's Jacob, suggests they commandeer all the transparent plastic storage containers fixed to the underside of the kitchen cupboards, and a few hours later, their freshly picked bilberries are lovingly sprinkled with salt.

So yes, they definitely do things together.

And still not. It's as if the boy refuses to let them get close to him. As if he's afraid they'll take something from him, disturb his position in the Place, make him alien, make him as different, as, deep down, he suspects he is.

It's true that the cousins speak a language he doesn't understand and do things he doesn't want to be associated with, like borrowing the unlocked bikes in the courtyard and leaving them here and there. It's also true that the rowan avenue is a small, enclosed world into which no one is admitted just like that, be they from Viksängen on the other side of the railroad bridge or from Tel Aviv on the other side of the globe.

But it's also true that they try to fit in as best they can, and that they pick up the language with surprising speed, and that by the end of the summer they move freely about the Place as though they feel entirely at home, and that they continue to the last generously offering to share everything with their inhospitable cousin, who lurks among the comics at Bertil's on the first floor of number 47 and pretends not to hear when they shout his name from the courtyard. *Berrrra* they call, the rolled *r*'s rasping in their throats, and they almost choke with laughter because they know that's what everyone calls Bertil and that's where their cousin's hiding.

They stay until the rowanberries turn red and school starts and nothing can get between the boy and his world any longer.

The boy's world and nobody else's. Not even his parents'.

Least of all his parents'.

Occasionally something happens to thrust him back toward theirs, and their shadows momentarily penetrate him, and a sensation of darkness and cold lingers on.

One winter's day, some children throw snowballs at their kitchen windows and shout "Jews." It's at number 45, where the apartment is on the ground floor, and the kitchen window faces the courtyard. The boy hears the snow thump on the window and sees his mother's face go white. Utterly white and utterly silent. She says nothing. Not to the children outside, nor to the boy in the kitchen. Nor to his father when he gets home from the factory. At least, not in the boy's hearing.

When the snow melts at the end of winter, the marbles come out. In the Place, marbles playing is the sign of spring. The monochrome stone marbles cost one öre apiece and you can buy them at the tobacconist's and they make your trouser pockets droop and bulge. Some kids keep their marbles in a special cloth bag dangling from their belts, weighing against their thighs. There are shiny metal marbles and multicolored glass marbles too. They're better for shooting than the stone marbles because they're bigger and heavier, but they cost more and are therefore not so often put at risk. Some people always seem to lose their marbles and have to make do with watching or trying to beg money for more. There's a lot at stake in a game of marbles, particularly the game where the object is to hit the pyramid. The pyramid consists of three marbles pressed into the ground and another one balanced on top. Whoever breaks up the pyramid gets to build it again and wins all the marbles that have rolled past it.

There are several ways of cheating at pyramid. The most insidious is to press the base of three marbles into the ground a bit too hard and a bit too deep, making the target area smaller, the pyramid more stable, and the top marble harder to dislodge.

Such a pyramid, the boy learns, is called a Jew pyramid.

He also discovers that there are marble Jews.

A marble Jew is someone who makes a Jew pyramid, or picks up more marbles than he has won, or collects his marbles in a pile rather than playing with them, or someone who just happens to get in the way of a player's frustration or disappointment. "Marble Jew" is a general insult for the duration of the marble season. "You goddamned marble Jew," usually.

The boy's rarely called a marble Jew because he's a useless marbles player, always losing his marbles, and rarely threatening or annoying anyone, but he goes ice-cold every time he hears the word "Jew" in one combination or another. He knows that Mom and Dad are Jews, and that he and his little sister are too, and the Klein family on the other side of the railroad bridge, and Auntie Ilonka at the other end of the rowanberry avenue. And even if he doesn't know what it means, he knows it has something to do with the shadows.

I wish I could make contact with him and explain a few things. That the Place cannot become his if it doesn't also become theirs. That he cannot make the Place his own if he doesn't know where he comes from. That he has a certain responsibility, small though he is, for the success of the Project.

I'd also like to ask him a few things. About language, for instance. About those early words in Polish. Where did he hide them? Are they perching like lost birds in his memory, waiting to be discovered? There's something about Polish that, much later,

I don't understand. The body recognizes the language, but the head does not.

Rudyard Kipling says in his autobiography that after eleven years at an English boarding school he returned to Bombay, city of his birth, and started to speak in whole, coherent sentences in a local Indian language he'd forgotten. The only catch was that he himself didn't understand what he was saying.

Maybe if I hadn't been in such a hurry to put their world behind me, or if I'd gone back to it sooner, I too would have been able to unearth a forgotten language, or at least a few coherent sentences, not just in Polish but also in Yiddish, and perhaps over time even to understand them.

And not only the languages, but also the worlds that went with them.

But the boy's far too small to be able to help me with such things and speaks too quietly for me to glean anything from what he says. Not like the twenty-year-old youth in a Jorge Luis Borges story who sits down beside the seventy-year-old Jorge Luis Borges one morning on a park bench outside Harvard and tells him loud and clear what it's like to be twenty and Jorge Luis Borges.

I'll have to make do with catching sight of him now and then. One evening in late summer I see him with the other children from our block by the swings at the Köpmansplan playground. He's not quite six, it's already starting to get dark, and he's not allowed to be out this late, but on this one evening all the children are out late and the playground is full of adults standing around talking in groups and smoking and waiting for a film to be shown on the big screen the Social Democrats have put up between the sandpit and the swings. In the film, a man's driving

41

his car on fields and meadows instead of on the roads. It looks like hard work and feels a bit menacing and the man gets angry and everything seems to be going wrong. The film is called *Tax-free Andersson*. The boy doesn't understand what it's about, but he sees the grown-ups of the Place standing there in front of the screen contemplating the car as it bumps over the fields and sees the glowing ends of their cigarettes leave traces in the gathering darkness and senses how they all worry about having no roads for the cars to drive on, and how they're all making a silent pact that in the Place where they live, cars will drive on roads and not on fields.

In my fourth school year I move from the yellow wooden house in Baltic to the school in the yellow-brick building in town, and from Miss Bergerman to Mr. Winqvist. It's a big step and one train stop away. Miss Bergerman cries for us as if we were her lost children.

The boy is now me. Or at least, I can no longer keep him at arm's length. I see him too clearly and recognize him too well and must take responsibility for the story he tells.

Mr. Winqvist the schoolmaster is gray-haired and extremely red-faced and scatters a few words of German into what he has to say, shouting *Herein!* whenever anybody knocks at the classroom door. For a brief period I'm Mr. Winqvist's favorite, praised when I answer questions, entrusted with helping a class-mate who has reading difficulties, and invited to tea and biscuits in Mr. Winqvist's cigar-scented apartment, where he gives me a fine old book as a present. One day Mom tells me Mr. Win-qvist is dropping in to see us that evening. I understand that this is a big thing, occasioned by the visit of a Polish colleague who wants to meet some compatriots and speak the language of his homeland.

I don't believe Mr. Winqvist has understood that my parents are Polish Jews, which is not the same thing as Polish compatriots.

I think he understands after the visit.

After the visit, I am no longer Mr. Winqvist's favorite. The reprimands and sarcastic remarks start raining down, and the blond twins take my place on the favorites' stand.

The book Mr. Winqvist has given me I read from cover to cover and like a lot. It's called *The Swedes and Their Chieftains* and is written by Verner von Heidenstam and smells strongly of cigar.

■

I want to write about the Place as I see it just then. And just then in this story is the time when a young man and a young woman, who have just got off the train on the road from Auschwitz, are living, working, and dreaming, just here. It's also the time when I, their first child, see the world for the first time and so see the Place as it will forever appear to me. It's the Place where the drifting ice floes on the Canal perpetually slip beneath your boots, where the first roach forever lies expiring on the quayside, where the fresh carp bream Mom has bought from the lift-netters on the shore of Lake Maren is still flapping in the newspaper on the draining board, where the first shy blush of shame has burned itself into my cheeks, where Mom and Dad forever press their young bodies into the soft sand of Havsbadet, smoking and talking and touching, and you hear the eternal

43

thud of bare feet on the creaking wooden piers and trampolines and the shrill sound-carpet of shrieking children and seagulls and the soporific sighing of the waves on the sand and the wind through the pines.

It's a world in which everyone who exists right then, right there, will always exist, albeit only in disconnected fragments of vivid sensations. What's seen for the first time has no history, no movement, it doesn't change, it can't be changed. The same apartment blocks, the same paved streets, the same barberry hedges, the same railroad bridge, the same station plaza, the same people moving beneath the rowan trees. Though over time open wounds of concrete and tarmac, highway interchanges, and port terminals have scarred the landscape, the fragments still lie there untouched.

Scattered and disconnected, but untouched.

In the lives of the two new arrivals, a place like this no longer exists. A place where they made the world their own, as I did.

Had there been such a place, they would have talked about it, would have given me a sense of its smell, its taste, taken me there, told me about the people who once lived there.

But they tell me nothing.

Where there must once have been a place like this one, there is now only silence.

Silence and shadows.

Whatever fragments of such a place lie hidden somewhere—and no human being lives without such fragments—someone or something has crushed them all too carefully and buried them all too deeply, in too-wide expanses of darkness.

THE WALL

So where did you get on the train? So many stations no one remembers anymore. So many places that no longer exist. So many trains to choose from. So many trains that stop too soon and for good.

So I decide for you.

I decide that you get on the train at Auschwitz.

I know it sounds dramatic, even striking, or in the worst case theatrical

And I admit that it's hardly commonplace to get on a train in Auschwitz, since Auschwitz is the place where all the trains stop too soon and for good.

And of course you get on a train *to* Auschwitz as well.

On reflection I think that's where I'll have you start your journey, at the railroad station outside the Łódź ghetto at the end of August 1944.

The exact date of your departure is a lost fragment. "*Eingeliefert* [delivered], 26. VIII. 1944, Auschwitz," is what it says on a handwritten list drawn up in the Ravensbrück concentration camp in April 1945. It's a German list, compiled by the SS, so they must have got the date from somewhere, but what does "delivered" mean? And how many days elapse between departure and delivery?

Can I write that you board one of the last trains from the Łódź ghetto to the selection ramp in Auschwitz-Birkenau?

The decision to liquidate the ghetto is announced on wall posters on August 2, 1944. The posters don't say that the ghetto is to be liquidated, but simply that it's to be moved elsewhere (euphemism is the SS empire's linguistic specialty), and that five thousand people must report for onward transport every day, each of them permitted to bring with them fifteen to twenty kilos of luggage, and that family members should ensure they all go together, "to avoid family separations." Those notified of their departure are to assemble at the central jail, situated within the ghetto fence, and will then be escorted to the station at Radogoszcz, just outside. The first transport leaves at 8 a.m. Those traveling are to be at the stated place by 7 a.m. at the latest.

Yes, that's what it says, in Yiddish and German, on the posters signed by Chaim Rumkowski. He's the chairman of the Jewish Council, and for the past four years he's been running the ghetto as a slave-labor factory for the Germans, and now he's been engaged by those same Germans to make the liquidation of the ghetto a calm and collected affair.

But no one in the ghetto is calm and collected. So many have already been transported onward and never heard from again. So many have been dragged away as if they were already dead. So many have been killed for refusing or for hesitating or for no reason at all, like flies swatted against a wall. So many recognizable clothes have turned up in the ghetto's textile factories. So many rumors no one's had enough imagination to believe or enough hope to shrug off.

So most people keep out of the way as long as they can, hiding in attics and cellars, trying to move from one hiding place to another, trying to convince themselves it will soon be over since the Russians have reached Warsaw, with the result that the euphemisms are exchanged for plain talk: *Wer einen Angehörigen bei sich beherbergt, versteckt oder verpflegt, WIRD MIT DEM TODE BESTRAFT* (Anyone giving shelter, a hiding place, or food to a relative WILL BE PUNISHED BY DEATH). German soldiers are sent into the ghetto, blocking off street after street and surrounding house after house, ordering the officers of the ghetto's baton wielding Jewish police force to drag the inhabitants out of their hiding places and take them to Radogoszcz. Early one August morning — the sun is low and the shadows are long — about thirty women and children are photographed on their way through the ghetto to the railroad station. I count nine Jewish policemen and one SS man escorting them. There's much to be said about the Jewish policemen, but the train is waiting for them, too.

No, no one in the ghetto is calm and collected, and once they get to the Radogoszcz station the euphemisms come to an abrupt end. The trains the former ghetto denizens must board are closed, lockable freight cars for the transport of cattle, the minimal openings for air sealed up with planks of wood and barbed wire. Boarding is via makeshift wooden ramps propped on makeshift wooden trestles. The passengers boarding are in their best clothes, as if for a long journey, the women in autumn coats, the girls in white socks and laced boots. August 1944 is an exceptionally hot month, but they have dressed more warmly than usual, just in case. They balance their loose bundles and their pots and pans insecurely on the steep, rickety ramps. You can see only their backs, not their faces, as they're swallowed one by one. The cattle cars fill up. The doors are bolted.

In one respect, the photograph lies. There's too much light in it.

You don't see the darkness. The darkness as they enter the cars and hope is extinguished.

Within twenty days, the seventy thousand remaining inhabitants of the Łódź ghetto have boarded the train at Radogoszcz. A hundred people in each cattle car equals seven hundred carloads, making thirty-five carloads per day. *Die Deutsche Reichs-bahn* has a severe shortage of freight cars in August 1944, and the more people you can squash into every car, the fewer cars you need. If everyone's packed in tightly, standing, you can get over 150 people into each car. The closed cattle cars of the German national railroad have a floor area of twenty-seven square meters, about 290 square feet. The German railroad authorities compile lists of the exact number of cars and trains they have to run between Łódź and Auschwitz and take payment accordingly, but I have no need to know the exact number, not in your transport nor in any of the others.

On August 28, Chaim Rumkowski boards the train at Radogoszcz without the slightest euphemism to support him.

On August 29, the last train departs from Łódź.

In the language that *delivers* human beings, the ghetto is thereby *liquidated*.

All that is left to clear away are the traces of those who have been *dispatched for delivery*.

The piles of abandoned bundles, the stench of starvation and death, the ruins of hope and of the will to live.

■

So I piece fragments together. If you're registered as delivered to Auschwitz on August 26, you must have boarded the train at Radogoszcz on August 25 at the latest, possibly a day or two earlier. It's only just over two hundred kilometers to Auschwitz, but in the Europe of human transports the railroad tracks are overused and the trains overloaded. Sometimes the trains grind to a halt for hours or even days. Some passengers survive the journey, others do not. Some remain human beings, others do not. So much has already been said about those days and nights in the cattle cars to Auschwitz. And so little. The Germans have no intention of letting anyone survive to say anything, and those who survive don't know what to say to be believed.

You've said nothing, and I have nothing to add.

The only thing I can say with some degree of certainty, thanks to the SS list at Ravensbrück, is that you board a train at Radogoszcz that delivers you to Auschwitz on August 26, 1944. But I don't know if you're registered as delivered the same day you get off the train onto the ramp at Auschwitz-Birkenau or not until a few days later. After all, the vast majority of those who get off the train from the Łódź ghetto are never registered because they're immediately sorted to one side (the left) to be murdered in the gas chambers and incinerated in the crematoriums, all traces of them expunged. The few who are not to be murdered just yet but are to be used as slave labor first have to be sorted again, assigned numbers, and registered as delivered. This must surely take time, possibly several days. If that's the case, then another fragment can be slotted in, a registration card from a later stop on the journey, which says that you're in the ghetto in Łódź until August 20, 1944, and in KL Auschwitz from August 21, 1944. That means you're in KL Auschwitz for a number of days without being delivered. Assuming it's necessary to make all the fragments fit together.

But that isn't necessary at all. In this context it makes absolutely no difference on precisely which day you reach Auschwitz. Your journey has no timetable and no direction. You have no exact dates behind you and no exact dates ahead of you. On your journey, exact dates have no function.

It's me they have a function for. I'm the one who needs them. I'm the one who needs every fragment that can possibly be procured, so I don't lose sight of you. A fragment that can't be erased, edited, denied, explained away, destroyed. A date. A list. A registration card. A photograph. The exact names and numbers of the days when your world is liquidated.

Because that's what's happening. These are the days when your world is liquidated. When the places and people in whose care you made the world your own are wiped from the face of the earth, blotted out of history, and expunged from memory. The last days in the ghetto are the last days when it's still possible to experience your world by smelling its scents, hearing its voices, touching it, missing it, fantasizing about it. The ghetto's a doomed world, a world of gradual degradation and destruction, a world of ever more unrealistic hopes, kept alive by increasingly implausible euphemisms, but it's a world that still has a past and a future. Just beyond the deadly fences of the ghetto, basically within walking distance, are the house at 36 Piłsudskiego where you grew up, the school you went to, and the places where your cheeks flushed, your eyes glittered, and your dreams were woven. The town's no longer called Łódź but Litzmannstadt, and the streets have been given German names instead of Polish ones; the houses and apartments where two hundred thousand Jews recently lived have now been taken over by Germans, and little by little all links to the past are being severed, and all links to humanity. So yes, your world is about to be wiped out, and day by day the ghetto is dying, but in apartment 6 at 18 Franciszkańska, near the corner of Brzezińska (which the Germans have renamed Sulzfelderstrasse), there are still some of the people who populated that world, and some of the objects that furnished it (nothing valuable, the Germans have stolen all that,

52

piece by piece, but still), and maybe a boxful of the links that consolidated it, and no doubt somewhere the photographs that immortalized it. Still living there are your father Gershon, your mother Hadassah, and your youngest brother Salek, and a short distance away, at 78 Lutomierska (Hamburgerstrasse), in apartment 29, your big brother Natek and his young wife Andzia, and in number 26 at the same address Andzia's father Majlech and mother Cywia. And somewhere out there, most recently heard of in Warsaw, your eldest brother Marek, who is also called Mayer. And with the Staw family in apartment number 3 at 18 Franciszkańska (Franzstrasse, the Germans have decreed), a very pretty girl two years younger than you called Halina or Hala, but more properly Chaja, and more affectionately Haluś or Halinka, and on whom you have a teenage crush, and who's sharing the apartment's single room with her father Jakob and her mother Rachel and her big sisters Bluma, Bronka, and Sima. In the kitchen there's yet another family. In the kitchen of apartment 5, on the third floor, lives Hala's eldest sister Dorka with her husband Jeremiah and their son Obadja, born on April 2, 1939, and still a baby when the ghetto is closed to the outside world on April 30, 1940.

Of course, your world can look like this only during the first days of the ghetto, when the two hundred thousand Jews of Łódź have just been forced behind the barbed wire, into *das Wohngebiet der Juden in Litzmannstudt*, and when nearly all of them are still alive and the transports haven't started yet and the dawn streets aren't lined with the previous night's bodies, with people who starved to death or died of typhus or killed themselves, and when the whole thing still seems too unreal to be true. Yes, this is what your world looks like when its root fibers are still attached to living people and memories and it's still possible to draw a family tree with an ever finer tracery of branches to ever more distant names, places, and stories, and no one yet knows that whole family trees can be chopped down and whole worlds liquidated.

On July 25, 1943, your father Gershon dies in apartment number 6. On July 26, 1943, Jeremiah, Obadja's father, jumps from the window of apartment number 5 on the third floor and succeeds, not without difficulty, in killing himself. On November 10, 1943, your youngest brother Salek dies in apartment number 6.

I also have their birth dates. Gershon is fifty-six when he dies, Jeremiah forty-two, Salek nineteen. I also have the exact dates on which Rosenberg after Rosenberg is dispatched from the ghetto for onward transport. Rosenberg's a common name in the ghetto, where it's spelled with a *z* instead of an *s*.

"*Ausg.* 10.3.42 Tr. 35" is written after the name of the porter Idel Rozenberg, who lives in apartment number 25 at 51 Sulzfelderstrasse (Brzezińska) and was born on 1.1.1897. *Ausg.* means *ausgeliefert*, dispatched for delivery, and Transport 35, like all the other transports of 1942, goes to the gas vans, the mobile gas chambers in Chełmno.

The list doesn't include this detail, but I know it's so.

On March 15, 1942, weaver Majer Hersz Rozenberg, who lives in apartment number 3 at 4 Kranichweg (Żurawia), is dispatched on Transport 31.

On March 25, 1942, schoolboy Mordela Rozenberg, who lives in apartment 10 at 1 Fischstrasse (Rybna), is dispatched on Transport 36.

On September 1 and 2, 1942, the ghetto's hospitals are emptied and the patients dumped into military trucks. Some are dumped out of the windows. Some try to run away.

Between September 5 and 12, an *Allgemeine Gehsperre* or general curfew is proclaimed: everyone is ordered to stay at home and no one is permitted to have guests and one block of apartments after another is forced to give up the old, the sick, and the children. Within two weeks, sixteen thousand people are dispatched from the ghetto, never to be heard from again.

On September 4, 1942, Chaim Rumkowski makes a speech.

I hope you don't hear it.

I hope nobody at 18 Franciszkańska hears it.

I don't know what anyone can hope for after hearing it.

But at the same time, I want everyone to know what Chaim Rumkowski said in his speech of September 4, 1942. So that everyone will know what sort of place it is that you're leaving behind when you board the train to Auschwitz in August 1944 and your world is liquidated.

Or is it already liquidated now?

It's a quarter to five in the afternoon and the sunshine is glaring and the day is still hot and loudspeakers have been set up in the square outside the fire station at 13 Lutomierska Street, and Chaim Rumkowski makes a biblical speech, without euphemisms. Or perhaps a speech with biblical euphemisms.

At any rate, a speech that cannot be misunderstood.

Or a speech that must be misunderstood if your world is not to collapse at once under the weight of its monumental futility and be liquidated on the spot.

"Fathers and mothers, give me your children!" says Chaim Rumkowski.

His white hair is tousled, his movements slow, his voice broken, but his words cannot be misunderstood, so they must be misunderstood.

55

He has received an order from the Germans to dispatch all the underage children of the ghetto.

And he is also to dispatch the old and the sick.

At least 20,000 Jews are to be dispatched.

He has come to inform the ghetto that he has decided to give the Germans what they demand. To "bring the sacrifice to the altar in his own arms." To "cut off the limbs to save the body," with his own hands.

Yes, those are the words he uses.

And says that if he doesn't offer up the sacrifice, the Germans will destroy them all.

But that if he does, some people will be saved.

What is there to misunderstand?

Chaim Rumkowski doesn't want to be misunderstood. Not this time. This is what he says:

I come to you like a bandit to take from you that which you hold most dear. I have tried by every means to have this order revoked, and when that proved impossible, to have it made less harsh. Just yesterday, I requested a list of all nine-year-olds. I wanted to try to at least save that year group, the nine-to-ten-year-olds. But I could secure no such concession. The only thing I successfully achieved was to save those aged ten and above. Let that be a consolation in our deep sorrow. There are in the ghetto many patients who can only be expected to live for a few days, perhaps a few weeks. I do not know if this is a diabolical idea or not, but I have to say it: Give me the sick. We can save the well in their place. I know how dear the sick are to each family, and especially for Jews, but when cruel demands are made, one has to weigh and calculate: who ought to be, can be, and may be saved? And common sense tells us that those who are to be saved must be those who *can* be saved and those who have a chance of being rescued, not those who in no circumstances can be saved.... Bear in mind that we live in the ghetto. We are subject to such great restrictions that we do not have enough for the well, let alone the sick. We give them our meager rations of sugar, our little piece of meat. And what is the result? Not enough to cure the sick, but enough to make ourselves sick. Naturally sacrifices of this kind are the most beautiful, the most noble. But there are times when choices have to be made: sacrifice those among the sick who have the least chance of getting well, and who can also make others ill, or save the well. I could not devote very long to thinking this over; I had to decide in favor of the well. In that spirit, I have issued instructions to the doctors: they have the task of delivering up all incurable patients, so that the well, those who want to live and can live, may be saved in their place. I understand you, mothers, I see the tears in your eyes; I feel what you feel in your hearts, you fathers who are obliged to go to your work even on the morning after your children have been taken from you, your darling little ones whom you were playing with only yesterday. All this I know and feel. Since four o'clock yesterday, when the order was first conveyed to me, I have been prostrate; I share your pain, I suffer your anguish, and I do not know how I shall survive this—where I shall find the strength to do it. I must let you into a secret: they demanded 24,000 sacrifices, 3,000 a day for eight days. I was able to reduce that to 20,000, but only on condition that all children under ten be included. Children of ten and older are safe. Since the children and old people together amount to only 13,000 souls, the gap must be filled with the sick.

I can hardly speak, I am exhausted, and will speak only of what I ask of you: you must help me carry through this *Aktion*.... A broken Jew stands before you. Do not envy me. This is the hardest order I have ever faced. I extend my broken, trembling hands to you and implore you: give me the sacrifices! So we can avert the need for even more sacrifices, and a population of 100,000 Jews can be saved! This is what they have promised me: that if we hand over the sacrifices ourselves, all will remain calm.

What more is there to say? Only a misunderstanding can maintain the world in which such a speech can be made. Chaim Rumkowski misunderstands nothing. The children, the sick, and the old are to be delivered up in order to be killed. This you must all understand. It cannot be misunderstood.

Nor can it be understood. The world in which something like this can be understood is a world no one in your world can imagine. Between your world and the world where parents are exhorted to sacrifice their children, children their parents, and the healthy the sick, there is a chasm that reason cannot bridge.

Only misunderstanding and lack of imagination—this is how I see it—can keep your world together after September 1942.

The inability to imagine a place like Chełmno. At one end of a manorlike building, "the castle," the entrance to the changing room and showers, at the other end the way out to the trucks that are docked to the outside wall, their airtight compartments snugly fit to the door openings. The biggest is a Magirus truck, made by Deutz AG in Cologne, which in 1942 has been declared a National Socialist model company, and which can load 150 living human beings. The two smaller vehicles, an Opel Blitz and a Diamond Reo, can load from eighty to one hundred each. Once the compartment has been fully packed, the smallest children sometimes packed on top of the adults, and the airtight doors bolted, the driver turns on the ignition and attaches an exhaust pipe from the diesel engine to the cargo area/gas chamber, and within five to ten minutes the cargo has been asphyxiated. Then the truck is driven to a camp in the Rzuchowski Forest, four kilometers away, where the dead bodies are unloaded, stripped of jewelry and gold teeth, and burned to ashes. After ten minutes of airing, the truck is driven back to "the castle" to get ready for the next load. Between September 3 and 12, 1942, a total of 15,859 people, young, sick, and old, are dispatched from the ghetto in Łódź and delivered to the gas vans in Chełmno.

I note down the exact figures and dates, in fact I scour the archives and sources for the exact figures and dates, because I want to reconstruct your world as you see it before it's liquidated, and I need something to build it with, and I don't know what else I can understand. But I soon notice that the exact numbers and dates merely reconstruct the widening gulf between what's happening around you and what can be understood. The ghetto's enclosed inside a wall of lies and euphemisms that no reason can penetrate.

Between January 16 and 29, 1942, 10,003 people are dispatched from the ghetto for onward transport and relocation. They're permitted to take 12.5 kilos of luggage each and are promised that they'll be able to exchange their ghetto currency for up to ten German Reichsmarks at the assembly point. Between February 22 and April 4, 1942, 34,073 people are dispatched from the ghetto. Between May 4 and 15, 1942, 10,914 are dispatched. Altogether, from January 16 to September 12, 1942, 70,859 people are dispatched from the ghetto in Łódź to be suffocated to death in the airtight compartments of the trucks that shuttle to and from the docking wall of a manor known as "the castle" in a small village sixty kilometers northwest of Łódź called Chełmno in Polish and Kulmhof in the language of the new masters.

I could have filled the rest of this book with figures and dates from lists detailing the dispatch and delivery of people who will never be heard from again, but apart from the fact that nothing can be understood from those lists, I also don't trust them. The figures are too precise, of course, and the abbreviations too arbitrary. *Ausgeliefert* is sometimes written *ausg.*, sometimes *a.g.*, sometimes just *ag*. Precise figures and arbitrary abbreviations are the crowbars of Nazi euphemism. They break up the established links between word and experience, between what happens and what is possible to understand. Why is 12.5 kilos of luggage the permitted amount? Why not ten, or fifteen? Why does the labor deployment, in a *Sonderaktion* (special action) for the "dejudification of the Warthegau" (*die Entjudung des Warthegaus*), require 1/8 liter of spirits per man per day? Why not a half liter, or a quarter? Amtsleiter Hans Biebow, the Nazi commandant of the Łódź ghetto, writes to the *Herrn Reichsbeauftragten für das Trinkbranntweingewerbe beim Reichsnährstand, Kleiststrasse, Berlin W32*, to request extra spirit rations and extra cigarette rations for the extra staff required to dejudify Warthegau—that is, the part of Poland now belonging to the German Reich, with its center a city now called Litzmannstadt, whose Jews are now being gassed to death in a small village called Chełmno, situated on the banks of the River Ner. The staff deployed for such a *Sonderaktion*, Biebow emphasizes, must unconditionally, *unbedingt*, be allocated an extra ration of spirits.

All this is somehow reassuring from a purely linguistic point of view: the fact that a man with the power to hire people for a *Sonderaktion* whose object is to dejudify Warthegau lacks the power to give them an extra ration of spirits. The fact that he repeatedly has to approach the high command of spirit allocations in Berlin and bow and scrape and attach certificates from the health authorities in Litzmannstadt testifying to the workers' need of spirits while on duty. Reassuring, because the long-winded sentences hint at some kind of meaning and the long-winded bureaucracy at some kind of order, but all of it, of course, entirely incomprehensible, since the words have been detached from their significance and the bureaucracy from its logic. Anyone with permission to transport 70,000 or 80,000 or, were it technically possible, 100,000 individuals to the gas vans in Chełmno ought not to have to concern himself with permission to dispense 1/8 liter of spirits a day to the extra staff that must be recruited to carry out the disgusting (yes, that's what it says, *ekelerregend*) work.

Not in the world as it has been understood until now.

∎

A man named Josef Zelkowicz is listening to Chaim Rumkowski in front of the fire station at 13 Lutomierska on that hot afternoon of September 4, 1942, and as usual takes notes on what he sees and hears. Zelkowicz's notes will survive the liquidation of the ghetto and the liquidation of Zelkowicz himself (in Auschwitz in 1944). Mortifying sobbing erupts, he notes, after the exhortation to mothers and fathers to deliver up their children. Piteous wailings erupt, he writes, after the declaration that the limbs must be cut off to save the body. Ice in every heart, he writes. Despair in every eye. Hands clenched convulsively. Faces rigidly contorted.

They all know. Little by little, the decrees have become brutal and the euphemisms have been stripped bare. Already in the second wave of transports, in February 1942, the promised exchange of money into German Reichsmarks is abandoned, and the travelers are brusquely told that the 12.5 kilos of minutely itemized luggage they've been urged to take with them to the assembly point are to be left behind when they board the train. The ghetto lies sleepless over the luggage left behind. And over the luggage that's sent back.

Everyone knows, but no one understands.

"The fact is," Josef Zelkowicz notes in September 1942, "that no one has even a vestige of doubt that the deportees from the ghetto are not being taken to any other location. They are being led to perdition, at least the elderly.... They are being thrown on the garbage heap, as they say in the ghetto.... If so, how can we be expected to accept the new decree? How can we be expected to live on after this?"

I don't think anyone has the right to ask that question in retrospect, but Zelkowicz asks it there and then. How can you go on living once you've been commanded to "sacrifice" your old, your sick, and your small children as a price for doing so? How can you go on living in a world where such a decree can be conceived and formulated? Let alone a world in which such a decree can be organized and implemented.

Many cannot live on. After each wave of dispatches comes a wave of suicides. People throw themselves from the windows, or hang themselves from beams and doorposts, or cut their arteries, or use poison, or take an overdose of some sleeping drug they've been fortunate enough to have access to, or get themselves shot by the German guards at the ghetto fence. That last one doesn't require much effort. The German guards readily shoot even those who don't want to be shot. All suicides are noted in the diary or daily chronicle maintained by the Jewish ghetto administration, without German knowledge, in premises on the third floor at 4 Kościelny Square. Thousands of typewritten diary pages, sometimes in Polish, sometimes in German, filled with observations and details of daily life in the ghetto, of deaths and births (!), of reductions in rations, of consignments of turnips and potatoes, of the lack of matches and fuel, of production quotas and actual production, of the weather, and of an old man, clearly ill, standing with an emaciated boy on a street corner, trying to sell something that looks like an onion. An escalating number of entries about starvation, transports, and suicides. Faced with the transports of September 1942, parents attempt to kill their children and themselves. Not all succeed.

Sixteen thousand people are offered up on those days in September, handed over for onward transport, according to lists compiled by thirty-eight people working twelve-hour shifts in the offices of the Jewish ghetto administration on the second floor of the building in Kościelny Square, plowing through the nineteen files that contain the ghetto register of inhabitants, copying thousands of family names and exact ages onto individual cards and sorting them by district and address before carrying them up to the Evacuation Committee on the third floor, which picks out the cards of those to be dispatched and sends them on to the Jewish ghetto police for execution.

Yes, this is what Josef Zelkowicz typewrites in Polish in the ghetto diary on September 14, 1942. Outside the diary, handwriting in Yiddish, he notes that everyone seems to have lost their senses. He also notes that the selection cards soon prove redundant because within a day or two the Germans lose patience and send their own people into the ghetto, ignoring the cards and picking the inhabitants out at random, shooting those who try to hide or refuse to obey or have the wrong expression on their faces. In the actions of September 1942, 600 people are shot by the Gestapo. Two of them in the backyard of 7 Żytnia Street, where the residents are ordered to file out for German inspection. Among them a mother and her four-year-old daughter. It's Zelkowicz narrating. The mother and daughter are holding hands tightly and smiling, the mother to show she's a viable survivor and the daughter because she's happy to be out in the sun. The German orders the mother to hand over her daughter. The mother hands nothing over and keeps on smiling. Mother and daughter are taken out of the line and given three minutes to think about it. Three minutes, not a second more. For some reason, the German is smiling, too. The ranks of neighbors are shaking with dread, but as discreetly as possible so as not to draw attention to themselves. When the three minutes are up, the mother and daughter are ordered "against the wall" and the German shoots them both, one pistol shot to each neck.

Zelkowicz tries to find words for what happens in the ghetto on those September days in 1942 but despairs of being believed. He senses that there will be those who, a few decades on, will claim it's all lies and deception. So at regular intervals, as if to pinch himself, he puts down in writing that this is really happening, that this is "one hundred percent factual," that it's happening before his eyes here and now, however inconceivable and preposterous it may sound to those who will one day read what he's writing. And actually, however inconceivable and preposterous what's happening may sound even to those who are living through it, here and now. When the only way to go on living is to fail to grasp what's happening. These are days when the people of the ghetto do not cry like humans, writes Zelkowicz.

They bark like dogs, howl like wolves, cry like hyenas, roar like lions. They don't cry like humans because the pain isn't a human pain that can be responded to with human tears. These are days when the ghetto is a cacophony of wild noises in which only one tone is missing: the human tone. Humans aren't capable of bearing such suffering. Beasts perhaps, but not humans.

So people don't cry.

Josef Zelkowicz strains his vocabulary and hunts for metaphors: people are shot "like mad dogs"; a woman who has just lost her three sons "laughs as wildly as a hyena"; a woman whose husband has just been shot before her eyes "hiccups like a crazed ostrich," and every hiccup "is a poisoned dart to the heart." In every apartment "a pocket of pus" is bursting, in every room there's "a roaring, rumbling, hiccuping, hysterical volcanic eruption," through every window and broken door "lava pours into the courtyards and streets. One dwelling infects the next, one house the next, one street the next. The whole ghetto quakes, churns, riots, runs amok."

With the "sacrifice" of the old, the sick, and the young children in September 1942, Josef Zelkowicz's world ruptures. He can't understand how the ghetto can live on after such a thing, still less how those responsible for selecting the victims could do so, and he's genuinely surprised, no, upset, in fact, to see that "the appalling shock" instead seems to transform itself into a kind of detachment. The brutal purge is hardly over before the struggle for survival resumes, as if nothing had happened. "People who have just lost their loved ones now talk of nothing but rations, potatoes, soup, and so on! It is beyond comprehension!"

The next entry in the ghetto diary: "During the first twenty days of September the weather was lovely and sunny, with only a few brief showers."

I don't know how you all go on living and perhaps I don't want to know, but I do know that you're still alive. That 85,000 people live on after September 1942, and that 73,000 survive until August 1944. That the Łódź ghetto is still in existence in August 1944, whereas the Warsaw ghetto is not.

In the Warsaw ghetto, life does not go on. In May 1943, the Warsaw ghetto is liquidated. In the space of two months, from July 24, 1942, to September 24, 1942, 270,000 people of all ages and conditions, no haggling over the old, the sick, and the young, are transported onward. Warsaw's Chełmno is called Treblinka. In Treblinka, the diesel engines are bigger and connected to stationary gas chambers in a purposely built block where many more people can be killed in a shorter time. No driving around in trucks through the woods; the bodies are burned in situ. It's more efficient that way. In the Warsaw ghetto, the chairman of the Jewish Council is Adam Czerniaków, not Chaim Rumkowski. When he's ordered by an SS-Hauptsturmführer, one Hermann Worthoff (who has just liquidated the ghetto in Lublin, whose Chełmno or Treblinka is called Bełzec), to deliver 10,000 people and a transport of children by July 24, 1942, he takes his own life. "I cannot send defenseless children to their deaths," he writes in his farewell letter.

Chaim Rumkowski doesn't take his own life. He lives on, convinced that by sacrificing the sick, the old, and the little ones, he can save the strong, the well, and those fit for work. He makes a calculation in which the survival of some becomes the overriding aim and the sacrifice of others the inevitable means of achieving it. He makes a calculation that he thinks will save the ghetto from something worse. He makes a calculation that is also the calculation of the Germans, which is to turn the victims into accessories to their own liquidation, which unquestionably makes Chaim Rumkowski an accessory.

This is the calculation that likely contributes to the fact that the Łódź ghetto is the only ghetto in Nazi-occupied Poland still not liquidated on August 2, 1944, when the Soviet army is only 120 kilometers away and some kind of survival seems conceivable.

Can we say that Chaim Rumkowski sacrifices his soul to save the life of the ghetto?

Can we say that he enters into a pact with the devil?

A lot of things like that have been said about the Jewish leaders who collaborated in the sorting and transport of their own people, and thereby contributed to the degradation and liquidation of the Jews. Much has been said about how they should have refused and resisted (as they did in Warsaw at the end, when it was too late anyway), about how they should have let themselves be killed rather than become accomplices in crime. Hanna Arendt calls their actions "the darkest chapter of the whole dark story." Primo Levi writes of Chaim Rumkowski, "Had he survived his own tragedy, and the tragedy of the ghetto which he *contaminated* [yes, this is the word Levi uses], superimposing on it his histrionic image, no tribunal would have absolved him, nor certainly can we absolve him on the moral plane."

In my view, Primo Levi is one of the few who have earned the moral authority to express an opinion about Chaim Rumkowski's morality. He immediately declares his reservations, citing the unimaginable moral challenge with which Rumkowski was confronted. The mitigating circumstances. To resist the Nazis' systematic degradation and debasement of their victims would have required "a truly solid moral armature, and the one available to

Chaim Rumkowski, the Łódź merchant, together with his entire generation, was fragile," writes Primo Levi.

Primo Levi writes this in 1986, in his final book before apparently taking his own life, and he asks himself what the rest of us would have done in Rumkowski's place. What today's Europeans would do, if they were put in Rumkowski's shoes. He finds the question still disturbing, and pertinent. He feels that something menacing is emanating from the Rumkowski story. That he can see in Rumkowski's ambivalence the ambivalence of our Western civilization, descending "into hell with trumpets and drums." That we all are like Rumkowski: "willingly or not, we come to terms with power, forgetting that we are all in the ghetto, that the ghetto is walled in, that outside the ghetto reign the lords of death, and that close by the train is waiting."

Primo Levi doesn't explain what he's alluding to.

Perhaps he's just expressing his growing sense of powerlessness in the face of amnesia and indifference. The powerlessness of those who have seen hell on earth but are able to find no words for it and still less able to convince posterity that hell is among us.

That powerlessness which in time will be yours.

No, too soon to write about your powerlessness.

■

In September 1942, Chaim Rumkowski, chairman of the Council of Elders in the Łódź ghetto, is presented with a choice for which I can find no historical equivalent and makes a decision that I lack the authority and ability to say anything about. So I say nothing, I merely observe that in August 1944, the Łódź

ghetto is still standing, whereas the Warsaw ghetto is liquidated. I merely observe that until August 25, 1944, or it could
be August 21, 1944, or whatever date at the end of August 1944
it actually is when you board the train of enclosed cattle cars at
the station in Radogoszcz (why am I so obstinate about these
dates?), most of the people in your immediate circle are still
alive. Your father Gershon is dead, as are your brother Salek
and your brother Marek, but your mother Hadassah is alive, and
your brother Natek and his wife Andzia, and the pretty young
girl from apartment 3 whom you're in love with and whose
name is Hala or sometimes Haluś or Halinka, and both her parents, Jakob and Rachel, and her sisters Dorka, Bluma, Bronka,
and Sima, and even Dorka's son Obadja, who's now five and has
survived the great sacrifice of the ghetto children. Five thousand children under the age of ten survive the sacrifice of the
ghetto children in September 1942 through being hidden away in
attics and under double floors and lowered into earth closets and
moved from place to place and, I assume, through connections
within the Jewish police, or through bargains of some kind, or
through luck.

Mainly luck, of course.

Is it Rumkowski's pact with the devil that's brought you this
far?

That is to say, this far but no farther.

In June 1944, the devil terminates the pact.

No, of course he doesn't.

No pact exists, and obviously no devil either. A pact has its
conditions. As has the devil. A pact with the devil is something
you can understand. In the Łódź ghetto, the conditions of the
pact are capricious, accidental, and couched in euphemisms in
order not to be understood.

So what exists is a new euphemism: "ghetto relocation." *Verlagerung des Ghettos*. What exists is a decision at the highest German level that the whole ghetto is to be liquidated and all its inhabitants murdered. No exceptions this time, no arguments about the economic value of the ghetto workshops, no calculations about the advantages of enslaving strong and healthy Jews instead of killing them. Here there remains not even the illusion of a pact. On June 16, 1944, the ghetto diary notes that the German commandant of the ghetto, Amtsleiter Hans Biebow, has stormed into the office of seventy-year-old Chaim Rumkowski at five in the afternoon and struck down his "pact brother" with a solid punch. No one understands why. Rumkowski is taken to the ghetto hospital but says nothing. Biebow presents himself at the same hospital, having damaged his hand. That day, Rumkowski has signed yet another proclamation, no. 416, dealing with "voluntary registration for work outside the ghetto." As usual, the headline, in heavy capitals: ACHTUNG!

No, no one understands it. Perhaps not even Rumkowski this time.

On June 23, 1944, the transports to Chełmno are resumed. On July 14, 1944, the Germans cease operations at Chełmno for fear of being caught in the act by the approaching Red Army.

At the start of August 1944, the first train runs from Łódź to Auschwitz.

As the proclamations become ever more threatening and the euphemisms ever more transparent, you all try to hide.

Statement by Hans Biebow on August 7, 1944: "If you force us to use violence, people will be killed or injured."

Bekanntmachung Nr. 426, August 15, 1944, signed Ch. Rumkowski: *Juden des Gettos!! Besinnt Euch!!* "Jews of the ghetto!! Consider!! Go voluntarily to the transports!"

Bekanntmachung Nr. 429, August 23, 1944, signed *Geheime Staatspolizei* (Gestapo): "Anyone found after 07:00 on August 25,1944, in those areas [of the ghetto] previously evacuated *WIRD MIT DEM TODE BESTRAFT.*"

On one of those last days in August 1944, as the Gestapo patrols have begun searching one building after another and anyone found is shot on the spot, you all come out of your hiding place for fear that the babies among you would give you away and you head toward the decreed assembly point outside the central jail at 3 Krawiecka (Schneidergasse). I don't know exactly who is accompanying you on this last walk through the emptied districts of the ghetto, how many of you there are, or whether you make it there on your own or whether you're "escorted" by the Gestapo, but I do know that among all those being gathered on this day for the transport onward are the last remaining links to that world you once made into your own. Had time stopped on this very day in August, I think to myself, and had the train at Radogoszcz never departed, and had the ghetto not been liquidated but instead liberated by the Red Army, which after all is only 120 kilometers away, then perhaps your world could have been brought back to life. Maybe then I could have had your journey start amid the fragrant smell of a meaty stew, slowly cooked in the oven in your mother Hadassah's kitchen, or in the warmth of the spring sun, shining on the blossoms in the cherry trees outside the house in Widawa where you were born on May 14, 1923, or in the noise and smoke from the heavy-brick textile factories around the vocational high school in Łódź where in the autumn of 1939 you began your studies to become a textile engineer.

Or perhaps even earlier, in the reflection of those people and places and events that preceded you in life and made you into who you are, and that I could have made contact with through the widening root system of memories and stories that has grown together with the people still surrounding you at the station in Radogoszcz.

You're sixteen years old when the Germans invade Łódź and you're forced into the ghetto and the world closes behind you. Sixteen years is a long time in a person's life, the first sixteen arguably the most important, for that's when we become the person we'll have to live with for the rest of our life. That's when we make our first connections with the world and have our strongest experiences and develop our deepest memories. A human being's story isn't complete without the story of what made him into what he is, or in your case, of what he's had the time to become before the world that made him is liquidated.

As long as you're all still at the station in Radogoszcz and haven't yet been ordered onto the narrow wooden ramps leading to the dark openings of the covered cattle cars, I imagine that such a story is still possible.

I also know that once the cars have filled up and the doors are bolted and the train pulls out, no such story is possible anymore.

Perhaps it became impossible even earlier, perhaps as early as those incomprehensible days in September 1942 when the old and the sick and the small children were sacrificed to the Germans so that the ghetto could live on.

Perhaps the world that existed before such things happened was a world where such things couldn't have happened—and therefore a world that could no longer exist.

So perhaps, there at the station in Radogoszcz, it's already too late. The most important people in your world are still alive, still waiting with their bags and bundles for the journey to nowhere, but their stories may already have fallen silent for good.

This I don't know, of course. I only imagine it to be so. I imagine that between the world as you understood it only yesterday and the world none of you can or wants to understand gapes a chasm that can no longer be bridged by memory.

Maybe I'm wrong. Maybe there's still a living family tree standing there among the bundles and bags, waiting for someone to investigate its foliage and root system. What were your grandparents' names? What did they look like? What did they do? Where did they come from? Who were your aunts and uncles? Did they have pet names, like Primo Levi's, who all have names starting with "Barba" and "Magna," including some names that can be traced back to Napoleon, since there's an Uncle Bonaparte on his mother's side who's called Barbapartìn, and who like all the Barbas and Magnas in Primo Levi's family chronicle has a character trait and a story attached to his name. Barbapartìn leaves the family because he can't stand his wife, so he has himself baptized and becomes a monk and goes off to China as a missionary. I read Primo Levi with envy and realize that for many reasons I will never be able to write a narrative like his.

I know your pet name, of course. You're called Dadek. You and your three brothers all have pet names. Dadek's a Polish pet name for David, Natek for Naftali, Marek for Mayer, and Salek for Israel. In Polish and Yiddish, and I assume in Italian too, diminutives are easy to form. They lie there on your tongue, waiting to pop out. As if it was in the nature of some languages to produce the soft diminutives that attach a note of solicitude and affection to the names of friends or relatives.

Dadek, Natek, Marek, Salek.

At the station in Radogoszcz, Dadek and Natek are still alive. And so is Hadassah. And so are Jankale and Rachela from

73

apartment number 3. And so are Dorkale and Bronkale and Blumale and Simale and Haluś or Halinka. And so is Obadja, whose pet name I don't know. And so are people in your world whose names, let alone pet names, will remain unknown to me.

But soon you have all climbed on board and the doors have closed and all thoughts of what stories might have been possible to tell, there and then, lose even their theoretical raison d'être. Once the train has left, I know for certain that this is where I must begin your journey.

I try to begin it earlier, but I fail.

Beyond the ghetto looms a wall I can't get past. A wall of darkness and silence. Almost no fragments at all.

Not now and not later.

THE CAROUSEL

In the spring of 1943, Czesław Miłosz writes about the carousel in Krasiński Park in Warsaw. It's a carousel that has been the subject of much writing and testimony. From the carousel in Krasiński Park in the spring of 1943, you can see and hear the liquidation of the Warsaw ghetto. The carousel doesn't stop while the ghetto is liquidated. Nor does the music. The Warsaw ghetto is liquidated to the music and laughter from a carousel in a park just outside its walls. This is on the days after Easter, and the last Jews in the ghetto have begun an uprising, and German soldiers are burning house after house, and the people whirling around on the carousel in Krasiński Park are enjoying the spring and the warmth as the last Jews of the ghetto are liquidated before their eyes.

> At times wind from the burning
> would drift dark kites along
> and riders on the carousel
> caught petals in midair.
> That same hot wind
> blew open the skirts of the girls
> and the crowds were laughing
> on that beautiful Warsaw Sunday.

Nothing new there, of course, it's well known that people are capable of living as if nothing's going on even when the most atrocious things are happening around them. In all wars, even the cruelest, even right alongside the fields of battle and slaughter, people try to live as if nothing has happened: to enjoy a meal, a night's sleep, a healthy stomach, a good laugh, a moment of forgetting. It's not always possible, and not everyone can do it, but life doesn't stop in the presence of death. Especially not there. In the presence of death, life itself can become the only thing of value. In the big diary of the Łódź ghetto, entries about death transports, fatal shootings, and suicides are interleaved with entries about grass growing, butterflies fluttering, and people streaming outdoors on a warm spring Sunday.

On Friday, April 23, 1943, a stork is sighted in the ghetto in Łódź, and in Warsaw the carousel in Krasiński Park whirls on.

■

While the Warsaw ghetto burns and the Łódź ghetto delivers up its children and the gas vans in Chełmno air out their compartments, feverish building activity is transforming the place where the man who gets on the train at Radogoszcz will eventually get off to start his life afresh. "Lofty pines, their crowns swept by the wind from the sea for many decades, are now succumbing to the woodcutter's ax," reports the local paper as a new part of town goes up in the Näset district below the red-brick station house at Södertälje Södra, where the big trains always make a brief stop on their way to and from the world.

The world's in flames, and in the little town of Södertälje, in the little country of Sweden, they're building houses and trucks as never before. Maybe not trucks so much as armored vehicles and tanks. Production of the SKP M-43 armored vehicle gets under way in late 1943, and production of the SAV M-43 assault artillery gun, consisting of a large gun mounted on a tank chassis, starts in March 1944. The chassis derives from a Czech tank that Scania-Vabis is building on license from Hitler's Germany, since Hitler's Germany has occupied Czechoslovakia, taken possession of the tank factory for its own use, and stopped the tank deliveries to Sweden.

What can one say? One man's meat is another man's poison?

No, that's too harsh, though I know there are those who think like that. The world in flames is, after all, out of sight for the people who happen to live here. There's no need for them to turn their heads away so as not to see. In their world, there are no houses burning in the next street, no neighbors being liquidated behind the carousel. They can imagine a summer following this one, and another beyond that, and feel the spring breezes from Havsbadet caress their cheeks, and hear the ax blows echoing through the pines, and be happy about all the houses that must be built to make homes for all the people coming to the little town to build all the armored vehicles that a world in flames demands. And eventually the trucks that will be in demand to help rebuild a world in ashes. In a place like this, the world can remain what it has always been and simultaneously become better than ever. The new houses rising in the cleared area below the railroad station all have laundries with washing machines and electric mangles, and the new apartments all have central heating and a bathroom and a kitchen or kitchenette, and between the kitchen and the hall a sliding, wood-veneer door, to save space. The installation of radiators and sinks in the Gondola quarter has unfortunately been delayed by a shortage of materials, by road haulage problems, and by military call-ups. A single day sees the call-up of twelve workers at the Edoff engineering firm, which is building houses both for the HSB housing cooperative and for itself, "and you can imagine how that might turn out."

The shortage of materials we can also understand; there's a war going on out there, after all, and the road haulage problems can be explained by the fact that the trucks have been called up too. But confidence is high, and the Gondola quarter is ready for its tenants to move in as scheduled, on New Year's Day, 1944, and the little town with the big factory is experiencing a boom, and there are far more employment opportunities than housing vacancies, and below the railroad station they're building not just a new town district but actually a new cityscape.

Yes, that's the word, cityscape. A bit unfamiliar still, but the language, slowly but surely, is adapting to the new frontiers. The apartment blocks in the new cityscape have two staircases and three floors, extending sideways rather than upward, but even so, the blocks are generally referred to as high-rise buildings. Buildings more than two stories tall are emblems of a new age, signaled by their name: high-rise. There are also plans for a sky-scraper in the area, that is, an eight-story tower block, which indicates the lofty ambitions for the emerging cityscape. None-theless, another ambition is that the apartment blocks are to be built "with such space between them as to make the living quarters light and pleasant." Admittedly, plans for a park are aban-doned to make way for more high-rise blocks, but who needs a park when the forest begins where the cityscape ends?

Summer 1943 sees the completion of the main street between the mushrooming rows of high-rises. Lofty ambitions here, too. On each side of the nine-meter-wide roadway are a pave-ment and a cycle path, each two meters in width, the pavement naturally farthest from the street. Between the cycle path and the street lies a protective strip of grass, two meters wide and planted with rowan trees. When it comes to the street paving, ambitions have had to be lowered a bit due to the war and the resulting asphalt shortage, and the cityscape must make do with paving stones. The stones have been given to the local authorities for free by the government, which has ample stocks of them, but they're more expensive to bring in and more labor-intensive to lay, and they simply don't feel quite right for a cityscape of the latest design. Paving stones cause more wear on automobile tires and are more uneven to drive on and would be out of the question in normal circumstances, but the circumstances aren't normal and the cycle paths are stone-paved too because heavy cycle traffic is predicted, especially in summer when the caravans of bikes down to Havsbadet are expected to use the new road through the new cityscape. The impression of a route through green spaces between the cityscape and Havsbadet is to be maintained as far as possible, and a strip of forest is to be retained between the railroad and the port area, although plans for the cityscape at Näset are as changeable, and sometimes as unreal, as the reports from the war that is said to be going on out there somewhere. Whenever possible, it seems, the local paper likes to feature news of current plans for the cityscape next to the latest war reports, a bit like the ghetto diary in Łódź, where an entry about the storks' arrival is followed by entries about the delivery of children to German transports.

On October 22, 1943, the front page of the local paper notes that the lively building activities at Näset have foregrounded the issue of a new junior school in the area. I read this with specific interest since it's my own future that's thus foregrounded. On the same front page, in the adjoining column, it's reported that all remaining Jews in the Netherlands have been arrested and taken to "the concentration camp in Westerborg." The camp is actually called Westerbork, and those taken there are soon to be forwarded to the gas chambers in Auschwitz-Birkenau, but there's no mention of that in the paper. What does receive mention is the new junior school's planned location on a hill near the separator factory in Baltic, where there's room for "a good-sized playground." On January 12, 1944, the paper also reports plans for a Sunday school and a kindergarten in "this hastily built part of town," and in the adjoining column reports that the Russians have launched an assault on the Crimea and that top Fascist leaders, including Count Ciano (pictured), have been executed in a prison yard in Verona.

What strikes me is how casually the two worlds coexist on these front pages: the small world and the large, the ax blows and the world fire, the survival and the destruction, the self-evident and the inconceivable. I'm also struck by how much of the inconceivable is actually published, sometimes splashed across the whole front page in big black headlines. On December 12, 1942, three columns are devoted to the fact that a million Jews have "died" in Poland. The statement itself is short and laconic, its source the Polish government in exile in London, and there's no explanation of how and why a third of the Jewish population of Poland has suddenly perished, but it's still worth pointing out that even inconceivable events are noted in print in the little town with the big truck factory. The next column reminds readers that the balloting to choose who will wear the crown of light in the 1942 Södertälje Lucia procession will close at nine that evening, and that the candidates will be on display at 7:30, and that this information "may be of interest to those who would like to see the seven young ladies before casting their vote."

On May 8, 1943, the paper notes that Södertälje "is holding its own as a summer resort," with the boardinghouses virtually fully booked from June to August, and two weeks later, on May 22, 1943, early season guests may read the following report in the same paper: "In the fog of war, the latest manifestations of Germany's persecution of the Jews stand out as a horrific symptom of the barbarism of our age. In Warsaw, the Jewish quarter was firebombed and the water supply turned off to hinder all efforts to fight the fire.... According to one source, which of course cannot be verified, two million Jews have been killed in Poland."

Jews are certainly not an everyday feature in Södertälje in the late spring of 1943, and it's by no means clear that any of the residents reading about the two million dead Jews have ever met a Jew in the flesh. The small town with the planned cityscape is at this time inhabited by sixteen thousand people, and in the small country as a whole there are only eight thousand Jews, and there's no evidence that many of them are living in Södertälje. In fact, you can hardly find any foreigners here at all. When Södertälje counts its foreigners in the national census of February 1939, it locates about fifty. The front page of the local paper notes—with a certain surprise (but still notes)—that "only four people [are] of Jewish descent." Or is it relief? The little newspaper makes no explicit admissions, but it has hitherto had very little positive to say about people "of Jewish descent." Or about the people referred to as *tattare* (a pejorative for "travelers"). On March 22, 1939, a month after the Census of Aliens, it's reported as the most natural thing that "a *tattare* pulled a knife at Tvetavägen." Pulling knives is what *tattare* generally do, we learn from the local paper. On December 5, 1941, readers are informed that "the knife-wielding *tattare* Torvald Lindgren, wanted since June for his knifing exploits, has finally been caught." *Tattare* and Jews are people whom the residents of the little town have learned over the years to view with fear and aversion. Jews do not pull knives but prefer slinking around the countryside, tricking gullible housewives into buying shoddy imitation goods at

83

exorbitant prices. "Beware of the fabric Jews!" warns the front page of the local paper on July 2, 1941. On the same page, German troops are heading for Leningrad. What proportion of the fabric Jews are also actual Jews remains unclear. The body of the article mentions an "itinerant salesman of foreign origin," whose crime, it's said, is that he sells some suit fabric worth 75–90 kronor for 170 kronor. It's far from clear whether or not a crime, in the legal sense of the word, has been committed at all, but that's not the point. The point is to warn readers, who belong to a nation of people "quite reserved and untalkative in their everyday dealings," not to let strangers into their homes and get carried away by a volubility that "exceeds all bounds." The same article notes that a "suit Jew" recently operating in the area "plied his customers generously with spirits he brought with him" and then "brazenly" took advantage of the liquid refreshment's effects. The increase in reports of dead Jews out in the world is matched by a decrease in the number of reports of Jews lurking about the countryside, though this does not prevent the local paper, as late as December 6, 1944, from putting on its front page the story of the "clever clothes Jew" who made raincoats from sheeting.

So it's a fair guess that there's an element of relief behind that phrase "only four people of Jewish descent." Particularly since the local paper, as far as this very issue is concerned, has a past. For a few years in the 1920s, when the *Stockholms Läns & Södertälje Tidning* is still two competing newspapers with the separate titles of *Stockholms Läns Tidning* and *Södertälje Tidning*, the editor of the *Södertälje Tidning* recurrently expresses strong opinions about "the Jews." His name is Elof Eriksson, and he's firmly convinced that "the Jews" run the world. And Södertälje too, presumably, even though at that juncture it would be difficult to find a single person "of Jewish origin" in the little town, and even though concern for Södertälje is hardly Elof Eriksson's most apparent interest. Eriksson's strongest opinions are reserved for "the intolerable party tyranny" and "all the dark and irresponsible forces working to break our nation apart for personal gain." In an editorial manifesto for the new year of 1923, the paper pins its hopes on Italy, "where a strong, popular nationalist movement—fascism—has enabled the land to cast off the heavy yoke laid on the people's shoulders by party bigwigs."

On the morning of November 22, 1922, the residents of Södertälje are able to read in their local newspaper that "there is a secret force in existence, a global government that leads and directs the political and economic development of the world over the people and governments."

On September 15, 1924, *Södertälje Tidning* pronounces it "an incontrovertible fact that the fate of today's world lies largely in the hands of the Jewish people, which directs and controls all capital and financial activity, whilst at the same time invisibly leading political and social, even purely revolutionary and 'anti-capitalist' movements among the people."

Elof Eriksson has a palpable respect for the power of "the Jews," pointing out that "those peoples who answered Jewish domination with desperate measures such as pogroms and racial persecution have suffered dire consequences...while... those nations that treated the Jews 'well' have been spared the graver misfortunes visited on the anti-Semitic peoples." The anti-Semitic peoples thus afflicted are the Russians, Germans, Hungarians, and Poles. Readers of *Södertälje Tidning* are informed on the morning of St. Lucia's day in December 1922 that the Poles for some reason have elected a "Jew president," against whom, however, the anti-Semitic masses have boldly risen up "in the battle for the racial purity of the Polish republic." Gabriel

Narutowicz is admittedly not a Jew, but he's an atheist and a liberal and has been elected as the first president of a free Poland with the support of "Jews, Germans, and Ukrainians," which explains why he's murdered by an upright fascist five days after coming to power. This "eruption of the anti-Semitic, nationalist movement" is reported in *Södertälje Tidning* on December 18, 1922, when readers are also reminded that it's time to renew their annual subscriptions, at a cost of a mere six kronor for "a free and independent newspaper, freely speaking the truth in all directions."

I follow the newspaper's truths into the new year. On November 9, 1923, the paper reports with satisfaction that Adolf Hitler has proclaimed a national dictatorship from a beer hall in Munich, and three days later, with irritation, that Hitler's revolution has been betrayed by a brazen "Judas kiss." Over the summer months, the front page features a list of "announced spa guests," complete with their titles and hometowns. On July 14, the list includes among others deputy manager Carl Gullberg and his wife from Gävle, stockbroker W. Doysk from Stockholm, Miss Margaret Setréus from Södertälje, and Mrs. Beda Våhlin from Lidingö.

I try to understand what is meant by "announced spa guests" and why their names are published on the front page, just as I try to understand what Elof Eriksson is doing in Södertälje. Does he live in the town? If so, where? Does he take walks in the park by the public spa in the summertime, raising his hat to the announced spa guests as they stroll by in their linen suits and summer dresses? Does he ever cycle out to Havsbadet on a summer Sunday to sit under a parasol and see the boats passing by out in Hallfjärden Bay on their way to and from the world? Is he at all interested in the reopened canal, which is twenty-four meters wide and six meters deep, and which passes beneath the newly opened, double-track railroad bridge, which is twenty-six meters high to allow for navigation and has a thirty-three-meter-long drawbridge span that can be opened for ships of a size never before seen in Södertälje?

Is he, in short, interested in the Place? As far as I can see, he writes very little about it. Admittedly, it's impossible to tell who writes what in the *Södertälje Tidning* because the articles are unsigned, but it's reasonable to assume that Elof Eriksson's fixation with forces far beyond the horizons of Havsbadet, the canal, and the railroad bridge increasingly monopolizes his pen. In September 1925 he leaves the *Södertälje Tidning* and presumably Södertälje too, if he ever lived there. He now launches the *Nationen* (The Nation), which comes out in Stockholm and establishes itself as Sweden's most crudely anti-Jewish publication. During the war, Eriksson goes to Nazi Germany to deliver lectures on Jewish world domination and publishes books in German about the powerful position of the Jews in Sweden, and should the Germans decide to invade Sweden, Elof Eriksson can put into their hands a detailed list of each and every Jew.

But not many of them in Södertälje, as we have seen.

On the other hand, Södertälje has nothing to do with Elof Eriksson's crusade.

Södertälje just happens to lie in his way.

Just as in August 1947 it happens to lie in David Rosenberg's way.

∎

Maybe something should be said about this: the town's tendency to lie in people's way. It's a long story, stretching back to the Viking age, so it's not really true that the Place has no history. The new cityscape below the railroad station is perhaps established in a historic backwoods, but not in a historic void. The new cityscape is located here because of the new railroad station, and the new railroad station is located here because ever since the Viking age, Södertälje has been a thoroughfare, situated on people's way to somewhere else.

It's not such a bad thing really, to be a place people have to pass through on their way to somewhere else. The Vikings, or whatever we like to call the people who passed through here a thousand years ago, were on their way from Constantinople to Birka, or from Sigtuna to Novgorod, or more generally on their way between the Baltic Sea and Lake Mälaren. Initially, this just happened to be where there was a shallow channel linking the two, and even when the land rose, turning Mälaren into an inland lake and the channel into an isthmus, the Vikings still gained time by dragging their keelless ships on rolling logs across the place first mentioned by name, Telge, in the travel writings of Adam of Bremen, a canon who passed through around 1070 on his way between the sees of Skara and Sigtuna. Perhaps he and his people made camp for the night, and perhaps he got the chance to observe the few people who lived here, and perhaps they contributed to Adam of Bremen's positive memories of Swedish hospitality: "They count it as the most shameful of all things to refuse hospitality to travelers, indeed they engage in an eager race as to who is the most worthy to receive the guest. Then he is shown all possible kindness, and for as long as he wishes to stay his host will take him to the homes of one friend after another. This gracious trait is one of their customs."

But it remains doubtful whether these particular memories stemmed from Adam of Bremen's transit of Telge; it seems likely that the few people living here made their living from passing travelers, and maybe even competed to make money from them, so they presumably had little reason to forge closer bonds with people who, when all was said and done, had only come to them with the aim of passing them by.

But it's also a delicate business, being a thoroughfare. The element of passage can easily grow to be more important than the place itself. The place can invest its greatest effort in being a place of transit, while its greatest fear is that the traffic will cease and the place be called into question.

There's nothing unusual, of course, about such a place, whose location is its raison d'être. Every town with a railroad station knows this, and it's not unusual for such places to wither away once the through traffic finds other ways around: when a water-way is drained, a railroad line rerouted, or a new motorway built; or when new means of communication are adopted; or when the need to travel from one particular place to another tails off or disappears. What's more, people who habitually pass through a place readily start to see themselves as its main characters and those who line their transit route as mere extras. Perhaps over time they even develop prejudices about people who prefer to stay put in the place they themselves prefer to pass through as smoothly as possible; they start to perceive these others as a bit less urbane, a bit less enterprising, a little slower, at worst a little more stupid. People and places that are shaped by being per petually seen in passing can for the same reasons accept the idea that they don't deserve much more.

Telge is born as a thoroughfare and shaped by its difficul-ties in remaining a thoroughfare over the centuries. So when that narrow neck of land grows wider, and the ships grow big-ger, and the favored thoroughfare becomes the longer but more navigable route via the rapidly expanding town of Stockholm, the dream of a canal is born.

When Södertälje canal is finally excavated and eventually opened in October 1819 and smaller vessels, after a break of about a thousand years, can again ply the waterway through Södertälje between the Baltic Sea and Lake Mälaren, the situation is very different. Building canals is in the spirit of the age, it's true, and a canal through Södertälje is considered a national interest, but to Södertälje the canal proves to be no guarantee of prosperity and rehabilitation.

In fact, the canal's a flop. It's pretty to look at and stroll along, of course, and possibly an attraction for those passing through, but the number of boats using it is far too small, and its costs outstrip the income it generates. The main traffic through the town is no longer by boat between the sea and the lake, but by horse-drawn carts and coaches, and before long by railroad, and in a distant future by car, between Stockholm and the world, that is, from one bank of the canal to the other. The wider and deeper the canal is dug, the wider and higher the bridge over the canal must be built, in order for one thoroughfare not to block the other.

As time goes by, it's no longer self-evident that the quickest route between Stockholm and the world must of necessity pass through Södertälje. New bridges and modes of conveyance open up new options for circumventing the pigs and the biscuit sellers of the town center and creating a straighter and quicker thoroughfare. Södertälje is perfectly placed for the shortest route by water between the Baltic Sea and the inner reaches of Lake Mälaren, but not for the shortest overland route between Stockholm and the world, which becomes obvious when it's time to put a new railroad line over the new canal and to build a new railroad bridge, and a straightening and shortening of the passage can be considered. The straightest route between Stockholm and the world hereby turns out to pass several kilometers south of Södertälje, with the result that the railroad station in Södertälje is built on the southern fringes of Näset and is given the name Södertälje Södra, which means Södertälje South. To get to the station that is given the name Södertälje Central and is located in the center of town, you must switch trains in Södertälje Södra.

Along the shortest and quickest rail route between Stockholm and the world, Södertälje becomes a railroad station at the edge of town, with a single spur to the town center.

In due order, then, the foundations for the future cityscape on the southern fringes of Näset are inaugurated: the railroad bridge, the railroad station, and the widened and deepened canal. On October 19, 1921, the first train runs on the new railroad bridge over the new canal to the new station at Södertälje Södra, where the pines are still standing below Platform 1.

This is not quite how it was envisaged, so no one knows as yet what to do with the pines. It was envisaged that the railroad would run somewhere else and the pines would be replaced by a social vision, but because it shortens the trip between Stockholm and the world by two minutes, Södertälje must exchange big dreams for petty adaptations, which become a definitive part of the place's history in the summer of 1943, when ax blows echo amid the heavily falling pines and the new, three-story yellow-and-gray apartment blocks are set out in rows along the stone-paved boulevard below the railroad and a cityscape of sorts rises up at a furious pace in the enclosed enclave between the canal, the railroad embankment, and the harbor.

The furious pace is set by the wartime market. In Södertälje, the wartime market is booming. From 1941 onward, all curves are rising. The boom starts before the war and accelerates from that point on. The war's good for Södertälje, which is growing after twenty years of stagnation. The war's good for the production of trucks, armored vehicles, and penicillin. The war's good for a town and a land of undamaged factories. The war's good for the small pharmaceutical company, which during these years quadruples its turnover and triples its staff and becomes a major industry. The war's good for the big truck factory, which during these years grows into a global business and needs to recruit people from far and wide.

It all comes as a surprise to Södertälje, which has not prepared itself for the role of rapidly expanding immigrant town or planned any housing for the new workers who stream in by the thousand. "Housing emergency" becomes a charged phrase in Södertälje during these years, and ending the housing emergency is seen as the final step in building the new and better society whose establishment will be completed as soon as the war is over.

Any way you look at it, the war's good for the building contractors; they go full throttle during these years and can only regret that the war prevents them from procuring the manpower and materials to go faster and build more. For the time being, the big truck company has to advertise in the local paper for rooms and apartments for its employees. "Rent guaranteed," it says. For the time being, the big truck company will also have to build bachelor barracks on its own property, basic accommodations for single male workers that cause a certain level of concern in the community, since the term "bachelor barracks" has a bad ring to it. Many marriages are postponed because of the housing emergency, says the local paper. Many fear that the housing emergency could lead to social unrest.

What's feared most, however, is the peace crisis—yes, that's what it's called—by which is meant a major slump as soon as the guns fall silent, or even a deep depression like the one after the previous war, when Södertälje's economy ground to a halt.

The war has been good for Södertälje and many people are anxious about what will happen when peace breaks out and the world is lying in ruins.

Be that as it may, there it is, the newly created cityscape below the railroad station on the other side of the new railroad bridge across the widened canal, waiting to come in your way.

■

You all are very lonely, I imagine. As lonely as the inhabitants of the Warsaw ghetto when they hear the music and laughter from the carousel in Krasiński Park. As lonely as the last people in a world that no longer exists, and which the people in the world that now exists have already forgotten.

Even before the fire is out, they've already forgotten the flames.

You're very lonely at the station in Radogoszcz.

It's full of people, of course: all of you who are to depart and who are now being squeezed together into the little assembly area in front of the cattle cars, and all the policemen and soldiers and dogs surrounding you, and the many inhabitants of the Germanized town of Litzmannstadt, who on this day, as on all days, are passing by in their separate world on the other side, and who cannot avoid seeing you as you mount the narrow wooden ramps and cram yourselves into the dark cars with the air vents covered by barbed wire and vanish from sight behind heavy doors that are slammed shut and bolted from the outside. Maybe they say something to each other about how much cleaner the town will be now that the ghetto has been liquidated and all traces of the Jews are gone.

The train, its cattle cars bursting with living people—the whites of their eyes are occasionally seen glittering through the sealed air vents—travels on ordinary railroad tracks through ordinary towns inhabited by ordinary people who occasionally look up from their ordinary activities to see what it is that's passing by.

In a cattle car rolling through the German camp archipelago, the narrator in Jorge Semprún's novel *The Long Voyage* has been able to get a standing place by the air vent and looks out over a world that is no longer his. On one occasion the train stops at Trier, a traditional German town in the beautiful Moselle Valley, which the narrator recalls from his childhood. At the station in Trier, he sees people gradually realize that this isn't a train like any other. They're talking agitatedly among themselves and pointing to the air vents in the freight cars, and a little boy who hears what they're saying shakes his head angrily and rushes off to get a big stone, which he hurls at the air vent with all his might, coming close to smashing the face of the man standing next to the narrator behind the barbed wire.

It's a long journey. People die on their feet.

Even young men die on their feet.

The young man standing next to the narrator dies on his feet, too.

I try to imagine the loneliness in the cars.

The loneliness of the moment when the door of the car is bolted behind you and the world as you'd recently understood it definitively leaves you.

Eighteen months later, in a letter to the young woman who is to be my mother, you write of "the nightmarish night in the railroad car on the way to hell."

That's all you write about the start of your journey.

THE ROAD

A lifetime later. At the opening of an art exhibit in Linköping, I meet Sara. Sara's a small woman with a shy smile and restlessly glittering eyes who comes up to my friend Peter, the artist, and asks if he can give her a lift to the funeral of her friend Ester the next day. The Jewish cemetery in Norrköping is over two hundred years old but still has some space left, Peter explains to me. It's a very nice cemetery, he adds, and free of charge, if you want to lie there.

No, Norrköping is not my place on earth, and hopefully not beneath it either, but tomorrow it will become Ester's place, and perhaps eventually Sara's, just as it has already become the place for many others who chose to make this their last stop on the road from Auschwitz.

I ask Sara Fransson, born Sara Leczycka in Poland on February 4, 1927, where she once came from, and she replies Łódź.

And then from Auschwitz, of course, she adds.

And then? I ask.

What do you mean, "then"? she seems to wonder. I survived Auschwitz, what else is there to say?

Yes, but by what road did you come from Auschwitz? I insist.

I seize every opportunity to ask about the road from Auschwitz, since every road from Auschwitz is an individual miracle unto itself, as distinct from the road *to* Auschwitz, which is a collective hell shared by each and every one. The road from Auschwitz follows the most shifting routes, veers off to the most unpredictable destinations, and comes through the most unexpected places. Those who are on the road from Auschwitz are all exceptions, just as every road from Auschwitz is an exception. And since the few who reach the end of the road alive have rarely traveled the same road, it's all too easy for the roads from Auschwitz to sink into oblivion.

Christianstadt, do you know anything about Christianstadt? asks Sara. Is there a place called Christianstadt? She was only seventeen on the road from Auschwitz and can't remember for sure if that was the name of the place, or even if it exists, but if there is a place called Christianstadt, then it's a place on her road from Auschwitz to Linköping.

No, I've never heard of Christianstadt, as I had once never heard of Vechelde or Watenstedt or Uchtspringe or Wöbbelin. And since I've set myself the task of digging those places out of oblivion, I also dig out Christianstadt, which proves to be a small town in eastern Germany that after the war becomes a small town in western Poland and changes its name to Krzystkowice and over time is reduced to a suburb of Nowogród Bobrzański. During the war there was a munitions factory in Christianstadt, owned by Deutsche Dynamit Aktiengesellschaft, DAG, previously Alfred Nobel & Co., which was the main reason the Germans set up a slave labor camp here in July 1944. The camp was sited at Schwedenwall, the Sweden wall, in the forests west of the town, and since the delicate and dangerous work of packing explosives into grenade casings was considered particularly suited to young women with deft fingers, the SS leadership in Auschwitz received a special order from the former Nobel & Co. in Christianstadt for female slave laborers. In late August or early September 1944, the order was dispatched by railroad freight cars, about ten carloads with altogether about five hundred women, recently delivered to Auschwitz from the ghetto in Łódź. The slave labor camp in Christianstadt was under the administration of the concentration camp at Gross-Rosen (today Rogoźnica in southwestern Poland), and when Sara Fransson much later writes down her memories, Gross-Rosen is the name she remembers.

The summer and autumn of 1944 is the time of hastily established slave labor camps in rapidly disintegrating Nazi Germany. The flow of civilian forced labor from occupied Europe is drying up, and German industry turns its gaze on the concentration camps. This is the time when the roads from Auschwitz open up. The war industry needs slave laborers, and the German annihilation machine is asked to provide them. The request is a source of some conflict, since the German annihilation machine needs to kill people, while the German war machine needs to keep them more or less alive. The conflict remains unresolved to the last. People are annihilated and people are delivered

It happens that German industrial managers turn up in person at the gas chambers and crematoriums in Auschwitz to make sure that Jews are being delivered rather than annihilated. Wherever German industries need slave labor, makeshift slave labor camps are set up, sometimes on the factory property, sometimes inside the factories themselves, sometimes in the middle of German cities and towns. Behind the retreating German front, a rapidly growing and increasingly incomprehensible archipelago of slave camps, through which the reluctantly opening roads from Auschwitz unfathomably fork and branch, unexpectedly changing direction and destination as German industries are bombed to pieces and the slave camps are of no use any longer, and the slave transports on their circuitous journeys are left with the primary task of removing all traces of themselves.

In front of me I have a list of names of places no one remembers anymore, or at least doesn't remember them the way you must have remembered them when, much later, you try to forget them.

Much later, I follow in your tracks on your road from Auschwitz.

On road number 191, between Neu Kaliss and Heiddorf, in Landkreis Ludwigslust, in the German federal state of Mecklenburg-Vorpommern, just east of the former border between East and West Germany, I am photographed. The photograph is taken through the windshield of a rental car, an Opel Astra with the registration number EU AO 2199, and my gaze is set on the distant view, as is recommended when driving, and therefore I don't see the camera that takes the photograph. Perhaps I should have seen it, or realized it might be there; my gaze, however, is focused not on speed cameras but on the well-kept villages that keep passing by in the snowy landscape, on their pretty, half-timbered houses, lining the road as I pass through, and on the sensibly dressed people making their way along the slushy pavements as if they all know exactly where they're going.

I don't know exactly where I'm going, because the road I'm trying to follow doesn't always lead where I expect, and sometimes doesn't seem to be where it ought to be. It's true that the road is narrow and winding in places, and that I'm apparently driving at eighty-two kilometers an hour on a stretch where the limit is fifty, but there's very little other traffic on the road and my thoughts are flying off in all directions, and one of the thoughts flying off is that not a single human being knows at this moment where I am and where I'm going.

Nobody except Frau Gorny at the traffic monitoring unit in Landkreis Ludwigslust in the German federal state of Mecklenburg-Vorpommern, it turns out. In a letter bristling with official crests, enclosing pictorial evidence, that finds its way with impressive speed to my home address in Stockholm, Frau Gorny brusquely informs me that on 4.3.2005 at 12:49 I infringed §55 of the law pertaining to violations of the public order, *Gesetzes über Ordnungswidrigkeiten*; I'm exhorted to admit my guilt by return of post and to pay what it costs (€225.60). It's a formal, correct letter, addressing me as "Highly esteemed Herr Rosenberg," and offers me the option of denying the charge within one week.

I have no intention of denying anything; the pictorial evidence is incontrovertible, but I do react slightly to the German legal terminology for my crime, where *widrig* in my language (*vidrig*) means "repulsive." This is not proportionate to the crime, in my view. Particularly not to a crime committed on this road, which is the road from Auschwitz to the town of Ludwigslust, in which the park between the palace and the city church is filled with the victims of Wöbbelin.

And particularly not in a language like this, with its documented capacity for concealing the most repulsive acts behind the most formal and correct terms.

■

Slave labor in the German camp archipelago goes under the formal designation of "prisoners' work contribution," *Arbeitseinsatz der Häftlinge*, and is administered by the SS Central Office for Financial and Administrative Affairs, *Wirtschafts- und Verwaltungs-*

103

hauptamt, called the WVHA for short, and superintended by SS-Gruppenführer Oswald Pohl. Formal applications from German industrialists for allocations of labor from Auschwitz are handled by SS-Sturmbannführer Gerhard Maurer, head of WVHA Department DII, responsible for prisoners' work contributions, but less formal approaches can be addressed to his superior, SS-Brigadeführer Richard Glücks, and on occasion highly informal requests go direct to Oswald Pohl himself. In the end, it's only the language that's formal. Repulsive acts know no formality.

In early September 1944—the exact date is unknown—two representatives of the Büssing truck company, Otto Pfänder (engineer) and Otto Scholmeyer (finance director) turn up at Auschwitz in person to select slave workers for the company's operations in Braunschweig. This is presumably not the formally correct procedure, since it is the SS that makes formal decisions about life and death in Auschwitz, but the links between the SS and German industry have grown more informal, as the production of goods has become increasingly dependent on the delivery of slaves. By autumn 1944, most large German companies are implicated in repulsive acts, demanding that the SS build them a slave camp at their factory gate.

The SS provides not just one slave camp but two for Firma Büssingwerke in Braunschweig. One is on Schillstrasse, in the center of Braunschweig, the other in the village of Vechelde, ten kilometers west of the town. The slave camp in Vechelde is an *Unterkommando* of the camp in Schillstrasse, which is an *Aussenlager*, or satellite, of KZ Neuengamme, which is the command center of the SS machinery for the swiftly expanding slave labor archipelago in the area between Hamburg, Hannover, and Braunschweig. In Schillstrasse, the slaves live in hastily built barracks, and every morning and evening they're marched a good kilometer under SS supervision through central Braunschweig to a big factory complex with the name H. Büssing in white letters on the curved facade of the brick-red main building. Most of the slaves wear the striped concentration camp garb, which is never changed and over time turns black with soot and stiff with dirt. All the slave laborers, including those who must drag themselves along, are marched through the streets of the town for all to see. No one in Braunschweig can be unaware of the formally correct atrocities that are committed in the truck factory in the midst of their city.

In Vechelde, Firma Büssing has set up a separate factory for the production of back axles. Since the past summer, it's housed in a disused jute mill in the middle of the village, a stone's throw from houses and gardens. There are no daily slave marches to disturb the idyll here, as the SS camp has been set up in one of the factory halls and the slaves sleep by their machines. One thing that may possibly disturb the residents of Vechelde is the weekly transport of corpses from the camp in Schillstrasse, as these are loaded onto the same vehicles that transport raw materials for the back axles from the factory in Braunschweig. In Vechelde, the back-axle materials are unloaded and any additional corpses are loaded, after which the combined corpses from Schillstrasse and Vechelde are transported another twenty kilometers to *Aussenlager* Watenstedt, where they are unloaded and buried. Emptied of corpses, the truck is then loaded with food for the slave laborers in Vechelde. Emptied of both corpses and food, the truck is then finally loaded with the completed back axles for the factory in Braunschweig. A most efficiently used truck, undoubtedly, but the Büssing factory is short on trucks for its own use, since all the trucks it manufactures must be delivered to the German state.

The death rate in the Schillstrasse camp is high; in late 1944, between eight and ten corpses a day are stripped naked, relieved of their gold teeth, allocated numbers, and packed in paper bags to await the transport of back-axle parts to Vechelde. The transport of back-axle parts is on Mondays. In the meantime the corpses are stored in a hut, where the corpses often make the bags wet, so they tear easily when they're being loaded onto the truck. Eventually, the bags are replaced by wooden boxes, each accommodating ten corpses. By January 1945, between four hundred and five hundred corpses have been transported from *Aussenlager* Schillstrasse to *Aussenlager* Watenstedt via *Unterkommando* Vechelde. I haven't been able to find any statistics for the number of corpses added each week in Vechelde, but that camp is smaller and conditions are better and the death rate is, for now, significantly lower.

I will thus dare to say that you're lucky, since *Unterkommando* Vechelde happens to be your first place on the road from Auschwitz. Of course, there's no need to keep repeating how lucky you are, so I shall say it only once. Luck, chance, and freak are the stones with which every road from Auschwitz is paved. There are no other roads from Auschwitz but those of improbability. You're loaded onto a train in Auschwitz and find yourself, utterly improbably, unloaded onto a freight depot platform in central Braunschweig for further delivery to *Unterkommando* Vechelde. You're part of a group of 350 Jewish men who were recently on their way from the ghetto in Łódź to the gas chambers and crematoriums in Auschwitz, and who by some blind fate have been nudged onto a route leading to a freight depot platform in the heart of Germany. You can't believe your eyes. "Some Sturmführer" asks if you're all hungry! You get your own plates to eat from! The Sturmführer personally (!) ladles out the soup, and asks if it tastes all right (!) and whether you'd like some more! You think you're dreaming. "After Auschwitz, this is Paradise," you write a year later, while the memory is still fresh, to the woman who is to be my mother.

In February and March 1945, Büssing's factories in Braunschweig are being bombed, and the slave labor camps are evacuated, and yet another circuitous journey through the camp archipelago begins, and hell makes its presence felt again.

It's on the trail of this journey, not far from its end, on the winding and solitary road to the pretty town of Ludwigslust, with my eyes staring vaguely ahead and my thoughts somewhere else, that I'm caught on camera, contravening the law against repulsive acts.

■

In Vechelde, all that remains of the Büssing factory for making truck axles is a Romanesque-style gateway of red brick and white marble. It takes a while to understand what it's doing there among the detached brick houses and box hedges that have sprung up all around, a lost factory gateway connected to nothing and leading to nowhere, until you come closer and discover the two memorial plaques on each side of it, one commemorating the jute mill and the other the slave labor camp. I'm not surprised. Anyone who knows at which points along your road from Auschwitz there ought to be a memorial plaque will most likely find one, and perhaps even a small monument if you search for it, and occasionally even a memorial museum. You have to hand it to the Germans, even in commemorating repulsive acts, they're conscientious. Touchingly conscientious, you might say. On the right-hand plaque, put up in October 1989 by *Gemeinde* Vechelde (the community of Vechelde), it says:

> Between September 1944 and March 1945 this former jute mill housed a concentration camp, under the command of the camp in Neuengamme, outside Hamburg. As part of the German defense industry, some 200 Jewish concentration camp inmates from Auschwitz, mainly of Polish and Hungarian nationality, were forced to work for the vehicle manufacturer Firma Büssing in human-destroying (*menschenvernichtenden*) conditions.

On the site of the slave labor camp in Schillstrasse there's a memorial monument too, in fact a whole memorial area. A rabbinical saying (*rabbinische Weisheit*)—"The future has a long past" (*Die Zukunft hat eine lange Vergangenheit*)—is written in large white letters on the wall of a modern factory building that happens to overlook the small walled enclosure where testimonies to the repulsive acts in Braunschweig have been put on permanent display for all to see. At my side is Dr. Karl Liedke, without whose help I would have found neither the road that leads here nor the memorials lining it. Dr. Liedke is my cicerone. He has drawn the map I'm following. It's useless as a driving map, but it's the only map in existence that shows your road from Auschwitz. It has dates and places and arrows showing direc-

108

tions and a green line showing the route absentmindedly crossing its own tracks among the red dots of the camp archipelago.

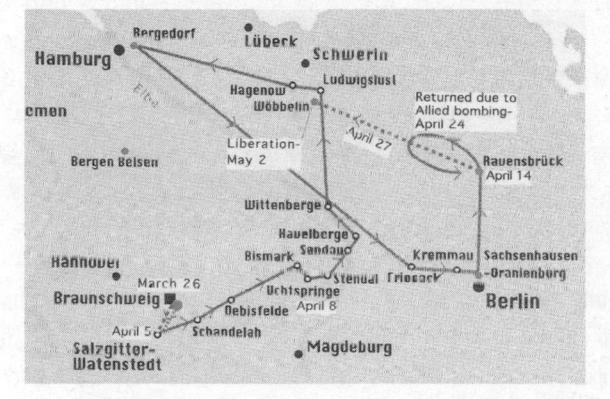

Perhaps you find it strange that anyone should devote several years of his or her life to mapping your particular road from Auschwitz, but no one who wishes to study the industrial history of the town of Braunschweig can avoid it.

Not all roads from Auschwitz have a Karl Liedke following their trail.

Karl Liedke is born in 1941 in Warsaw as the youngest son of an ethnic German father and an ethnic Polish mother and grows up in postwar Poland, where for understandable reasons, ethnic Germans are not in favor. When Germany invaded Poland, the father was recruited by the Polish army as a Polish citizen, and after the German victory, by the German army as an ethnic German, which turns out to be reason enough for vengeful Poles to have him killed in the wake of the war. In Karl Liedke's earliest childhood memory, his father is wearing a uniform and his mother won't answer the boy's question about which uniform it is. Later in life he's trained as an industrial economist.

In the summer of 1981, Karl Liedke gets permission to go on holiday to France but travels instead, as planned, to West Germany, a country to which he as an ethnic half-German would never have received permission to go, but where as an ethnic half-German he's received like a long-lost son. West Germany's need for Polish-educated industrial economists in their forties is somewhat limited, however, and after a long search for work, Karl Liedke takes a job with a historical research society in Braunschweig. His task is to carry out a financial feasibility study for a proposed museum of the industrial history of Braunschweig. Karl Liedke's study shows that while such a museum would not be financially viable, the industrial history of Braunschweig is well worthy of further study and in fact urgently demands it.

It's the Poles, I believe, who awaken Karl Liedke's lust for research. In the industrial history of Braunschweig, or indeed in any German industrial history, Poles cannot be avoided. In June 1944, over two million Poles are employed by force in German industry under the euphemism "civilian workers," *Zivilarbeiter*. The only civil aspect of the civilian worker system is the name. The civilian workers are housed in camplike barracks, live under prisonlike restrictions, and work in slavelike conditions; they're obliged to wear a *P* on their clothing to prevent them from using public transportation or going to restaurants or swimming in pools strictly reserved for Germans.

Not only Poles are forcibly conscripted as civilian workers. Little by little, the factories of Germany fill with civilian workers from all over German-occupied Europe and with prisoners of war from the battlefields in the east, and when the fortunes of war turn and the supply of civilian workers and POWs runs dry, with Jews from Auschwitz who are still fit to work.

The Auschwitz Jews represent an emergency solution, since the Jews have been brought to Auschwitz to be killed, but necessity knows no law. In September 1944, the German war industry finds itself in circumstances of direst necessity, and beneath the oily black smoke from the crematorium chimneys stand engineer Pfänder and finance director Scholmeyer, choosing or rejecting from among the still-able-bodied Jews who have just been delivered from the liquidated ghetto in Łódź.

Any study of Braunschweig's industrial history will find it difficult to skirt around the formal delivery from Auschwitz of 1,000 to 1,200 Jews from the Łódź ghetto for slave labor in the truck factories of Firma Büssing.

Karl Liedke does not skirt around anything in the industrial history of Braunschweig, particularly not an activity like this, visible and familiar to all the residents of Braunschweig for as long as it lasts. He wants to know everything that happens to the little trickle of Jewish men still deemed fit for work who are delivered as slaves to Büssing's factories in Braunschweig in September and October 1944. As a result, your particular road from Auschwitz is supplied with an incorruptible and tireless investigator who ascertains how you all are selected, how you survive, how you're transported, and, when necessary, how you die.

He also investigates the silence afterward. In December 1945, under the supervision of the British occupying forces, the German police look into the slave activity at the Büssing factories. The man in charge of Büssing at the time, Rudolf Egger, says he had no reason to concern himself with the high death rate at *Aussenlager* Schillstrasse, "firstly because mortality in wartime is hardly surprising, and secondly because it was not my area of responsibility."

On July 4, 1946, the public prosecutor in Braunschweig, Dr. Staff, writes to ask the British occupying authority whether the

111

results of the police inquiry are to be presented to a court of the Allied occupying forces or to an authorized German court. Almost two years later, on March 1, 1948, the War Crimes Group (Northwest Europe) decides that the findings of the inquiry into slave labor at Büssing will not be presented to any court at all. Instead, Rudolf Egger becomes the chairman of the Braunschweig Chamber of Industry and Commerce, and a few years later he receives permission from the federal state government to add Büssing to his surname, for his services to the nation.

On February 25, 1957, Firma Büssing Nutzkraftwagen Ltd. claims in a letter to one of your surviving fellow prisoners from *Unterkommando* Vechelde, a man in Paris named Henryk Kinas (who is demanding reparation for his unpaid labor in the factory), that Rudolf Egger-Büssing personally made sure you all got more food and better clothing than the SS regulations allowed, thereby running the risk of being arrested by the local SS, *von den örtlichen SS-Stellen verhaftet zu werden*, on suspicion of sabotage.

Yes, that's what the letter says, signed by Rudolf Egger-Büssing himself, and also—for the sake of appearances, I assume—by a Dr. Schirmeister. Payment of any damages to Henryk Kinas is consequently out of the question. If anything, he should rather be grateful for the management's courageous solicitude for his well-being.

In short, by 1957 the time has arrived for Rudolf Egger-Büssing to shamelessly claim the status of hero and benefactor.

The road from Auschwitz is lined with such shamelessness, I should tell you, with people who initially say they heard and saw nothing and in any case had nothing to do with it, and then say they opposed what they neither saw nor heard. Nothing to be surprised at, unfortunately, since a blatant lie is a well-tested weapon against the memory of something too many people have seen and heard for it to be forgotten. A blatant lie loosens the ground beneath what can't be forgotten and turns it into a quagmire. In its defense against such a weapon, therefore, memory must time and time again mobilize its collected arsenal of witnesses, documents, and relics to fortify, time and time again, the loosening ground beneath it.

There are those who testify against Rudolf Egger-Büssing's shameless discovery of his heroic contribution to the well-being of slave laborers, among them truck driver Erich Meyer, who was employed by Firma Büssing to take back-axle parts from the factory in Braunschweig to the factory in Vechelde. In the police investigation of 1946, Meyer says that in the same truck he also took paper bags and wooden boxes with a total of four hundred to five hundred dead bodies from *Aussenlager* Schillstrasse to *Aussenlager* Watenstedt.

Further testimony against Rudolf Egger-Büssing is provided by the memorial stones in the cemetery at Jammertal, outside the former camp at Watenstedt, to which Dr. Karl Liedke takes me one chilly day in March when a virginal layer of snow is covering the names of those who didn't know how to make the most of Firma Büssing's care for their well-being. I carefully brush the snow aside from Paweł Diamant, Tadeusz Goldman, and Jakob Urbach.

A final testimony against Rudolf Egger-Büssing is the fact that even two SS officers from the main camp in Neuengamme, inspecting the satellite camp in Schillstrasse in January 1945, feel impelled to order the immediate transport of two hundred slave laborers, sick or unfit for work, to the concentration camp hospital in Watenstedt.

The Jews among them do everything they can to avoid the transport, having learned in Auschwitz that in a concentration camp, hospital is a euphemism for gas chamber. The non-Jews, however, particularly the Frenchmen and the Russians brought here from Neuengamme and not from Auschwitz, can imagine nothing worse than *Aussenlager* Schillstrasse and see the transport of the sick as a gift from above. One fellow prisoner, a French doctor called Georges Salan, is surprised by the Jews' reaction: "You have to have seen it with your own eyes," he writes,

> the cunning, trickery, and desperate energy they employed to avoid going.... None had any desire to be labeled sick any more. The same individuals who recently stood in never-ending queues at the end of the working day to request a day's dispensation from work, their legs and feet so swollen with edema that they could hardly walk, suddenly summoned their last drop of strength to look as though they could still be good for something (*pour donner l'illusion qu'ils sont encore bons à quelque chose*).

This is what Georges Salan writes on page 163 of his book *Prisons de France et bagnes allemands* (French prisons and German slave camps), which is published as early as 1946 and could thus have served as evidence for the prosecution in the trial of Rudolf Egger that never takes place.

In Rudolf Egger's defense, it could nevertheless have been argued that the slave labor camps at Firma Büssing were superior to Auschwitz. That they in fact offered salvation from Auschwitz. That by comparison with Auschwitz, they were paradise. That in any event they were camps where death was not an end in itself but at the very most a regrettable setback to production. At Firma Büssing, the goal was trucks, as distinct from Auschwitz, where the goal was annihilation. Had engineer Otto Pfänder and finance director Otto Scholmeyer not presented themselves underneath the smoke from the crematoriums and personally selected a thousand or so men fit for work and assigned them for onward dispatch and delivery to Firma Büssing in Braunschweig, Auschwitz might well have been the final stop for them too.

And that's how it is. Auschwitz-Birkenau is the intended terminus for all of you. Ever since May 1944, the trains of cattle cars have been heading straight to Birkenau, practically straight to the gas chambers. From a newly constructed ramp, you can see the four crematorium chimneys rising toward the sky from behind a thin curtain of foliage. From mid-May to mid-July 1944, a steady stream of transports unload here a total of 437,000 Hungarian Jews, of whom 320,000 are immediately selected and sent down the short path to the changing rooms and shower rooms, and a few hours later have been reduced to smoke and ashes.

It is to this terminus, purposely built for the reception, killing, and disposal of thousands of people every day, that the last Jews of the Łódź ghetto are brought in August 1944, and it's here that two-thirds of those who boarded the train in Radogoszcz get off and are never heard from again. Of the approximately 67,000 people transported from Łódź to Auschwitz, only about 22,000 survive the initial selection process and the gas chambers. Of these, some 1,200 able-bodied men are selected in three separate instances in September and October 1944 to serve as slave labor for Firma Büssing in Braunschweig. Anyone thereby asserting that this particular group of men may owe their lives to Firma Büssing is not wholly wrong. Not all of those selected survive Firma Büssing, and not all of those surviving Firma Büssing survive the evacuation and the liberation, but compared to Auschwitz, Firma Büssing can be said to have been a sort of paradise, after all.

Yes, this is roughly how a defense for Rudolf Egger, later Egger-Büssing, could have been constructed. It could perhaps even have been reinforced by witness statements of survivors, mainly from the factory in Vechelde, where at times something approaching job satisfaction and camaraderie is said to have occurred, and where something akin to human feelings is said to have been shown by German foremen and civilian workers. Those working hard enough to exceed the rigidly set quotas could even be rewarded occasionally with coupons to be cashed in for cigarettes, pickled gherkins, and beetroot, and the most proficient workers could even advance to more specialized tasks. One of your workmates in Vechelde, M.Z., proudly told me much later how skilled he grew at the lathe, turning the casings for drive shaft housings; how in a twelve-hour shift he could turn casings for fifty drive shaft housings, to be mounted in fifty trucks; and that his German foreman, whose name was Hans, occasionally showed his appreciation by sticking an extra bit of bread to the lathe. And in fact a year later, you yourself write: "The first four weeks at Vechelde quite bearable, no problems with the food."

There's no denying that beatings occurred, that the food situation deteriorated over time, and that an SS guard used to station himself outside the privy to deliver a kick in the balls as a deterrent to anyone needing to go. There's no denying that you

116

were slaves, and that many died, but I can imagine a clever lawyer might nonetheless have succeeded in turning Rudolf Egger, later Egger-Büssing, into something of a hero.

All this is belied, of course, by the fact that the operation was built on, and entirely dependent on, the most repulsive of acts. Without Auschwitz, no slaves for Firma Büssing. Without the transports of Jews to the gas chambers, no able-bodied Jewish men for engineer Otto Pfänder and finance director Otto Scholmeyer to pick from. At a trial, Rudolf Egger might possibly have been able to claim that Auschwitz was beyond the scope of his responsibility, but he could hardly have claimed that he was unaware of the nature and conditions of the place from which Firma Büssing recruited its slave labor in the autumn of 1944. Nor does the fact that he was never brought to trial mean that the occupying Allied authorities deemed him innocent of war crimes, only that they deemed him to be more important for the reconstruction of the economy than for the restoration of justice.

The same calculation did not apply, however, to the head of Steinöl Ltd., Prof. Solms Wilhelm Wittig, who had a slave labor camp built for him by the SS at Schandelah, outside Braunschweig. What happened in *Aussenlager* Schandelah did not differ substantially from what happened in *Aussenlager* Schillstrasse, but the two hundred or so prisoners who died at Schandelah while working as slaves for Steinöl Ltd. came largely from the main camp at Neuengamme and not from Auschwitz, and they died principally while mining oil shale rather than making trucks and were primarily non-Jewish citizens of the victorious Allied states, rather than stateless Jews from the Łódź ghetto, and perhaps it was this last little difference that ruined the calculation for Prof. Solms Wilhelm Wittig. On January 2, 1947, he was put on trial in front of a British military court and a month later sentenced to death by hanging for "treatment of Allied state citizens in contravention of international law." Another factor that may have influenced the calculation was that operations at Steinöl Ltd. were of no postwar value, as there was no further demand for synthetic gasoline, whereas operations at Firma Büssing were considered to have a bright future. Admittedly, Prof. Wittig had his death sentence commuted to a twenty-year jail term from which he was reprieved in May 1955, so basically the same calculation applied to him as to Rudolf Egger, but the commandant of *Aussenlager* Schandelah, SS-Unterscharführer Friedrich Ebsen, was hanged with three of his subordinates on May 2, 1947, in Hamelin prison. It should here be noted that Friedrich Ebsen took his orders from the commandant of the Schillstrasse camp, SS-Hauptscharführer Max Kirstein, who was neither hanged nor sent to prison for his actions. Had there been a trial of Max Kirstein, it would have been revealed that he had a particular predilection for abusing his Jewish captives, referring to them by the abbreviation "3F," *faul, frech, fett* (lazy, insolent, fat). If he was feeling talkative, he sometimes extended this into a whole sentence, incorporating 4 Fs: *Wenn ein Jude zu viel frisst, dann wird er fett und faul und schliesslich auch frech* (If a Jew stuffs himself he grows fat and lazy and in the end insolent).

So no sentence was ever passed on the repulsive acts in Braunschweig. People were enslaved, used, and destroyed, but no one was held to account. The shameless lie triumphed, as did the shameless calculation weighing the value of truck produc tion against the value of justice—but as a wise rabbi has now been allowed to point out from a factory wall in Braunschweig, the future has a long past.

In the memorial area at Schillstrasse, Rudolf Egger-Büssing's past has caught up with him. On three gray boards, made of unbreakable acrylic and screwed tightly to a wall topped with sharp spikes to deter vandals, Christoph Egger-Büssing writes of his grandfather: "The facts are incontrovertible. I belong to a family that profited, directly and indirectly, from National Socialism. My grandfather was responsible for the exploitation of concentration camp inmates at Firma Büssing. The camp that was built beside his factory was a scene of inhumanity, a *Schauplatz von Unmenschlichkeit.*"

These are hard words from a grandson, particularly a grandson who also says that he loved and admired his grandfather. "The child in me cannot comprehend to this day," writes Christoph Egger-Büssing, "how Rudolf Egger-Büssing the private individual could allow the business leader of the same name to do what he did."

Diese Verstörung wird bleiben. The harm is done and will endure.

He makes a point of saying that we can't simply assume such harm will be remembered. That the easier reaction is blatant lies or convenient silence, that he himself would prefer to have kept quiet rather than speaking out, and that amnesia has time on its side.

They're fine words, and perhaps essentially true, and that's why I regard Dr. Liedke with a kind of love or tenderness as he walks quietly at my side, patiently showing me the memorial plaques and stones that line your road from Auschwitz and might not have been placed there had Dr. Liedke not been on hand to produce his painstakingly excavated fragments, documents, and testimonies.

With Karl Liedke's research in my briefcase and his map in my hand, I leave Braunschweig in March 2005 to follow the continuation of your road through the German camp archipelago in March 1945.

■

Maybe first I ought to say something about Auschwitz. At least about how you get out from there. Everyone knows, or ought to know, how you get there. It's unimaginable in its own way, but no mystery to posterity. You arrive in a barred and bolted cattle car that pulls in to a platform built in the spring of 1944 at walking distance from the gas chambers and crematoriums in order to speed up the murder and annihilation of Europe's Jews. You're transported in the same car as the rest of your family, along with what remains of the family from apartment number 3 at 18 Franciszkańska, among them the eighteen-year-old girl, really a woman now, the one you call Haluś and are in love with, who on this "nightmarish night on the way to hell" falls asleep with her head in your lap. I find it hard to imagine how anyone can fall asleep on such a journey, but then I find it hard to imagine such a journey at all. At any rate, that's how you recall the journey to Auschwitz in the letter you write on January 15, 1946, in a place very far from hell, to the young woman who is to be my mother: "You had fallen asleep on my lap and when you woke up, you burst into tears. That's how I saw you in my imagination and that's how I see you today."

Maybe Haluś really did fall asleep on your lap. Or perhaps you just remember her falling asleep there because that's how you have to remember her once you've been parted and you've lost each other and you've been ordered to join separate columns five abreast, men in one column and women and children in another, to be sorted onward into hell.

About the arrival much has already been said. What happens to you and Haluš happens with monotonous inconceivability to hundreds of thousands of people, who to the last cannot or will not understand what sort of place they've arrived in. On the ramp in Auschwitz-Birkenau, your mother Hadassah is sorted out for the gas chambers, as are Halus's mother Rachel and father Jakob, and Haluš's sister Dorka and her five-year-old son Obadja, as are most of the remaining Jews from the Łódź ghetto.

For them Auschwitz works as planned. Nothing remains. Not even a registration card with a name or a number. No numbers for those who shall never have existed. Death in the gas chambers is collective, anonymous, naked, and painstakingly shrouded in euphemisms (changing room, shower room, etc.), stage props (signs, birches, Red Cross vans, etc.), and unfathomability.

Unfathomability above all. A large part of the success rests on that.

The unfathomability.

From the smaller group, those not selected for the gas chambers, death makes a temporary, tactical retreat. The daily "maintenance" of the swelling camp requires thousands upon thousands of new slave laborers, the majority of whom starve to death, work to death, are beaten to death, get a bullet in the back of the neck or a phenol injection in the heart, or are reselected and sent to the gas chambers. On the platform in Auschwitz-Birkenau a certain Dr. Josef Mengele is also waiting, routinely selecting living human beings for deadly medical experiments. Subordinated to Auschwitz-Birkenau, moreover, is a growing archipelago of *Aussenlager* serving an expanding circle of German industries that build their entire operations on the selection of slaves from among the people delivered to the gas chambers. The largest business involved in this system is the IG Farben chemical industry conglomerate, which has been given its own camp in Auschwitz, Auschwitz III-Monowitz, also known as the Buna camp after the Buna works, the name of the factory that produces synthetic rubber and synthetic fuel and where some 30,000 slave laborers are worked to death.

Those selected to work themselves to death generally get a number tattooed on their forearm and are entered with pedantic precision into the registers of the SS bureaucracy. Every day at Auschwitz there are excruciating, hour-long roll calls, where the prisoners are assembled in straight lines so a check can be made on who's living, who's dead, who's missing, and who's too weak to work and therefore must die. Of the 405,000 people given a registration number on arrival at Auschwitz, 340,000 die. Of the 67,000 Jews delivered from the Łódź ghetto, 3,000 are given registration numbers in Auschwitz, while 19,000 are allocated to a no-man's-land between slave labor and gas chamber and left unregistered until further notice.

You belong to the latter group. You don't get a number tattooed on your forearm. For some reason, unknown until further notice, you're allowed to live as part of a not yet fully processed human reserve. Since May 1944, the Birkenau II extermination camp has had separate sections for people being kept alive while awaiting full processing. In the former camp for Gypsies (section BIIe), its 3,000 inhabitants having been fully processed in the gas chambers on August 2, 1944, there are vacant barracks, as there are in section BIIb, where 7,000 men, women, and children from the Theresienstadt ghetto, the so-called family camp, were kept until they too were fully processed, at night, between July 10 and

12, 1944. The not fully processed Jews from the Łódź ghetto are kept in the standard hellish conditions, or perhaps even worse, as they're forced to sleep outside, or on the floor, or sitting in long rows with the prisoner in front pressed between the legs of the prisoner behind. Nor are they given their own spoons and bowls, which is a precondition for survival in Auschwitz-Birkenau. The daily starvation rations of "soup" must be eaten without spoons from a bowl shared by four, however that is to be managed. A spoon and a bowl of your own is one of the differences between hell and paradise. Another is the smell of burned flesh. Everyone bears witness to that smell, including you. You all bear witness to the smell and the black smoke and the nightly flames from the tall chimneys a few kilometers away, all of you who survive the days and nights waiting to be fully processed in Birkenau II, where the gas chambers go full throttle and the crematoriums can't keep up and bodies have to be burned in huge pits in the open air.

This is probably one of the reasons for the delay in fully processing you: the pressure on the crematoriums. Another is the pressure from the fast-growing camp archipelago beyond the province of Auschwitz-Birkenau. Virtually every industry of any size in the now surrounded Germany is crying out for slaves. In the autumn of 1944, the camp archipelago extends new branches even farther into Germany, with almost every German concentration camp acting as a central command for countless outer camps and under camps and subdivisions that must be filled with slaves, but the only remaining slave reserve of any size is the Jews who are being delivered to the gas chambers in Auschwitz. In the late summer of 1944 some 30,000 Jews, mainly from Hungary and Poland, are set aside for possible onward delivery. Not all those set aside are delivered, and not all who are delivered survive, but being set aside for onward delivery is the first step on the road from Auschwitz.

I don't know how you keep track of the days and nights in Auschwitz. I understand how hard it is to keep track of such things when one's in a state of shock and the days and nights seem to blur together, but eighteen months later you write in a letter that you were in Auschwitz for twelve days. You also write that the sorting of prisoners starts immediately and that prisoners are shifted from barrack to barrack and disappear from view as the sorting proceeds, and that after a day or so you're separated from the Szames brothers. That's all you say about the Szames brothers, but Haluś, to whom your letter is addressed, clearly knows who they are, so I assume that you all must have known each other in Łódź, and that you all have arrived at Auschwitz in the same transport, and that with the Szames brothers yet another link to the world before Auschwitz disappears.

I assume that's why you mention it.

It must be noted, however, that you're not alone in Auschwitz. If you were alone, I find it hard to imagine that you'd be selected for onward delivery, and still harder that you'd survive. The pickers and choosers of Birkenau II pick the biggest and strongest and those who make the most convincing case for possessing the required skills. Now you may be as fit and strong as any young man could be after four years in the ghetto and twelve days in Auschwitz, but you're slight of build and not very tall or particularly pushy or enterprising—if you'll forgive me for saying that. So I can't imagine that you would have made it through the intrusive checks and interrogations at the selections for onward delivery on your own. One of the selection procedures involves setting up a wooden bar and rejecting all those who don't reach it. I'm not sure you would have reached the bar, nor am I sure you would have made a convincing case for being an experienced welder or lathe turner or electrician or whatever skill was demanded at the moment. There were people who made it through anyway, by a mixture of enterprise and desperation, but I think you made it because you weren't on your own. After the selection on the ramp, you still have your brother Naftali or Natek at your side, six years older than you, with more experience of life and, I think, a stronger survival instinct. Or at any rate, I think your survival is a compelling reason for him to survive. I think it's he who pulls you with him out of Auschwitz.

Many stories of survival are stories like that: one person pulls another along with him.

Being alone is a cause of death in Auschwitz.

It's just the two of you now, nobody else.

On the third day in Auschwitz, you come across Beno.

"You wouldn't have recognized him," you write in that letter to Haluš.

He'd grown so fat you could hardly see his eyes. I was still exhausted from the overture [the arrival at Auschwitz], felt punch-drunk and was reeling about like an idiot, and Beno made the whole thing worse. I simply didn't recognize him, he'd got into such a brutal way of expressing himself. This is what he told me: "Everyone except my sister ended up in the chimneys. Our lives are worthless, all you can do is enjoy eating and drinking, because we won't get out of here alive whatever happens. You know what, David, I don't believe in those transports. I bet they go to the chimneys, too." I told him it was all the same to me, I was still going to sign up for a transport, and things would have to take their course. I wanted to get on a transport as soon as possible, at any cost.

And in another letter: "There's not a lot to say about Beno. He didn't behave well at all, not that he harmed anybody, but there was a time, my first days in Auschwitz, when he could have helped me quite a bit but didn't. He pretended not to notice me."

This Beno has evidently been in Auschwitz for some time and knows what's going on there and has been promoted to some kind of Kapo or guard and gets plenty to eat at the expense of his fellow prisoners, and seeing him in Auschwitz affects you deeply. Among all the things that happen to you in Auschwitz and that you want to tell Haluś in a letter dated from Alingsås on March 10, 1946, the Beno episode looms large. You write more about your encounter with Beno than about anything else. I can only guess why that might be, and my guess is that you and Beno not only knew each other in the ghetto but were close friends, perhaps best friends, or at any rate close enough for his behavior to affect you deeply, and that the image of the fat, brutal Beno in Auschwitz still haunts you. Especially as Beno eventually turns up at the camp in Braunschweig, having left Auschwitz along the same narrow road as you.

It's your reaction to Beno that tells me you wouldn't have come through Auschwitz on your own.

Particularly the fact that in the letter, you forgive him.

Forgive him for what? If you had been a person capable of surviving Auschwitz on your own, there would have been nothing to forgive. What Beno did to you was what being alone did to people in Auschwitz.

Being alone was lethal in many ways.

"What he did means nothing anymore," you write to your Haluś. "I forgave him long ago."

On the twelfth day in Auschwitz, your brother and you, Natek and David Rosenberg, manage to get onto the first transport of Jewish men from Auschwitz to Braunschweig. To the very last, you're convinced you're going to a coal mine in Silesia. There are many rumors about where the transports are going, and of all the possibilities, a killing coal mine in Silesia may be the least bad. To Haluś you write: "After 24 hours the journey ended, and when we got off the train I couldn't believe my eyes, we were standing in a freight depot in the suburbs of Braunschweig."

At the end of March 1945, when the Büssing factories are bombed out of use, the slave camps in Braunschweig are evacuated. As ever more factories in Germany are bombed out of use, the slaves who can no longer be put to work in them are transported onward, primarily to other camps with factories still in operation.

When there are no factories left, the slave transports are left with no purpose—other than to erase all traces of the slave operation itself.

This is when hell reasserts itself.

First, your group is evacuated by truck to *Aussenlager* Salzgitter-Watenstedt, which in conjunction with Salzgitter-Drütte and Salzgitter-Bad supplies slave labor for the production of steel and ammunition in the Reichswerke Hermann Göring. The reason the Reichswerke Hermann Göring is still in operation is that production has largely been moved underground. You're put to work for two weeks, clearing the underground factory floors from falling debris after Allied bombing raids, but soon even the subterranean machinery for the production of German artillery shells is stopped, because American artillery shells have started falling on the factory complex.

Twenty-four hours before American troops occupy the Reichswerke Hermann Göring, you and some 1,600 other prisoners are loaded onto a train of open freight cars for immediate and chaotic evacuation to other parts of the camp archipelago. Every remaining prisoner in Watenstedt is loaded on board. The sick and the dying are brought from their sickbeds and wards on trucks, piled on top of each other like planks of wood, and then distributed among the freight cars. There can be no explanation for this precipitate evacuation, which includes the weak, the sick, and the dying, other than the intention to remove every last trace of you all.

It's the night of April 5–6, 1945, and there's a month to go until the German surrender, and the road from Auschwitz is still long. On the train pulling out of the station at Salzgitter-Watenstedt is the French doctor Georges Salan, who in Braunschweig had wondered why the Auschwitz Jews so desperately tried to avoid being allocated to transports of the sick. Maybe now he's not wondering anymore, because this is evidently a transport of the sick, and clearly a deadly one to boot. At any rate, death will be a logical consequence—and ultimately the purpose—of the conditions on the train. In every car there are between 50 and 60 prisoners, writes Salan. In every car there are between 80 and 90 prisoners, you write. There's food but no water, writes Salan. There's neither food nor water, you write. Maybe there are classes on this train, one for Jews and another for the rest, which makes no difference in the long run, because on the train everyone falls ill, and more and more are dying. There are no latrine buckets in the cars, so the prisoners relieve themselves in the food containers and try to dispose of the contents overboard, with varying degrees of success. Those who die are put in the last car of the train. There are many dying as the train with the open freight cars meanders like a Flying Dutchman through the German camp archipelago, searching for a camp or a grave to dump its cargo in.

That's how Salan describes it in his book.

That's how you describe it in your letter to Haluš in March 1946:

> We went from one camp to the next, and none of them were willing to take us. Men dropped like flies along the way. We got as far as the outskirts of Berlin, but no one wanted us there either, we had to turn around and go back, Oranienburg, Sachsenhausen, everywhere was crammed with prisoners [you use the German word *Häftling*]. Finally, on the ninth day, we got to Ravensbrück, 1/3 of the people had died on the way there. And the rest looked like ghosts.

You name some of the places along the train route, but there are more. In fact, the train is crossing large parts of northern Germany in a triangle between Braunschweig, Hamburg, and Berlin. With nearly twenty open freight cars crammed with the sick, the dying, and the dead, it presumably causes some stir among people who see it pass by, stopping at station after station in the hope of unloading part of its cargo. So the train stops at Schandelah, Oebisfelde, Bismarck, Uchtspringe, Havelberge, Ludwigslust, Hagenow, and Bergedorf, which is a borough of Hamburg. This last stop indicates that the transport is ultimately intended for KZ Neuengamme, the main concentration camp for all the satellite camps in the Braunschweig and Salzgitter area, but KZ Neuengamme is full to bursting. So the train turns back east, toward Berlin and the Sachsenhausen-Oranienburg concentration camp, which also, as you note, is full to bursting with *Häftlinge*. After nine days (I cannot fathom how you keep track of time), the train reaches the Ravensbrück concentration camp, ninety kilometers north of Berlin.

It's April 14, 1945, and this is where you're all unloaded.

It should be noted, however, that you're not the first to be unloaded. At about ten in the evening of April 8, the train with the open freight cars from Watenstedt makes an extended stop in Uchtspringe. The local district doctor, Dr. Behnke, notes down the following: "On board the train there were 66 dead bodies. Transport leader SS-Rottenführer Winkler and Dr. Mittelstedt, an accompanying Polish doctor, no. 3506, asked my permission to bury the bodies, which were in various stages of decomposition. The destination of the train was not known to me. The bodies were buried on Monday 9 April in a mass grave at Kiesberg."

■

With Dr. Liedke's map on the front seat beside me, I follow in the tracks of the train. It isn't easy following railroad tracks in a car, especially if those tracks have in places been repositioned and straightened out, and the stations that once dotted the line have been left behind on overgrown lots, with rusting rails and collapsing station houses.

That's why it takes me a while to locate the old station at Uchtspringe, where 66 corpses were unloaded on April 8, 1944. The new station, a naked platform with no station building on a straightened fast track between Hannover and Berlin, is located a bit outside of Uchtspringe. I find the old station house roughly where I expect it to be, along the still detectable embankment running through the town, and the station house is indeed on the point of collapse. The roof has sagged inward, the gray plaster has flaked off, the windows are boarded up, the canopy that extends over the waiting area by the former platform is damp and rotten. On the front of a half-timbered, red-brick storehouse, the name Uchtspringe still stands out in big black letters on a white background, but a newer sign put up by the German Railroad Authority, Deutsche Bahn, warns against entering the station area. *Unfallgefahr. Betreten für Unbefugte verboten.*

It is at this station, on this platform, within view of practically the whole of Uchtspringe, that a train of open freight cars loaded with 1,600 concentration camp prisoners, all sick and dying in varying degrees, "stops for a considerable length of time" (Dr. Behnke) while 66 bodies are taken off and buried.

After liberation, American troops open the mass grave to identify the dead, but find that all means of identification have been removed—by SS-Rottenführer Winkler personally, according to Georges Salan. The bodies, still nameless, are then reburied one by one.

I search for the memorial dedicated to them that ought to be in Uchtspringe.

I search for other memorials in Uchtspringe, too. The little town is still dominated by its large psychiatric hospital, attractively set in a beautiful park, and today serving as the federal state of Sachsen-Anhalt's central institution of forensic psychiatry, Landeskrankenhaus für Forensische Psychiatrie Uchtspringe. In the 1930s it bore the name Landesheilanstalt Uchtspringe and was one of the Third Reich's main centers for forced sterilization and the killing of lunatics and other inferior human material. Between 1934 and 1941, 765 patients were forcibly sterilized at Uchtspringe. Between 1940 and 1945, some 500 patients, most of them children, were murdered at Uchtspringe with drug overdoses. Between July 1940 and July 1941, 741 patients from Uchtspringe were transported to the gas chambers built at the psychiatric hospitals of Brandenburg an der Havel and Bernburg in the state of Saxony-Anhalt, where they were murdered as part of the German euthanasia program T4.

Since September 15, 2004, there's a memorial dedicated to them in front of the ivy-clad main building dating from 1894, a bronze plaque on a rough-hewn granite stone, bearing the words "To the women, men, and children who were humiliated and killed in Landesheilanstalt Uchtspringe, or sent from here to their deaths." It's emphasized that this took place under National Socialism, *während des Nationalsozialismus*.

A completely different time, we are to understand, with completely different people.

Why did it take so long for a memorial to appear?

I look for the memorial to the 66 men from your train who are buried here and find a reddish-brown sign with a cross and the word *Kriegsgräberstätte*, "War burial site," with an arrow pointing up a small hill. I trudge up the 250 snow-covered meters of the scarcely discernible path from the road to the top and find a narrow walkway lined with small thuja trees, at the end of which stands a brick-built grave monument with a polished plaque in black stone. Sticking out of the snow at the foot of the monument are the pine twigs of a wreath. On the black plaque, six words are engraved: HIER RUHEN 66 OPFER DES FASCHISMUS. "Here lie 66 victims of Fascism."

I'm touched by the exact figure. From a train carrying some 1,600 prisoners, of which a large but forever inexact number will die before journey's end, the exact number of the bodies unloaded at the Uchtspringe station has been preserved by history and carved into stone by the good citizens of Uchtspringe, at a time when the town was part of the German Democratic Republic (DDR). Even if you didn't know that Uchtspringe was once part of East Germany, and might perhaps be surprised to learn it, since it was American troops who liberated Uchtspringe and tried to clarify the identities of the 66 bodies in the mass grave, the text on the grave monument leaves no room for doubt. For the good citizens of the DDR, National Socialism was the history of another Germany. Theirs was an unbroken struggle against "fascism," which was the shameless lie that for four decades undermined the memory of what actually happened. In

DDR history, it was another Germany's train that made a longer stop at Uchtspringe, and another Germany's doctors who prescribed death to more than a thousand of their patients in Uchtspringe.

Historical coincidence determined how the event would be remembered. In the month following the end of the war, the armistice lines between the armies of the victorious powers were tidied up a little, and some of the troops were moved around. On July 1, 1945, American troops moved out of Uchtspringe and Soviet troops moved in, and sixty-six men in a mass grave were transformed from victims of the German Reich to victims of "fascism."

I decide not to follow the train on its long detour from Uchtspringe via Wittenberge to Bergedorf in Hamburg, and drive directly to Ravensbrück.

Dr. Liedke gives me a copy of the Ravensbrück list. Well, not the whole list, but the page with your name on it. Of the documents from the slave camp archipelago, it's the only one I have that bears your name. It's a handwritten list compiled by the SS in Ravensbrück, and on it you appear as David Rosenberg and your brother Natek as Nathan Rosenberg, first Natek and then you. Rosenberg is spelled with an *s*, Natek appears as Nathan rather than Naftali, and your date of birth is 1926 rather than 1923, but it's undoubtedly the two of you on the list. You're entered as numbers 315 and 316. Prisoner category: Polish Jew. Birthplace: Widawa. Delivery: Auschwitz 26 VIII 1944. Dispatch: Wattenstedt (*sic*). Old prisoner numbers (from the SS registers at Neuengamme): 50648 and 50649. New prisoner numbers (for the SS registers in Ravensbrück): 18300 and 18301. Beside the prisoner numbers is a firmly penciled check mark, although not by the non-Jewish names. If I didn't know what I know, I'd assume that the Jews thus marked were selected for a worse hell than the rest, but in Ravensbrück the unimaginable happens: the Jews are selected for a better one. I don't know if the check marks on the list apply to that particular selection, but it may well be so. At any rate, the checks entitle the Jewish inmates to a food parcel from the Red Cross.

It's April 14, 1945, and the front is approaching, and the stated aim of the increasingly deadly prisoner marches and transports through the German camp archipelago is to wipe out all traces of themselves; or as Himmler himself puts it on April 18, 1945, to ensure that no prisoner falls into enemy hands alive.

Kein Häftling darf lebend in die Hände des Feindes fallen.

Given another month, they might have done it. Of the 700,000 or so concentration camp inmates entered in the SS registers in January 1945, a third die in the final months of the war; dropping like flies, as we hear in testimony after testimony, not only yours. Toward the end, this is the sole remaining purpose of the evacuation transports: to make you disappear from the world.

And then, in Ravensbrück, after nine days on a train of open freight cars with a special car in the rear for the dead, your names are checked for a five-kilo food parcel from the Red Cross.

The Jews, specifically.

How is it possible? Ravensbrück is a concentration camp (mainly for women). In Ravensbrück, the SS is in absolute control. In Ravensbrück, prisoners are dying in vast numbers, 50,000 of them altogether, and from February 1945 onward in a newly installed gas chamber. In March and April 1945, 25,000 prisoners are evacuated from Ravensbrück in order to disappear. In

Ravensbrück, too, no prisoner is to fall into enemy hands alive. SS men who check off Jews, especially, for life-saving food parcels are not only going against Himmler's express orders, but they're also sabotaging what to the very end remains the overriding mission of the SS empire: the annihilation of the Jews.

Who has the authority to order such a thing?

Himmler himself, it turns out. In the last months of the war, SS-Reichsführer Heinrich Himmler is playing a double game of life and death with a Swedish count named Folke Bernadotte. Himmler thinks he's playing for his own life after the surrender, and Folke Bernadotte, head of the Swedish Red Cross, thinks he's playing, at least initially, for the lives of Norwegian and Danish citizens in Himmler's concentration camps. With the war still raging, these people, in columns of white buses with Swedish flags and red crosses painted on them, are to be evacuated to life, not to death. More pressure is then brought to bear, widening the operation to include Danish and Norwegian Jews as well, and toward the end of April gravely ill women from Ravensbrück. At the same time, a Swedish representative of the World Jewish Congress, Gilel (Hillel) Storch, a Jewish businessman from Latvia who has managed to escape to Sweden, is simultaneously negotiating with Himmler, the Swedish government, and the International Red Cross about sending food parcels to surviving Jews in the German concentration camps. "In the Ravensbrück camp there are 35,000 Jewish women literally starving to death," writes Gilel Storch on March 19, 1945, in a letter to legation counselor Hellstedt of the Royal Department for Foreign Affairs in Sweden.

As you no doubt realize, this is a story in itself, and it's really not about you or any of the Polish Jewish men aboard the meandering train of freight cars from *Aussenlager* Watenstedt, but in

Ravensbrück the food parcels and your road from Auschwitz just happen to cross paths. Those food parcels are a big thing, probably decisive to your survival, and the events associated with them remain vivid in your memory eleven months later, in that letter to Haluś:

Here [in Ravensbrück] they started talking about some parcels from the American Red Cross, and, believe it or not, the following day actually handed out parcels, each parcel to be shared by two. People went sort of crazy with happiness, and no wonder. A few weeks before the end of the war and here's a dirty, hungry Häftling tucking into American chocolate, biscuits etc.

On the third day we were given another parcel, and news started to spread that the Jews were going to Sweden, but nobody believed it. I thought to myself that people had been so overwhelmed by the food parcels that they were starting rumors and gossip.

But people weren't talking through their hats this time, either, because a few days later we hear somebody shouting: "*Alle Juden.*" This was hardly music to my ears, for what could they possibly want with all the Jews, but we had no choice but to fall in. We were then 800 Jews among 6,000 [inmates] of other nationalities. An SS man gave us a speech: "At roll call tomorrow morning, the Jews are to stand to one side. You're going to Sweden. The Swedish Red Cross will come and get you."

Right away I thought of Biebow's speech in the ghetto: "Now we'll have some new guests arriving." Actually I could have hidden and stayed behind, because I'd met a German Häftling I knew from the previous camp, and he was now a barrack guard. He said that if I didn't want to go, I could stay. But he also said there was nothing to be afraid of, because the story about going to Sweden was true. I believed him because I knew he was a good friend, so why sit there in a camp if I could be free in a few days.

137

But still it was completely incomprehensible.

Could it be possible for a Jew to survive the war?

The next day we were taken from the camp [in freight cars], and for the journey we were each given three American parcels and could have had more if we'd wanted. So how could we not believe it?

On the parcels it said, American Red Cross *durch Vermittlung Schwedischen Roten Kreuz—an den Ältesten der Juden in Ravensbrück*. And in some of the parcels there were cans of meat labeled "kosher." Now we were certain we'd been rescued.

At midnight, the train stopped. A civilian we recognized as a Kapo (this time a German Jew) came into our car. He wasn't wearing his prison suit any longer, but normal civilian clothes, with a white armband. He spoke to us in German, and this all took place in the presence of the SS men who were escorting us: "I've heard there are various rumors circulating among you, that you're dubious about all this (the journey to Sweden), that you're afraid and talking of crematoriums, etc. Put all that out of your minds. The hours of this war are numbered. You see these SS men (and he pointed at them)? They still have their rifles, but you can be sure they'd like to throw them away now. They're no longer our enemies. Let us not blame anyone, though it's true that your children, mothers, fathers, and so on have been burned in the crematoriums. But they aren't guilty of this. The whole of Europe is in ruins, don't avenge yourselves on the Germans, they're not the only ones guilty of this war, the whole world has gone mad, everyone is guilty. Englishmen, Americans, etc."

During this speech the SS men stood with heads lowered. Kapo Meyer (that was the name of the German Jew) told us all to stand up and sing "Hatikvah"[the anthem of the Zionist movement]. Just imagine, three weeks before the end of the war, 800 Jews on German soil singing "Hatikvah" and SS men presenting arms (that's what it looked like in our car). People were moved to tears.

I must hurry up with my story, I'm afraid I'm already boring you.

Allow me here, before you resume boring the woman who will become my mother, to insert one detail about the food parcels. Though it's true they're labeled RED CROSS, my guess is that the labels do not say AMERICAN RED CROSS but INTERNATIONAL RED CROSS, as anything else would hardly be possible; this is Nazi Germany, after all, still at total war with America, and it's hard enough to understand how even this much is possible. Again, a story apart. Not that it matters, not now and not then, but just so your account jibes with my documents. You're quite right about the Americans' being behind the food parcels, but they're operating primarily through a body called the War Refugee Board, set up by President Roosevelt on January 22, 1944, and tasked with taking immediate steps "to forestall the plan of the Nazis to exterminate all the Jews and other persecuted minorities in Europe."

One such step is to finance the 40,000 parcels of kosher food that in February 1945 are warehoused at the port of Gothenburg and which, through the mediation of Gilel Storch and others, are handed over to the International Red Cross to be transported by rail, primarily to the Theresienstadt, Bergen-Belsen, and Ravensbrück concentration camps, and expressly for distribution to Jewish inmates. Some 7,500 of the parcels from Gothenburg reach Ravensbrück sometime in April. I assume that toward the end of your journey, one or two of these parcels save your life. Each parcel contains twenty Camel cigarettes, vitamin tablets, a bar of soap, half a kilo of dried milk, chocolate, biscuits,

139

half a kilo of margarine, a can of corned beef (marked kosher), a can of cheese, and a can of tuna fish.

The food parcels not only save lives, they also kill. Starving bodies cannot suffer the shock of solid food. Hunger must be controlled to be vanquished. Not everyone is capable of such control, and a can of corned beef, however kosher it may be, is no child's plaything. "There are evidently different methods for killing people; by gas chamber or by Red Cross parcels," notes Dr. Georges Salan, counting 58 Jewish prisoners dying from the food parcels in Ravensbrück.

The train carrying the singing Kapo and the SS men presenting arms never completes the announced journey to Sweden, but you don't explain why. This is where you hurry up with your story a bit so as not to bore the woman who is to be my mother. Dr. Liedke's investigations reveal that the trainload of Polish Jews from Łódź sets off from Ravensbrück in the direction of Hamburg on April 24 but comes under attack from Allied bombers and is forced to turn back. The German railroad lines are common bombing targets in the last weeks of the war. I find it hard to fathom how you can gloss over something like that, but I'm starting to realize that on your road from Auschwitz, the cancellation of a train ride to freedom is just another wrong turn in the growing chaos of war, where no one knows what's real or unreal anymore: food parcels, death transports, liberation, annihilation, the Red Cross, the SS, truth, lies. I imagine the only things that really exist for you on that train are the food parcels in your hands, but I'm not sure everyone's convinced that even those are real. Nor am I at all sure whether you and the others on the train realize what's happening, or why the train is turning back, or even that it's doing so. Trains have a tendency to shunt to and fro, to move from one track to another, without necessarily changing their destination. Maybe your two stays in Ravensbrück blur into one, with the food parcels being the all-suppressing link between the two. Maybe all days, dates, and events are blurred together. The last white buses leave Ravensbrück on April 25 under the command of the Swedish lieutenant Åke Svenson. That same day, a "Swedish" train leaves Ravensbrück for Hamburg with 4,000 women loaded on fifty freight cars, but the train disappears in the fog of war and is found four days later outside Lübeck, where its engine has broken down. When the trucks are unbolted, four women are found dead while others are in a very bad state and have to be taken to a hospital, but this "ghost train" is nonetheless able to continue its journey to the Danish border with 3,989 surviving Ravensbrück women. The train carrying the singing Kapo and the arms-presenting SS men apparently left a couple of days earlier, yet it does not, as far as I've been able to establish, feature in the narrative of those who were saved from Ravensbrück. The ghost train of Lübeck is there, but not the train with the singing Kapo. If you were on the way to Sweden, as you were expressly told, why is there no record of it other than your story and Dr. Liedke's story and, I assume, the stories of all the others who share the experience, on a train from Ravensbrück, of a Jewish Kapo intoning the new Jewish national anthem in front of SS men presenting arms?

Maybe the Kapo and the SS men got their trains muddled up.

Maybe you and the others weren't on your way to Sweden.

Maybe there was never any intention of rescuing you at all.

Be that as it may, there is certainly no intention of rescuing you when you leave Ravensbrück a second time.

"Instead of Sweden, we were sent to Wöbbelin," continues the letter you fear might bore the woman who is to be my mother.

I like your concise, low-key style. You really are doing your best not to bore your reader.

The story of Wöbbelin can hardly bore anyone.

■

The rail route from Ravensbrück to Wöbbelin runs due west, first through an area of lakes with long stretches of deciduous woodland and narrow forest roads, then through increasingly open agricultural countryside with small villages and towns along the roads, which are still narrow but now lined with poplars. When traveling by car, however, one can go west from Ravensbrück only by first going north for about ten kilometers and then taking the exit for Wesenberg and Mirow, and it's not a straight route, particularly if you want to avoid the Berlin-to-Hamburg superhighway, which I do. Between Ravensbrück and Wöbbelin there are plenty of minor roads to go astray on, roads where in moments of inattention one runs the risk of being caught on camera.

It's actually the road to Ludwigslust I'm taking, since Wöbbelin is too small to appear on my map. Wöbbelin is five kilometers north of Ludwigslust, so if I find the one, I ought to find the other. Ludwigslust has been called a gem of a town, as its name perhaps hints. At the end of the eighteenth century, the Mecklenburgian Grand Duke Christian Ludwig had a palace built here to satisfy his lust for hunting. Around the same time, he had a church built at an appropriate distance from the palace, perhaps to set limits to his lusts.

Ludwigslust is indeed a gem. Both the palace and the church are still standing, and the area between them has long been an

142

open common, lined with old linden trees and well-preserved half-timbered houses. The only thing disturbing the idyll, on closer inspection, are the two hundred flat gravestones in four straight rows, fifty stones per row, lying along the walkway between the linden trees, two rows on each side. Half the stones are engraved with a cross and half with a Star of David. That's all. No names, no dates, no explanation. The stones are pale gray granite, and for particular reasons especially thick (eight centimeters) and extremely heavy (fifty-five kilos), and sunk deep into the ground, and provided with a graffiti-proof glaze. In short, they would be awkward to remove, and difficult to vandalize. For a gem of a town to have its most central place covered by gravestones is, after all, rather unexpected—and not entirely uncontroversial, either.

Especially not as the graves were dug once upon a time by the residents of the town themselves, at the command of American troops.

The forced digging takes place on May 7, 1945. While the world is celebrating the German surrender, two hundred dead bodies from Wöbbelin are lying in rows between the palace and the church. They are all wrapped in commandeered white cloth, carried to the freshly dug graves by Germans ordered to do so, and laid out on simple field stretchers, their tormented, emaciated faces left clearly visible. Every grave is marked by a white wooden cross. A voice-over on the documentary film of the mass burial announces that fifty-one of the two hundred graves are marked with a white Star of David, but none of these stars is seen in the film. What we do see are the residents of Ludwigslust, eyes lowered and heads bare, filing past the shrouded bodies. The townspeople are all well nourished and well dressed, in many cases even dressed in their best, and do not seem to have grasped yet what is happening. Some women dressed in black are seen hesitantly placing flowers on some of the bodies, as if not quite knowing whether this is the appropriate thing to do, or as if at the last moment they are recoiling from the exposed faces. In his burial address, the American military chaplain, Major George B. Woods, hammers home their guilt and shame: "Within four miles of your comfortable homes 4,000 men were forced to live like animals, deprived even of the food you would give to your dogs.... Though you claim no knowledge of these acts you are still individually and collectively responsible for these atrocities."

The contrast between death in Wöbbelin and life in Ludwigslust is grotesque and provocative, and the impulse to hold the well-nourished and well-dressed to account is hard to suppress. Revenge hangs in the air. Anger seeks an outlet. The decision to turn the prettiest place in Ludwigslust into a cemetery and memorial site answers a demand. The well-nourished and well-dressed are to be taught a lesson they'll never forget. Never again shall they be able to stroll under the linden trees in the parkland between the palace and the church without being reminded of the atrocities in Wöbbelin.

That's the idea, but it doesn't turn out that way. Less than a year later, just as in Uchtspringe, the American troops are replaced by Soviet troops, and within a year or two the white wooden crosses and Stars of David are gone, and soon the blatant lie (we knew nothing and could do nothing) settles like thick grass over the memory, and had it been up to the good citizens of Ludwigslust in the German Democratic Republic, set free from history, the grass on the graves would have been left to grow higher and higher.

When the lawn between the palace and the church is nevertheless dug up again, it's because people with good reason to remember the atrocities in Wöbbelin are suddenly able to return. A good ten years after the fall of the Berlin wall, Leonard Linton, a former corporal in the 82nd Airborne Division of the US Army, returns, and in November 2000 he launches a scheme to have the graves restored. Half the work is to be paid for from public funds and half by private donations, and what might still be lacking he'll pay from his own pocket. Linton quickly gains a hearing from the local politicians of another era, and on April 22, 2001, the new, heavyweight, graffiti-resistant granite stones are laid out between the palace and the church, at exactly the same spot where once the wooden crosses and Stars of David stood. The day before, hundreds of neo-Nazis had marched through the streets of Ludwigslust and, stopping just a few steps away from the still unmarked grave lots, demanded honor and rehabilitation for the SS (and by extension for the perpetrators of Wöbbelin). The need for heavy granite and graffiti-proof glaze is thus dramatically illustrated.

On May 2, 2001, the fifty-sixth anniversary of the liberation of Wöbbelin, the graves in Ludwigslust are rededicated in the presence of, among others, some ten of the Jewish men from the

Łódź ghetto who were dispatched from Auschwitz in September and October 1944 to the Büssing factories in Braunschweig and in April 1945 were loaded aboard a train in Ravensbrück that was said to be taking them to Sweden but took them instead to a place called Wöbbelin. They're all visibly moved by the commotion and, it seems, still somewhat surprised. Fifty-six years is a long time, and they may be wondering why nobody's been in touch before, and I sense that they feel like pinching themselves now and then as they walk past the newly laid gravestones between the palace and the church in Ludwigslust and it gradually sinks in that the well-nourished and well-dressed have once again, this time of their own volition and apparently for posterity, allowed the memory of the atrocities in Wöbbelin to be etched into the prettiest part of their town, so none of them will henceforth be able to stroll with their children or grandchildren under the linden trees beyond the palace lake without running the risk of being questioned about the graves.

Unless it's winter, of course, and a layer of newly fallen snow covers everything, and they'll have to know exactly where to brush the snow off a bit so that the question about the graves can be asked.

In the long run, who wants to remember Wöbbelin?

At the Hotel Mecklenburger Hof, in the bar decorated with hunting paraphernalia, I get into a conversation with a man and a woman of about forty who have fallen in love, and have obtained separate divorces, and are having a drink to celebrate their good fortune. He's an engineer from the West and she a nurse from the East, and they've just moved here, so it doesn't seem the right time to bring up the graves in the park.

When I leave Ludwigslust the next morning, it has stopped snowing. You won't need a map for Wöbbelin, the woman at the reception desk assures me. Just continue a few kilometers along the road from the hotel. You can't miss it.

■

Wöbbelin isn't on the American troops' map either. They don't know of any place with such a name, still less that it's a concentration camp, when they enter Ludwigslust on May 2, 1945. Only after they spot three naked, emaciated men in a broken shop window, trying to swap their striped prison clothes for something better, is the existence of Wöbbelin revealed. The camp has been abandoned by the SS during the night, and some of the inmates have managed to "go shopping" in Ludwigslust, and around noon, troops from the US 82nd Airborne Division move out to the north, following directions.

"One could smell Wobelein [*sic*] Concentration Camp before seeing it. And seeing it was more than a human being could stand," writes the American commander, General James M. Gavin, in his memoirs.

Aussenlager Wöbbelin in the Neuengamme archipelago is one of the last concentration camps to be set up in Nazi Germany. It's in existence for ten weeks, from February 12 to May 2, 1945. Its main and before long sole function is to kill off its inmates. In Wöbbelin there are neither armament industries crying out for slave workers, nor a system for exploiting them otherwise, nor a system for keeping them alive, nor a system for putting them to death. Wöbbelin is hell, organized as the absence of every human necessity. Within the newly unfurled barbed wire and the hastily erected watchtowers, a few unfinished brick barracks stand in the late winter chill; the roofs leak, the windows have no glass, the doorways no doors, and the floors no floor-boards; the prisoners sleep on the ground, with nothing to lie on or to cover them, many of them wearing only their prison clothes, stiff with dirt. There's scarcely any water (one polluted pump for the whole camp), scarcely any food (initially a kilo of bread and half a liter of "soup" to be shared among ten prisoners with no plates or cutlery, afterward less and less, and toward the end nothing). An overflowing latrine pit soon forces everyone to relieve themselves anywhere but there, and the total lack of washing facilities soon leads to deadly epidemics.

In the course of ten weeks, at an accelerating rate, more than a thousand of the five thousand prisoners in Wöbbelin die. At the beginning of April, some forty are dying every day, but by the end of the month, when you arrive, between eighty and a hundred. A few more unliberated days and the camp would have fulfilled its mission. Until the middle of April, the corpses are dumped into newly dug mass graves in the sandy heathland beyond the forest, a few kilometers from the camp and not far from the railroad track that links Wöbbelin to the rest of the dis-integrating camp archipelago. It happens that living bodies are thrown into the mass graves as well. In the piles of dead bodies, one or two are still breathing.

"Living skeletons were scattered about, the dead distinguish-able from the living only by the blue-black color of their skin," writes James M. Gavin.

Another difference between the living and the dead is that the living sometimes eat the dead. Not that there's much on the dead worth eating, but cannibalism in Wöbbelin is a known and certified fact. Toward the end of April, there are too many bodies to be moved to the mass graves, so they're piled up in one of the barracks instead. In a photograph taken at the liberation, most of the dead are lying naked, or rather, stripped of their clothing. In another photograph, the living are wearing double layers. Yet another difference between the living and the dead in Wöbbelin.

For you, the difference between life and death is the food parcels.

The food parcels and the timing.

At the time of your arrival, liberation is a week away.

You need only to survive a week in Wöbbelin to survive the war.

I'm not sure you would have survived a week in Wöbbelin without the food parcels.

To my knowledge, the transport from Ravensbrück to Wöbbelin is the only transport in disintegrating Germany where prisoners en route to their planned disappearance eat corned beef and smoke Camel cigarettes on the train. I learn of comparable transports on which the prisoners drop like flies and are buried here and there along the embankments, for example in the town of Sülsdorf on the railroad line a few dozen kilometers north of Wöbbelin, where 217 women and 129 men in transit from *Aussenlager* Beendorf are buried; those who survive all the way to Wöbbelin aren't in much better shape. Death in Wöbbelin is continuously reinforced with the dying delivered by the transports.

The food parcels are and remain a mystery to me. If you're not bound for Sweden to survive but for Wöbbelin to disappear, why the parcels? Is the whole thing just a grotesque joke? The Nazis specialize in grotesque jokes. In euphemisms and grotesque jokes. Why aren't the food parcels confiscated? How are you able to hang on to your food parcels in a camp where the living are eating the dead?

149

I find it hard to visualize you with a food parcel in Wöbbelin, but as you know, there's a great deal I find hard to visualize.

You write that it's the food parcels that save you in Wöbbelin, particularly the cigarettes. You write in your letter to the woman who is to be my mother that you have two hundred American cigarettes in Wöbbelin, and you make it sound like a small fortune. Clearly, you don't want to give her the impression that you've had a particularly hard time on your road from Auschwitz: "As you can see from what I tell you, things weren't all that terrible. I somehow sense that you've been through worse."

This is what you sense, since she's not telling you anything about *her* road from Auschwitz. Letter after letter, and she tells you nothing. Your sense is that someone who doesn't tell has something unspeakable to hide. The fact that she doesn't tell fills you with anxiety. I believe that *you* tell in order to make *her* tell. But think of it, how much do you actually tell her? Almost nothing about your days in Wöbbelin. In Wöbbelin "they had it in for us" is as far as you go in terms of detail. You write about the leaky huts and the "terrible" hunger, but say nothing of the living dead.

It suddenly dawns on me what you mean by the verb "to bore." To bore is to tell someone something you don't want to burden her with. To bore. To speak of the unbearable.

So you tell what's bearable to tell. The liberation, for example. On May 1, 1945, the Americans are on the outskirts of Ludwigslust and the Germans make one last attempt to follow Himmler's orders. In the afternoon you're ordered to board yet another train of open freight cars. A hundred and thirty of you to a car, you write. You also write that you all knew what was at stake:

If that train reached its destination, we'd had it. We stood in the cars all night. On the morning of May 2, we heard the guards telling each other the Führer was dead. At ten o'clock they hustled us back to the camp, and at twelve we were free. I just can't say any more about all this, but when we meet again, which will be soon, we'll have lots to tell each other.

That's all you write to the woman who is to be my mother.

You don't write about things no one's going to understand anyway.

You don't write about the unbearable.

The day after the liberation of Wöbbelin, the local population is ordered to view the camp. There's a photographic record of this event. A young woman with a coat and handbag is looking in horror at the dead bodies on the ground and has put one hand to her heart; another holds her hand to her mouth and stares at the camera, eyes open wide; an elderly man with a stick and a peaked cap looks doggedly straight ahead. Wherever they direct their gaze, the dead stare back at them. Hundreds of dead people. Piles of dead people. The 3,500 prisoners still alive at Wobbelin stare back at the townspeople too. Many of the surviving prisoners are incapable of moving from the spot, let alone taking their revenge on the well-nourished and well-dressed people filing past them. One or two get their hands on a well-dressed local's jacket or coat, but that's all. Some try to welcome their liberators with cheers and national anthems, but most lack the energy. Many die during the liberation and many more after the liberation; those still alive are cared for in a makeshift hospital in an aircraft hangar on the edge of Ludwigslust and, once the hangar is full, in one of the permanent hospitals and nursing homes in the town and surrounding area. "The comfortable bed in the little palace in the town of Ludwigslust" is how you describe the hospital or nursing home where you're treated for typhus over the course of several weeks before continuing your journey.

Wöbbelin isn't the end of your road from Auschwitz.

■

In Wöbbelin there's not much for the previous night's newly fallen snow to conceal; all traces of the former camp have been erased long since. Only a memorial stone of unhewn granite at the side of road 106 from Ludwigslust and an information board with a map on the edge of a sparse copse of birches mark the location of the camp. I suspect the birches date from the liberation, and I'm amazed at how small an area it is, maybe thirteen or fourteen acres in all, and how easy it is to expunge the traces of hell, and how close it actually is to the mass graves. The graves too have been taken over by trees, a meager wood of young pines, and the only thing to mark what's hidden beneath them is an engraved memorial plaque on a flat slab of stone on the edge of the wood. I clear away the four-inch layer of snow that has covered the inscription like a blank page and read:

> Here lie the victims of a camp that was situated just a few hundred meters east of this spot. They died of starvation, illness and brutal mistreatment. We do not know their names but we shall never forget them.

How long will anyone remember the victims of Wöbbelin? The memorial stone is new, as is the signpost pointing through the trees to the mass graves. There's another stone, visibly older and more like an ordinary gravestone, standing discreetly a little farther in among the pines, the words engraved in it already rendered illegible by dirt, moss, and neglect. Again, the new memorial plaque seems to be covered in some kind of graffiti-proof substance, the snow slips off so easily.

In Wöbbelin, if one can talk of being in a place one's immediately out of, the memory of the dead in the camp is shared with the memory of the nineteenth-century German poet Theodor Körner, in a building erected in 1938 to honor this cultural icon of the Third Reich. Theodor Körner wrote romantic poetry in which he glorified and heroized war, and he died in a manner befitting his writings, in a skirmish between Prussian militia and a French baggage train near Wöbbelin (to be more precise, at a place by the name of Rosenberg) on August 23, 1813. In the nineteenth century his grave monument, a lyre crossed by a sword, became a place of pilgrimage for German nationalists, and during the Nazi era an official cult site, where German recruits were gathered to swear their oath to the Führer. This ceremony—the *Waffenübernahme an der Körnerstätte*—took place for the last time in mid-March 1945.

This is not to say that every poet revered by the Nazis deserved such a fate, it's only that Goebbels ended his infamous speech at the Berlin Sports Palace on February 18, 1943, *Wollt Ihr den totalen Krieg?* (Do you want total war?), with a verse by Körner: *Nun, Volk, steh auf, und Sturm, brich los!*—"Now, people, rise up, and storm, break loose!" It was also indisputably the Nazis who built the red-brick building in Wöbbelin with the words *Unserm Theodor Körner* (To our Theodor Körner) in wrought-iron letters on its front wall. In one part of the building, a permanent exhibition commemorating the German nationalist writer of heroic poems;

in the other part, since 1965, a permanent exhibition commemorating the victims of the German nationalist insanity his poems to some degree inspired. The latter is a powerful display with all the photographs and documents one could possibly ask for, such as to leave no visitor in any doubt of what confronted the liberators of Wöbbelin and to ensure that the memory of the atrocities will remain more than graffiti-proof. Yet in the house the Nazis built, no spatial distinction is drawn between the memory of a poet who died in 1813 and an atrocity that occurred in 1945 (both are allocated the same amount of space), which makes me fear for the memory of the latter.

On the front wall it still says only *Unserm Theodor Körner*.

In the long run, who wants to remember Wöbbelin?

A stone's throw from the pine woods that cover the mass graves, the double-track railroad from Ludwigslust to Schwerin runs past on newly laid concrete sleepers. The siding that led to the camp has been demolished, as has the old railroad line; only a walled-up, red-brick station building is left standing desolately by the embankment. No trains stop at Wöbbelin anymore.

However, as late as November 26, 1946, a reminder is sent from the Eisenbahn-Gesellschaft Altona-Kaltenkirchen-Neumünster to Herrn Oberfinanzpräsidenten Hamburg concerning a bill of 1,728 German Reichsmarks for the conveyance of 2 officers, 84 men, and 576 prisoners from Bahnhof Kaltenkirchen to Lager Wöbbelin Bahnhof Ludwigslust, on April 16, 1945. "This bill," the railroad company emphasizes, "has been neither wholly nor partially withdrawn or annulled."

I turn the car around and take the plane back to Sweden.

Sweden is where you're heading, after all.

154

∎

Exactly why you're going to Sweden isn't clear. It's true that you once thought you were on the way to Sweden, on the train from Ravensbrück with the singing Kapo and the SS men presenting arms and the food parcels of corned beef and Camel cigarettes, but there's no indication that the road from Wöbbelin leads to Sweden. The road from Wöbbelin leads to an American field hospital in Ludwigslust, and to a convalescent home in Schwerin, and to the Bergen-Belsen camp for human wrecks from the German camp archipelago.

This camp is not to be confused with the concentration camp next door, which has been burned to stop the spread of epidemics. The Bergen-Belsen concentration camp is liberated by the British on April 15, 1945, and while the world for a short time is receptive to the unbearable, it's the unbearable images from the liberation of Bergen-Belsen that the world is seeing.

As the years go by, the displaced persons camp, as it is called, becomes unbearable in another way, because for many of those displaced here, there seems to be no way out. Their old world no longer exists, and the new world is none too eager to let itself be theirs. By the end of 1946 there are still 250,000 Jewish survivors in European camps for displaced persons waiting for somewhere to go. The Bergen-Belsen camp remains in operation until 1950.

On the map of the displaced, the road to Sweden hardly figures at all. Nearly all of them pin their hopes on the road to America or Palestine. That's also true for most of those who in June and July 1945 are allowed to take the road to Sweden, at the request of the United Nations Relief and Rehabilitation Administration. UNRRA is up and running as early as November 1943, but for as long as the war lasts, neutral Sweden will have nothing to do with it. After the war, the situation appears in a new light, and on June 1, 1945, the Swedish government decides to give temporary refuge to "some ten thousand children and invalids" from the refugee camps of Europe. "The Swedish government feels unable to turn down a request of this nature," explains Gustav Möller, minister for social affairs, to the Lower House of the Swedish Parliament on May 25, 1945. He emphasizes that the refuge is of limited duration, a matter of months, until the health of the sick has improved enough for them to move on elsewhere.

It's plain that he's addressing a public opinion not altogether congenial to his project.

On what grounds you're selected for one of the transports to Sweden remains unclear. You've been ill, of course (typhus), and when you're liberated you weigh eighty pounds, and you have nowhere to go, but the same is true for many others. Perhaps the mysterious promise made at Ravensbrück plays some part; somehow, Sweden's already on your map, and perhaps as a consequence, you're on Sweden's. The Jewish men from the Łódź ghetto who survive the selection on the ramp at Auschwitz-Birkenau, and the slave labor at the Büssing factories in Braun-

156

schweig, and the meandering death transport from Watenstedt to Ravensbrück, and the black hole of Wöbbelin, are virtually all transported to Sweden through the good offices of the Red Cross in the summer of 1945.

David Rosenberg. Entered July 18, 1945. Passport control, Malmö.

THE STOP

There are still some places to rescue from oblivion. One of them, strangely enough, was mine before I discovered it had once been yours. It's actually more than strange that the place has been both yours and mine, a most improbable coincidence, in fact, bordering on the impossible. After all, it's a place that can hardly be detected on the map, even with a magnifying glass. In any event, it's a very small place on the edge of a very big forest that stretches for miles in this sparsely populated country, where elk are more common than people and the narrow forest roads are seldom frequented by anyone except the few who for some inscrutable reason live and work here. But it's a place of great beauty, especially in summer, when the black water behind the hydroelectric dam on the River Ore glitters invitingly against the clear blue sky above the pine trees, and the air fills with the scent of needles and resin, and sunlit fields and pastures peep through the trees, and the small village on the shore of Lake Ore nestles in the gossamer green of unfurling leaves on dazzling white trunks of birch.

The little place is called Furudal and is situated in the vast forest belt between Rättvik in Dalarna and Bollnäs in Hälsingland; as I say, it's not a place you might accidentally pass through on the way to somewhere else, but a place you come to only if you know in advance that this is exactly where you're going, which few people have a reason to know. Before May 1974 I had never heard of Furudal, but I did know in advance that it was where I was going, first by train to Rättvik, then by bus through Ovanmyra, Boda, and Gulleråsen to Furudal, and Furudals Bruk, the estate of a former ironworks a bit farther to the north. In the old manor of the estate, at the edge of a dark forest by a black pond, I was to spend two weeks taking a crash course in French, with the blessings and support of my then employer. It was all beautifully planned, and the conditions for intense language learning were probably the best, but Furudal became important in my life for mainly nonlinguistic reasons (French still eludes me). Quite simply, I fell in love with the place, which largely had to do with the fact that I fell in love with a woman in this place, meaning that in this very place my life took a turn. Such places tend to linger on in life even after one's links to them are broken and life has taken a few more turns. In this case, my link to the place wasn't broken. For many years I returned to Furudal, motivated by a number of apparently unconnected reasons, though the underlying and unifying reason must have been an invisible attraction to the memories the place evoked.

So you must understand my astonishment, I might even say shock, when, a lifetime later, I'm confided with a yellowing bundle of handwritten letters dating from the winter and spring of 1946. I say confided because they're mostly love letters. They're the letters you write to the woman who is to be my mother after you've found out she's alive and you can no longer imagine life without her. These are joyful letters and desperate letters and letters of life and death, and the letter on top has the dateline Tappudden-Furudal, which I don't have to know Polish to understand. "Tappudden-Furudal 15/1 46," it says in the top right-hand corner. Your handwriting is small but clear, every letter distinct and separate, almost like printing, and I read the heading over and over again, wondering for a moment if there might be more than one Furudal in Sweden, but I already know that Tappudden

162

is a point on Lake Ore and that your Furudal must also be my
Furudal and that this is precisely where you are when on January
15, 1946, you receive a postcard, sent to you by the World Jewish
Congress, which passes on greetings from a certain Hala Staw,
to whom you can write via Komltet Żyd at 32 Śródm. in Łódź or
via A. Borensztajn in Hohne Belsen, b. Celle, Camp 3, R.B. 1/16.
There's no explanation of who this A. Borensztajn might be and
the dual addresses are a little confusing and perhaps not entirely
reassuring, as neither provides an unambiguous street with an
unambiguous number where you could immediately go and
knock on the door and take your beloved Haluś in your arms and
never let her go again; but there's no doubt that in this particular
place amid the vast forests between Rättvik and Bollnäs, your
young life takes yet another turn. The letter you write in duplicate that very day and send off to both addresses registers for all
time the overwhelming effect of a postcard in Furudal:

Haluś, can you imagine what happened to me!?

I was so overcome I couldn't get a word out. I ran home to the
barracks and read the card again, and then again, and again, and
again…until the words finally dislodged themselves from my
breast:

Hala's alive! Hala's alive! Hala's alive!

You've been in the aliens' camp at Tappudden-Furudal for just
over two weeks when it happens.

Yes, that's what the official papers call it, the aliens' camp.

One of the papers notes that you're part of the contingent of
Polish Jews transferred on December 12, 1945, from the aliens'
camp at Öreryd to the camp at Furudal. There are seventeen of
you, and the head of the Öreryd camp asserts that you have all
been provided with a set of winter clothes and pocket money

until December 31, 1945. To ensure that there's no duplication of provisions or payments, I assume.

A copy of the contingent list is to be duly signed by the head of the camp in Furudal and sent back to the head of the camp in Öreryd. So no one in the contingent disappears, I assume.

You're duly arranged in alphabetical order, from Apelbaum Juda to Zylberszac Mozes, and somewhere in between is Rozenberg Dawid and Rozenberg Naftali, Rozenberg with a *z*, Dawid with a *w*. You're not intended to stay in Sweden, so there's no reason to start spelling your name any other way. "Transit migrants" is the term that's been coined for people like you, which means you have the government's permission to recuperate here for a while before continuing your journey to somewhere else.

In the months following the end of the war, nearly thirty thousand survivors from German concentration camps are permitted to recuperate in Sweden. Some never do recuperate. Some soon continue their journeys to somewhere else. Some soon go back to where they came from, giving rise to yet another term applied by officialdom to those who have come to recuperate, *repatriandi*, which means people who can be expected to have a home or at least a homeland to return to. Of the thirty thousand transit migrants or *repatriandi*, however, ten thousand are Jews, which soon turns out to mean that most of them have nowhere to return to, and of course nowhere else to journey on to.

About the difference between Jews and *repatriandi* there's initially some confusion, or even downright ignorance, among the Swedish authorities, and about the difference between Poles and Polish Jews as well. The authorities eventually learn to know better, which presumably is one of the reasons why in late December 1945 most of the Polish-Jewish men in the aliens' camp at Öreryd are transferred to the aliens' camp at Tappudden-Furudal, and most of the Polish-Jewish women to the aliens' camp in Doverstorp.

In Öreryd, all "former concentration camp clients" (yes, that's what they write) are categorized as Poles, whether they're Jews or not. This isn't a very good idea, for among some of the Poles there's a tradition of anti-Semitism that hasn't necessarily been softened by the fate of the Polish Jews. Among the former concentration camp clients there are also some who were perpetrators, and some who were both victims and perpetrators, and it happens that victims are directly confronted with their former tormentors, which isn't good for camp discipline. Subsequently, the idea of putting the Jews and the Poles into separate camps comes up, and this rouses the indignation of a leading Swedish opinion maker, Alva Myrdal, who writes in the weekly magazine *Vi* (no. 35, 1945):

> If the tendency to segregate were to triumph, we would have to acknowledge that this is the first introduction of the ghetto in Sweden—a terrible calamity and a horror that a democratic society cannot tolerate. We must not unleash such racial hatred and racial fear: we must do all we can to conquer them by education and information.

Which, as we have seen, does not prevent the aliens' camp at Öreryd from being almost emptied of its Polish Jews in December 1945, so that a postcard sent there to Dawid Rozenberg must be forwarded to the aliens' camp at Tappudden-Furudal.

You're transferred to Öreryd on August 10, 1945, after three weeks of quarantine in the small university town of Lund.

165

Öreryd is located amid the vast forests of Småland, between Jönköping and Gislaved, and it too is a place hard to find on the map if you don't know where to look beforehand, which is presumably an important reason why a camp for Norwegian refugees is opened here on March 16, 1941. At any rate, such a camp is not exactly something that Sweden would want to advertise to Germany, which at that point looks likely to win the war and therefore should not be needlessly provoked. Further camps for Norwegian refugees are consequently set up in equally undistinguished and hard-to-find places with names like Holmudden, Bäggböle, Voxna, Skålmyra, Bäckehagen, Älgberget, Stråtenbo, Gottröra, Mälsåker, Mossebo, and Tappudden-Furudal.

Yes, as you can see, Tappudden-Furudal is also initially a camp for Norwegian refugees and part of a growing Norwegian-Swedish camp archipelago. As the winds of war change direction in 1943 and 1944, the camps are turned into bases for the training of Norwegian "police reserves." The training is organized by the Norwegian exile government in London and carried out with the consent of the Swedish government, with the aim of creating military and police units that in the case of a German surrender shall be capable "of restoring Norwegian law and justice as soon as possible."

The story of the Norwegian training camps on Swedish soil is a reasonably heroic one that many people will have good reason to remember, and memorials, to the extent that they're erected on former camp sites, are dedicated to the Norwegians. Since 1994, the old ironworks in Furudal is home to a Norwegian veterans' museum, and in Öreryd in the summer of 2008 a musical theater performance was put on to commemorate the years when the Norwegians came to town, and Elsa's cafe was the center of world politics, and Sweden made some contribution to

166

the right cause, after all. On a rough-hewn stone on the site of the former camp, a plaque reads "Öreryd refugee camp 1940–46," and another conveys the gratitude of the Norwegians "for the good reception and kindness shown to us in the war years."

Far fewer people remember the Poles. Actually, no one really remembers the Poles, still less the Polish Jews, who in fact do not officially exist, since they go by the name of Poles or Polish *repatriandi*. When the well-known Swedish journalist and writer Jan Olof Olsson (Jolo) happens to be passing through Öreryd in April 1972, he visits the churchyard by the white wooden church, where among the stones for departed shopkeepers, manufacturers, farmers, and stay-at-home daughters he finds two iron crosses engraved with clearly foreign names. "No dates, nothing more," he notes. "Just these strange names in the Öreryd graveyard. The names are Polish. How did these two get here?"

The people with the Polish names get to Öreryd by train and bus in July and August 1945, after the Norwegian police reserves, just a day or so following the German surrender, have marched off "with flags flying and music playing" toward the railroad station in Hestra. Unlike the Norwegians, who are viewed by the locals as brothers or cousins of a sort, the people with the Polish names are viewed as foreigners first and foremost. Contacts between the villagers and the camp residents cool and drop off. The language barrier doesn't help, and neither does the anxiety about—one might even say fear of—what the foreigners may bring with them. Pretty much everyone knows a bit about where they come from and what they've been through, and that presumably they're all scarred in some way. Rumors of scuffles, fits of madness, and cases of suicide filter out into the little community around the white wooden church, and in any case the word is that the foreigners' stay at the camp will be only a short one, because these are transit migrants or *repatriandi* who will soon be moving on to somewhere else.

So why make the effort?

Even those who make the effort don't always have an easy time of it. On August 2, 1945, the Christian daily *Svenska Morgonbladet* publishes an article signed B.J. and titled "Our Guests from German Torture Camps":

> Brought together in camps of varying sizes surrounded by tall, barbed-wire fences, with only forestry workers' primitive barracks or similar to live in, they are isolated from the outside world for week after week, month after month.... When the author of this piece tried to telephone one such camp in the Stockholm area...the female operator replied that the telephone number of the aliens' camp "was unlisted."...
>
> These guests in our country, invited by the Red Cross, should have the right not to be seen as mere numbers in an impersonal mass of "*Lagerschwestern*" [camp sisters]. It is the isolation from "ordinary people" that really gets on their nerves.

Only the kindest of people should be allowed to have anything to do with these—often Jewish—victims of Nazism. One can hardly call the head of one such camp kind who when asked by a visiting member of the women's corps if she could go and say hello to her friends, replied: "There is too much mollycoddling of these unpleasant refugees." When she told him that she had got to know "these refugees" as charming and grateful, and that moreover one had to bear in mind that most of them had seen their parents and siblings consigned to the gas chambers of Auschwitz, he interrupted her curtly: "That has nothing to do with it."...

We must remember that these are living people whom we have committed ourselves to rescuing, not a mere collection of numbers from miscellaneous clusters of German barracks.

On August 17, 1945, *Svenska Dagbladet* reports that forty "inmates" at Öreryd ("Polish camp in Småland") panicked and set out on a march to Stockholm to protest against the camp conditions, and that the police stopped them at Mossebo, about five kilometers north of Öreryd, and that they were presently under arrest in Jönköping, awaiting further proceedings. "The forty who did not want to stay apparently fell prey to some kind of concentration camp psychosis. They are all very young, in the age range 16–20. They claim, among other things, that they did not receive sufficient allocations of food or tobacco in the camp."

On August 29, 1945, the head of an unnamed aliens' camp writes in the daily *Göteborgs Handels- och Sjöfarts-Tidning* (*GHT*) that the only "more general dissatisfaction" he has noted relates to food:

As a rule, this is because they are unused to Swedish food—they find black pudding and fish balls particularly hard to come to terms

169

with, and most of them find it impossible to appreciate the Swedish habit of putting sugar in all kinds of dishes.

A more intractable problem is how to teach the refugees not to waste food; some kind of hoarding instinct seems to force them to store up supplies, which then go dry or moldy and eventually end up in the pig bucket.

The refugees' unstable emotional state provides fertile soil for what might be termed camp psychoses, which take various forms. Sometimes it is individuals suddenly feeling themselves unjustly treated or persecuted by other camp residents, sometimes a general sense of alarm spreads rapidly, with anxieties about the future, the fate of relations....

For the most part, however, the Swedish press doesn't write very much about the aliens' camps and the people who populate them. In community after community, Auschwitz temporarily moves in behind the local co-op store but leaves little trace in public life. Only rarely do journalists take the opportunity to visit the camps and interview the people who inhabit them and provide an account of their experiences and thereby also try to understand why some of them sometimes behave as they do. It's as if a curtain of silence has descended between the world the visitors bring with them and the world that surrounds them. Or a curtain of anxiety, perhaps, that the two worlds will prove incompatible, or at least will not readily tolerate meeting each other. I note this anxiety also in Alva Myrdal's otherwise enlightened view of the camps: anxiety that the darkness inside the residents will infect the enlightened society around them. "The victims of brutality themselves become brutalized," she writes.

When life is reduced to its bare minimum, primitive selfishness is the only natural response.... Women whose reason should tell them

170

that they will get enough food, and that there will be food for the next meal and for the next day too, cannot believe it because of their old terror. They save every crumb left over from the table. They pick dandelion shoots and other things to eat. They collect the pigs' potato peelings. They rake up every dry little pea that has fallen on the ground. They even continue to steal from the camp stores.

The question is raised: what are we to do with such people? In two articles in *Expressen* (June 22 and 25, 1945), they're described as animals. The writer maintains that "most of them survived thanks to those more or less animal qualities that Western society otherwise tries to keep in check: trickery, cunning, lying, obsequiousness, pilfering, and selfishness, combined with a certain brutal will to live."

She's consequently concerned about who would eventually want to employ them: "It won't be easy for them to adapt, and it won't be easy for their employers. The latter will presumably require more tireless understanding and generous humanity than the average employer can muster."

The writer doesn't specifically identify the Jews as the problem here (in fact, quite the opposite); most of the women in the camp she visits (Doverstorp), and on whose conduct she bases her conclusions, are non-Jewish Poles. The vast majority of people living in the archipelago of aliens' camps in Sweden in the summer and autumn of 1945, it should be noted, are non-Jews.

Sometimes, however, the Jews are specifically identified as a problem, as in an article signed G.B.G. in *Göteborgs Handels- och Sjöfarts-Tidning* on September 5, 1945:

Swedish employers are not, as many may imagine, particularly accommodating when it comes to taking on Jewish workers. The present writer has considerable experience of the difficulty of finding decent work for such workers. Only textile workers seem to be accepted. With its low wages, the textile industry has taken on many refugees who have not been able to find any other work.... We know from experience that the Jews will not take on just any old work except in cases of extreme necessity. Business is in their blood, and of the other professions, that of tailor is the most attractive to them....

If these young Jews are now to become Swedish citizens, it should be made clear to them that they must set their sights on careers other than business....

Assuming these young Jews are now to be trained as, say, workers in manufacturing industries, carpenters, painters, etc., a new problem presents itself, namely how the Swedish trade union movement would react to the prospect of Jewish workmates.... One can occasionally sense a certain unwillingness, even among Swedish workers, to work with Jewish comrades.

I do wonder how many of all these problems with the Jews G.B.G. had already identified before having anything to do with actual Jews, if indeed he ever did. At any rate, none of these problems appears to stop the more or less Jewish Poles in Öreryd from soon being in great demand as forestry workers in the vast forests surrounding the camp, and as agricultural workers on the farms nearby, and as workers in the numerous manufacturing companies in the region. In a letter to the camp administrator at Öreryd dated November 9, 1945, the chairman of the local council in the small town of Norrahammar, some forty kilometers to the north toward Jönköping, pleads for permission for the refugee David Szpiegler to be granted an extended leave of absence from the camp, "so his job is not put in jeopardy," since he has "shown himself both competent and hardworking, and is liked by the management." David Szpiegler has found his job at the Norrahammar works, which produces iron ranges, pots, and pans, through the mediation of Mr. Åke Roström, who also arranged board and lodging for him and is said to invite him to his home on a daily basis, "to keep him informed about work and other matters."

"As I am also there on a daily basis and have learned much about the refugees' sad situation, I hope that the best possible provisions can be made for him," the chairman of the Norrahammar council ends his written plea to the camp administrator at Öreryd.

There's a recurring tendency to stress the sadness of your existence and the occasionally strange way some of you behave. It's much rarer to see anyone stress the fact that the sadness of your existence has very little to do with conditions in the camp, still less with conditions in Sweden. Rather, you keep pinching yourselves each morning when you find a Swedish breakfast laid out for you in the dining room, followed by a Swedish lunch and a Swedish dinner, and even if there's too much sugar in the food and a few of you squirrel away a bit of it here and there, Sweden must still seem like paradise to most of you.

I know you had thought of yourself as being in paradise before, but this paradise here will still be standing in the morning. And the morning after that. Admittedly, it's a paradise that seems at times unfamiliar and hard to understand, and the shadows that follow you all will follow you into this paradise as well, but nowhere in the letters you write to Haluš during this time do I find a word of criticism directed at conditions in the camp or in the country.

If it didn't sound so trite, I'd say you're grateful, deeply grateful, and for brief periods happy, too.

Happy and unhappy.

As in the letter your brother Natek sends from Öreryd on December 21, 1945, just before the Polish Jews are to be moved to Tappudden-Furudal. The all-eclipsing shadow in Natek's life is the uncertainty about what has happened to his wife Andzia (Chana) since they were parted on the ramp at Auschwitz-Birkenau.

The letter is addressed to Sima Staw in Łódź.

There's a rumor that Sima Staw has survived Auschwitz and gone back to Łódź and might be able to answer the question of whether Andzia is alive or dead. But the rumor's false. The letter instead reaches the hands of Sima's sister, the woman who is to be my mother, and it's through her that I much later find it in my own hands.

In parts, it's undeniably a desperate letter: "I implore you, tell me everything, no matter what it is. This uncertainty is draining me." In parts, nevertheless, it's a letter from paradise:

> Sweden's a country where there is no anti-Semitism. And as if that weren't enough, there's no "Jewish question" at all. The standard of living is very high. The ideal of class equality has, quite simply, been achieved. There is no unemployment and no one goes hungry. And anyone who wants to work can do so, and live well from it, and if I had my wife here, my happiness would be complete. Sima! For God's sake, don't let your answer tarry!

While so many answers still tarry, some of you cycle the eight kilometers to master bricklayer Manfredsson's in Hestra to pick potatoes. This is on the morning of September 26, 1945, and the formal request for the delivery of four named individuals from Barrack F arrived two days ago from the aliens' section of

174

the labor exchange in Öreryd. I suspect the aliens' section is the only section there is at the labor exchange in Öreryd. The unspoken requirement for the job of potato picking is that you know how to ride a bike, which not all of you do. Nor, it transpires, do you all know how to pick potatoes. Each of you has been promised four kronor for the work, but the plants are not pulled up properly and lots of potatoes get left in the ground and the two-wheeled barrow on which you've loaded the potatoes tips over and has to be reloaded. What's more, you eat like horses and the master bricklayer has to send his children out for more food.

I learn all this much later when the story is told to me by M.Z., who was the one who had to learn to cycle overnight, but who on the other hand knew more Swedish than the rest of you and had to do most of the talking as you sat around the table at Mr. Manfredsson's house.

It's a fond memory, I realize, that wobbly, late-summer bike ride through the countryside of Småland to your first job since the slave camps, even if I'm not quite convinced by all the details of these memories. Especially since so much else I ask about, things that seem more important, has been forgotten.

When I ask M.Z. about the potato picking, fifty-nine years have elapsed, and only fragments of this memory are left.

So I prefer to stick to the documents, as you know, and a written record of the potato picking in Hestra is to be found at the Swedish National Archives in Stockholm, Riksarkivet, as is your application to the State Aliens Commission on September 19, 1945, for permission to travel to the aliens' camp in Gränna to visit your cousin Helena Wiśnicka.

I can't deny that I'm surprised to find such an application, since I've never heard of such a cousin before. I'm not even sure such a cousin exists. Especially not after having read your letter to Haluś of April 6, 1946, in which your trip to Gränna is revealed in another light. The letter's written in an increasingly dejected mood; three months have passed since the postcard in Furudal and Haluś is still in Łódź, and you are still in Alingsås, and the formal barriers to your reunion seem to multiply by the day. You've been worrying about Haluś's state of mind ever since she wrote in her last letter that she'd started avoiding people. You immediately interpret this to mean that she's sitting alone with her thoughts: "You mustn't do that Haluś! Sitting alone with your thoughts is terrible for people like us!"

And as if to share her solitude in some way, you tell her about the time when you, too, were sitting alone with your thoughts, which happened to be the time of your trip to Gränna.

It was in my early days at Öreryd, when I still had no idea of your existence. We shipwrecked people certainly don't lack reasons to lose our spirits. If the weather was nice we tried to forget by swimming and rowing at a nearby lake, or by walking in the forest and picking mushrooms. It was much worse when the weather turned bad, it was enough to drive you mad, and there were lots of rainy days like that. I had to get away for a few days, at any cost. I had no money for travel, nobody to visit, and nowhere to go. I cut down on cigarettes (in the camp we were given 5 kronor "pocket money" that was supposed to cover cigarettes and other small expenses) and I saved up a few kronor. Then I got on a bus without any real plan and went to the nearest town, Jönköping (known for its picturesque setting and its match factories). I wasn't really supposed to travel because I still had no passport, but I didn't care. The town is on a huge lake, with lovely hills all around. I was so dazed by it all that I forgot who I am and how I ended up here. After I'd wandered around for a couple of hours I felt so uneasy, so foreign (I couldn't talk to people, I only knew a few words of Swedish) that I was on the verge of going back to Öreryd that same evening. But I put the thought out of my mind when I met two Hungarian Jewish women. They told me that in Gränna, about 60 km away, there was a Polish camp, and that I could get there by car, or by boat across the lake. So I went there, thinking I might meet someone who knew something about your fate.

When I got to Gränna it turned out there wasn't a camp there after all, instead there were women billeted at hotels and boardinghouses (Gränna is a well-known spa and tourist resort)—Polish women, at that. I didn't even have time to look around me and see which way to go before I suddenly hear someone calling: "Dawid! Dawid! My God, who is it that I see! Dawid's alive!" And there in front of me is Estusia (red-haired Estusia, from the post office). Her first words were: "Where's Hala, have you had any news of her?"

What happened next is hard to describe. Girls came streaming in from all directions and looked at me like a creature from another planet. All around me I can hear voices: "Has this guy been in a concentration camp? God, how is that possible, he looks like a normal human being, *ein emes jiddisch jingl.*"

I was rooted to the spot and didn't know what to do with myself or what it was all supposed to mean. But suddenly it dawned on me that these women had come to Sweden before the end of the war (through the Red Cross), and therefore hadn't witnessed the liberation. Which served to explain why my appearance came as such a pleasant surprise to them. A few hours before they left for Sweden they'd been lined up for roll call at Ravensbrück, opposite the men (I happened to have been one of those men, or should I say walking corpses). They kept me talking until late into the night, wanting to hear every last detail of the liberation.

177

The next day I went back to Öreryd. Before I left I had to make a solemn promise that I would come back for Rosh Hashana [Jewish New Year] and that I would bring a few more men with me, because they were planning a traditional New Year celebration, and without men it sort of wouldn't work because they wanted to have the prayers, too [for a Jewish act of worship you have to have a *minyan*, that is, a gathering of ten Jewish men].

I kept my word and took a whole gang with me to the celebration. Since then, men keep going there from Öreryd and vice versa. That way, by simply asking around, many people have found out what happened to their relatives and friends. We took our turn and organized dances and invited the girls from Gränna to them. In short, we started having a bit of a social life again. And thanks to my first escapade in Gränna, there are now six couples. They're scattered all over Sweden. Only one of the couples lives here in Alingsås.

At about this point, the mood of the letter darkens. It's palpable. The words lose their bounce. Shadows fall between the lines. The reunion which only a moment ago seemed to be a matter of course is now vanishing beyond the horizon. From Poland, only those cleared for continued travel across the Atlantic are now allowed to enter, you write. Obtaining admission to Sweden from the DP camp at Bergen-Belsen has also become "very difficult." "As regards the possibility of my arranging the formalities, it's nonexistent for the time being."

And Haluś hasn't even made her way to Bergen-Belsen yet. She's still in Łódź.

Tomorrow you'll give it another go and try to find out exactly how things stand in Bergen-Belsen, and try to talk to people who have just arrived from there and who are still in quarantine in Helsingborg.

Today, you're too tired to write anything more.

"I'm in a terrible state of mind," ends the letter about the merry trip to Gränna.

From time to time, the weekly physician's reports from Öreryd record the medical consequences of terrible states of mind. In the early hours of June 21, 1946, dentist Abraham Goldman takes his own life by cutting his wrists and sticking a knife with a four-centimeter blade straight into his heart. Nine months earlier, in the report of September 27, 1945, it's noted that the said Abraham Goldman hadn't been able to produce certification of his dental qualifications, but that he'd been vouched for by two "Poles" in the camp and an application therefore had been sent off to the Royal Board of Medicine asking permission for Goldman to practice as a dentist in Öreryd.

To judge by subsequent reports, permission has been granted and the temporarily precarious state of the "dentist question" clarified.

What doesn't get clarified, at least not permanently, is Abraham Goldman's state of mind.

"In his last weeks he was melancholic and preoccupied with suicidal thoughts," writes the Öreryd camp physician in his report of June 28, 1946.

By this time, you and Natek are long gone from Öreryd, and long gone from Furudal too. You leave the Swedish archipelago of aliens' camps for good in early February 1946. About Furudal, you write that the area is beautiful, and that it's covered with a thick layer of snow, and that camp life is monotonous, although "those who enjoy winter sports have no trouble pass-ing the time."

You yourself learn to ski in Furudal.

No one forces you to leave Furudal. You've simply "had enough of camp life and want to work."

You also want to stay in Sweden, at least for now. On September 1, 1945, while still at Öreryd, you both apply for Swedish aliens' passports. You emphasize in the strongest terms that you don't want to return to Poland, that you don't want to be categorized as *repatriandi*, that you want nothing more to do with Poland. Your brother is even more adamant on this point and encloses a separate sheet with a handwritten declaration in Polish, and alongside it the translation, typed in Swedish: "My entire family, which lived in Łódź before the war, has been mur-dered by Hitler's brutes. If I were to return to Łódź now, my whole life would be a string of tragic memories."

Under the handwritten signature of Naftali Rosenberg, someone (the translator?) has typed the word "Jew" in brackets, perhaps to explain or clarify, but the answer is slow in coming, and on December 10, 1945, the two of you write another letter to the State Aliens Commission, this time without any typewriting go-between, and this time in German.

BITTE, in capitals at the top.

BITTE. We are two brothers, both qualified textile engineers, who would be able to get jobs at a textile factory in Marieholm if only we had our passports. Favorable treatment of our request, *die gün-stige Erledigung unserer Bitte*, would make it possible for us to start living a normal life. We want to stress that we have no intention of returning to Poland as our whole family in Poland has fallen victim to the Hitler regime, *ist dem Hitlerregime zum Opfer gefallen*.

You write politely, rounding off with thanks in anticipation and yours faithfully, but no aliens' passports are forthcoming as far as I can tell, which however doesn't prevent you from checking out of the aliens' camp in Tappudden-Furudal on February 2, 1946, and checking into Friden Pension in Alingsås, where two days later you embark on an apparently normal life as textile workers at Alingsås Bomullsväfveri. It's a hard job, working under a lot of time pressure at clattering mechanical looms on large factory floors, and since you've both presented yourselves as qualified textile engineers (which is truer of your brother than of you), it's maybe not quite what you'd hoped for. On the other hand, you're eager to convince the woman who is to be my mother that your entry level in the Swedish labor market is a purely temporary one and only to be expected, and that Sweden is paradise, all the same. In your first letter from Alingsås to Łódź, on March 7, 1946, you write:

> The Swedes unfortunately take priority for the better positions, which is quite understandable, though in Sweden nobody is ashamed of their job and nobody is choosy. The Swedes are a hard-working people and work is considered a blessing. No wonder, as an average worker lives better than a small businessman in prewar Poland. In some industries a worker earns (almost) as much as an engineer. I can earn as much as about 75 kronor a week. You can live all right on that, dress decently, afford proper accommodation, etc. Natek works at the same factory. For now we're living at a pension, i.e. we get food and lodging. We'd rather have an apartment of our own but accommodation is difficult here. Even so, I think it will happen soon. The pension is fairly expensive, and what's more we don't like the food (Swedish food isn't particularly tasty). Once we're set up on our own we'll be able to make our own breakfast

and supper and eat lunch at a restaurant. Can you imagine, Swedes sprinkle sugar on their herring, and drown their meat in cream. They add sugar to almost everything. We work in two shifts. One week from 5 in the morning to 1.30 in the afternoon, the next week from 1.30 until 10 at night.

You ask what my plans are. I want the same as you, Haluś, which is to hold you in my arms as soon as possible.

I would like to fly away to you at this very minute—there actually are flights from Stockholm to Warsaw—but you know very well what the obstacles are.

The only thing we can do is to get you to Sweden, and it would happen all the sooner if only you could get to Bergen-Belsen.

That's how most of the letters from Pension Friden in Alingsås to Hala Staw in Łódź end. With "if only."

If only you could get to Bergen-Belsen.

If only you could claim to be someone's wife or child. Claiming to be someone's sister or brother isn't enough, as you know.

If only from the start, I had declared you my wife.

If only from the start, you had declared me your husband.

If only you could get in touch with so-and-so who knows so-and-so who knows the best way to get from Łódź to Bergen-Belsen and from Bergen-Belsen to Sweden.

If only I could get a Swedish family to guarantee the ten thousand kronor required for an entry visa from Poland.

If only I could join the crew of a Swedish ship in Gothenburg and smuggle you aboard in some Polish port, Gdynia maybe—there's a lot of smuggling going on there, you know.

The tone is generally one of forced optimism: things will fall into place, you'll see; new options have opened up and so-and-so has just arrived from Bergen-Belsen without any family ties here at all; tomorrow I'm going to talk to so-and-so who is right up to date on the best way to go about it; everything's ready for when you get here, you know, with a job and a place to live all organized; and there's so much I haven't had a chance to tell you, and so much you haven't had a chance to tell me; and I can't see the point of having both survived hell if we're not allowed to share paradise.

There are times when you can't convince even yourself, and sometimes I get the feeling you aren't even sure whether the woman who is to be my mother actually wants to join you in Sweden or whether she'd prefer that you join her in Poland, which tends to make you desperate as well as decisive. In a disconsolate moment you write that it might be best for you to go to her in Łódź after all, that your longing for her is unbearable, that you can't stand the idea of being apart from her much longer. In your decisive moments, and they are many, you put a great deal of effort into convincing her that she has to leave Poland, that Poland is no place for people like her and you, and that it's definitely not mere selfish convenience that's deterring you from leaving paradise at once and coming to her side:

> You mustn't think that the decisive factor for my not coming to Poland is the drop in living standards that would lead to. The way things look now, there's no way back for a Jew. I've talked to people who have just come to Sweden from Poland illegally, via Gdynia. They were two Christian Poles who had already been in Sweden, then returned to Poland but have now come back here. When I told them I was weighing up the idea of going to Poland they looked at me as if I was mad....
>
> I don't want to build a new life on the ruins of our homes, and what's more, at a time when everything around is malign or even

hostile toward us. And this, even despite the fact that in Łódź I might be able to arrange things better for myself, live better, i.e. get a job in my own profession. But it can't be helped, I would rather be an unskilled worker here than have to listen to comments like "So where are all these Jews coming from now, I was sure we'd got rid of them?"...

I'll say it again: it's in "our" own best interests for you to come to me, even though it isn't easy to put into practice. How can I even think of coming back, when we keep hearing about murders of Jews? Right now they're talking on Radio Warsaw about the murder of 5 Jews in Krakow. So why should I drop everything and go to where I'm hated and despised?

In your letters, you try hard to present life in Alingsås as fully normal, yes, even as bright and promising. After only a few months, you're able to report that Natek has landed a new job at the textile factory, in the stockroom of the dyeing section, with the prospect of promotion since textile dyeing is his speciality—which goes to show that even foreigners have the chance of "a first-rate job." You write of the Jewish-Polish colony and its gatherings, of your trips to visit new friends in the land of the vast forests, of the new language, which you learn not so much from your two lessons a week as from talking to Swedes, "and I'd be lying if I didn't tell you: including Swedish women."

You begin one letter by telling about the two letters that were waiting for you both when you got back from work, one from Haluś to yourself, dated February 5, 1946, and one for Natek. The letter for you has taken seven weeks to get there, and I can well imagine the dark misunderstandings that can arise from such postal service. The letter to Natek brings the answer to his question about Andzia:

When he'd finished reading the letter, he wasn't able to utter a word. He just sat there staring listlessly at the same spot. I went out of the room because I could feel something was happening inside him and he needed to be alone. Up to that point he hadn't let any bad thoughts get near him. In fact just the opposite, he'd tried hard to behave in an easygoing, lighthearted way and had even allowed himself brief flirtations now and then. But I knew very well that it was all self-deception, and in fact he told me himself that if he didn't keep up the show he'd soon be in bad shape. With Andzia he could have been happy, because there was no other woman he could ever truly be in love with. He still thinks it's thanks to her that the sun is peeping out from the clouds.

You can't imagine the effect the letter had on him.

Then a detailed account of a burlesque linguistic misunderstanding is suddenly allowed to take up most of the rest of the letter:

Coffee is the Swedish national drink, and they take cakes and biscuits with it. When Swedes offer you coffee, you can't say no, or they're mortally offended. So we come in, take a seat, and our hostess kindly invites us to help ourselves. As we begin drinking and eating, the hostess turns to us and says: *varso gut dupa*, but since we weren't familiar with Swedish customs, we didn't know what she meant, and she repeated it several times, *varso gut dupa, varso gut dupa*. There were three of us, Natek, me and another fellow. We all burst out laughing and couldn't stop, and our hosts laughed with us. They wondered what we were laughing about and our hostess said we had to explain what was so funny, and was even ready to defend herself. There was nothing for it, we had to tell her that the word *d—* [an explicit four-letter word] is not a very nice one in

185

Polish. Once she had heard it, there was no stopping her, she was splitting her sides with laughter. It turned that what she'd said was *varsågod och doppa*, which means "Do feel free to dunk." Swedes have the habit of dunking their biscuits in their coffee, in fact it's such standard practice that it has its own special name. Since then, Swedes have been avoiding the word, but only in Polish company of course.

Here you seem a bit shocked as you realize how your pen has run away with you—"Haluś, what am I doing, what good is this nonsense to you?"

At this point you're interrupted in your letter-writing by a visit to your room. A workmate and his girlfriend have come to tell you they're getting engaged, which prompts you to offer them, "elegantly," some fruit and wine—"Haluś, can you imagine me as a host?" But once the guests have left you start feeling sad and eventually have to throw out your brother, who's been sad all evening and should rather go and see a movie to banish the darkness inside, and as so often, the letter ends in shadows. "Haluś, what's to become of us?"

The biscuit-dunking story is a glade of brightness in a forest of shadows.

Life in Alingsås is a life of waiting for answers that tarry, in the meandering stream of people who come and go on their way to somewhere else, in the restless motion between the shadows of memory and the glades of forgetfulness. Pension Friden is located at Torggatan 8, which is about as much in the center as you can get in little Alingsås, but for the people who come and go across its creaking floor, it's a place on the outskirts, or rather a no-man's-land between a world that is no longer and a world that is still unreal.

A waiting place, in fact.

A waiting place for a connection not yet established.

Hardly a life you would call normal, if by normal you mean a life with a past and a future.

It's hardly normal to wait for a connection that may not exist.

At any rate, there's no given term for people in your category. The official documents are stamped RED CROSS REFUGEES, but refugees you are not.

If only you had been. If only you had fled while there was time.

But you didn't flee, you were transported, which is something else, particularly if the purpose of the transport is annihilation.

You aren't immigrants, either, not in your own eyes, nor in the eyes of Sweden. You haven't come here of your own free will or under your own steam, but again by being transported, from one camp to another, from a camp in hell to a camp in the land of the vast forests, which out of a combination of magnanimity and guilt has offered you a temporary stop while you're waiting to journey on to somewhere else, and which therefore designates you as transit migrants or *repatriandi*.

For people who haven't fled, and haven't migrated, and have nowhere to be transited or repatriated to, and who are still waiting for answers that tarry, and who until further notice live a life without a past and without a future, there's no ready-made term and no ready-made policy, either, which is hardly surprising. Whoever could have imagined that in the course of a few short summer months, Sweden would take in over ten thousand individuals for whom no ready-made category exists in the Swedish language?

As time goes by, the term "survivors" starts to be used, initially as a statement of fact, survivors as distinct from the perished, but gradually as a category in its own right, a term for people whose main attribute is that they're alive when in all probability they should be dead. Those to whom this term primarily applies are people who declare themselves to be Jews and who prove to fit particularly badly into the official categories of transit migrants and *repatriandi*. Already on July 3, 1945, an editorial in Sweden's main daily newspaper, *Dagens Nyheter*, notes that the minister of justice has received a request "for the benefit of a large group of stateless individuals" to

> set aside the rule requiring a minimum of ten years' residence to qualify for Swedish citizenship.... Among the UNRRA refugees that the Red Cross has been bringing here for some time, there are a number of people with highly uncertain futures—for example Polish Jews with no links to home—fearful that they will be sent from one anti-Semitic environment to another.

Jewish concentration camp survivors become, in short, a human category all their own. Shipwrecked, you call them in one of your letters. Floating wreckage, I read somewhere else. Some of the shipwrecked still fear that in all probability they should be dead and therefore declare themselves as something other than Jews, which makes it somewhat difficult to keep a tally.

Some of them see forebodings everywhere.

Förbjudet att luta sig ut, says a small metal plate screwed to the window frame in every Swedish train compartment, forbidding passengers to lean out.

Some of the survivors see only the letters spelling *jude* and draw their own conclusions.

Some of them keep on being afraid even after they understand.

I go through a plastic bag of small and somewhat dog-eared photos from your time in Alingsås. Many of them are group photos of young people cautiously pressing together, smiling into the camera, often with a glass in their hand, and a cigarette. Some are holding each other. Some are kissing. Some look a little distant. Most are under thirty, I would guess, though many look older. Most are dressed up, some are even elegant. You're always elegantly dressed, I must say. Nice jackets, several of them, I note, a pale check in the summer pictures, usually with a wide bow tie, sometimes an ordinary tie; your shoes are polished, the cut of your trousers impeccable, your shirts well ironed. You care about your appearance, I can see that, and you're eager for Haluš to like what she sees. Apart from anything else, you want her to see that you're earning enough to dress "decently," as you put it. "In the next day or two I'll get a new photo taken and send it to you. I don't look all that good in the last one. I've lost 6 kilos in Sweden, though I don't really know why. We aren't short of anything here, it's like the good old days before the war."

No, you aren't short of anything, and you look very good despite those six kilos you're worried about, not very tall, that's true, but slim, with finely chiseled features. You're rarely smiling in the pictures and your eyes often have a slightly absent look (posing is not your best sport), but no one seeing you at those parties and on those outings in and around Alingsås in the spring and summer of 1946 could possibly see anything other than a handsome young man with his life ahead of him. Especially not in the photos where you're all posing on warm summer jetties and rocky shores and the sun is shining and the sea is

189

glittering and for one captured instant you all look as if you've known one another for a long time and have belonged here for a long time and are only doing what young people with their lives ahead of them do.

But soon faces will disappear, and farewells be said, and names be forgotten, and what seemed like a lasting fellowship will turn out to have been a haphazard and brief encounter between people who just a while ago had never met, and who just a while ago couldn't imagine a place like this, and who for a single captured instant have only one another to share the world with. I see you holding one another, touching one another, looking at one another as if you'll never have to part again. But I also see that you're clinging to one another, bearing one another up, convincing one another that the waiting will be over soon, and the connection soon established, and the journey on to somewhere else soon resumed. Sweden may look like paradise and for a while feel like paradise to the young people in the yellowing pictures of parties and outings in and around Alingsås, but most of them are dreaming impatiently of the next leg of the journey, including your brother, to judge by another yellowing document: "wishes to travel to Palestine" says the record of a police interrogation at Öreryd on August 22, 1945.

Perhaps you do too, before the dream of Haluś overtakes everything.

As late as September 1946, 45 percent of Jewish survivors in Sweden want to travel on to Palestine, 28 percent to the United States, 8 percent to other destinations. Only 16 percent want to be repatriated. Only 3 percent want to stay in Sweden.

Some 650 Jewish survivors, most of them young women, eventually tire of waiting for legal openings for the journey onward, and at the end of January 1947 they board a ship in the harbor of Trelleborg. The ship, the *Ulua*, is a Honduran-registered former American coast guard vessel weighing 880 metric tons. The passengers, who arrive on two specially chartered trains, are said to be between eighteen and thirty, mostly women. The voyage has been organized by the Jewish Refugee Welfare Association, whose representative in Trelleborg, Mr. Gunther Kohn, finds the *Ulua* in such a poor state that he wants a committee of passengers to approve conditions on board before departure. "A quick look at the ship's facilities explains why Mr. Kohn is letting the passengers voice an opinion before they are crammed on board," writes the local paper, *Trelleborgs Allehanda*. In any event, it's "scarcely suitable for accommodating even 600 passengers for a number of days. The steerage has been fitted with a kind of cross between bunks and shelves, made of rough wood, on which the passengers are expected to sleep."

The departure of the *Ulua* on January 24 makes the front page:

It was a singing ship that put out from the quayside in front of the Trelleborg harbormaster's office at 3:30 in the afternoon—sailing toward an uncertain fate at the center of international politics. During the day, 661 Jewish emigrants had boarded the "ghost ship" *Ulua* and in the current cold weather had stayed below deck, but just as the vessel was putting out from the quay, the Jew passengers came swarming up from steerage like ants from an anthill, and it became clear just how overcrowded the ship was. As the *Ulua* swung its stern toward the hundreds of Trelleborg residents on the quay, the emigrants started singing a song of farewell, which could still be heard as the *Ulua* passed the outer section of the middle bridge.

The ship's official destination is South America, but after a violent storm in the Bay of Biscay and emergency repairs in an Algerian port, the *Ulua* puts in at an unguarded beach outside Taranto in southern Italy and under cover of darkness takes seven hundred more Jewish survivors on board. With over 1,350 passengers crowded above and below deck, the ship approaches Palestine on February 27, 1947, level with Haifa. There she's sighted by British reconnaissance aircraft, and two British mine-sweepers attempt to force her to stop. The *Ulua* responds by hoisting a "Jewish" flag and making for the coast at full speed. Along the sides of the ship, passengers push out wooden beams and sit in the lifeboats to obstruct boarding. Two British naval officers and ten seamen nonetheless succeed in boarding by the stern, but the swell in the wake of the ship sweeps their boat away, and when their tear gas runs out, they're overpowered by the passengers and forced to jump overboard. At the next attempt, twenty-seven soldiers get themselves aboard and fire warning shots over the passengers' heads while the *Ulua* steams toward the coast at twelve knots, reaching land just south of Haifa with the British soldiers still literally clinging on and within sight of a British army base at the foot of Mount Carmel. Nine passengers manage to swim ashore and get away; the rest are taken to Haifa and then transferred to a British internment camp on Cyprus.

Thus ended the journey onward for 650 individuals, some of whom might well have had their pictures taken on sunny jetties and rocky shores in the land of the vast forests, momentarily thinking they were in paradise, but to whom the idea of staying on had remained alien, perhaps even frightening. None of them could possibly have been unaware of the risks of such a voyage. The illegal conveyance of Jewish survivors to Palestine on defective, undersized, and overloaded ships was a high-risk enterprise that could end well or in disaster, or in a British internment camp on Cyprus, or sometimes in a British internment camp in Germany.

Yes, this must not be forgotten, the British had the gall to do even that. In the summer of 1947, four thousand Jewish survivors of the much mythologized *Exodus* were taken to a camp in Poppendorf, just outside Lübeck, after having come within sight of the coast of Palestine. Nobody could be unaware of the fact that this was how the journey onward could end. The picture of Jewish survivors being taken back to a camp in Germany was published the world over, even on the front page of *Stockholms Läns och Södertälje Tidning* on September 13, 1947.

Maybe someone shows you the picture—someone who already knows who you are and where you've come from.

But there I go, anticipating your life.

It's so easy to do, and so unnecessary.

Time enough for that.

193

The place is still Alingsås, the time is the summer of 1946, and you're still waiting for an answer that's tarrying, and in the land of the vast forests there's a debate going on about what to do with people like you. It can no longer be assumed that people like you can move on. That much has become obvious.

But it can't be assumed that you can stay, either. In the land of the vast forests, the inhabitants aren't used to the idea of thousands of people with wildly foreign languages and cultures suddenly taking up residence behind the Co-op at the forest edge. Only recently, even a dozen was unthinkable; jobs would be stolen, cultures destroyed, and the pure Swedish breed contaminated. Such views have not vanished completely, even if a deepening blush of shame now attends them. It may seem astonishing that such views persist at all, given that the land of the vast forests is crying out for people to man its unscathed cotton mills and truck factories. But xenophobia is old and ingrained, while the hunger for labor is new. On September 15, 1945, an editorial in the *Dagens Nyheter* sounds a note of warning about letting "the Polish-Jewish refugees" stay on:

> If they hear that Sweden feels obliged to let them stay permanently, they will presumably be more than delighted. But the social workers who counsel them must beware of fostering that idea. It does not chime in with the authorities' intentions, nor does it harmonize with opinion in informed Swedish Jewish circles. On the contrary, those circles urge caution in equating *these herds* [italics added] with the stateless group of the prewar years. They are concerned that the former will be indiscriminately let loose on the labor market. They also maintain that there should be careful checks on their conduct and a critical assessment of their professed demands.

Clarifying the position and future prospects of these groups is a matter of urgency. No doubt it will at least prove necessary to introduce a reasonable waiting time with provisional solutions, a waiting time that may well prove quite difficult. We are not used to dealing with people so alien to Swedish attitudes and standards. The feat of humanitarian rescue is worthy of honor. The rescue work that still remains may prove harder, above all because it must seek to extract the individuals from the mass.

Does it surprise you that such things are written? Or does it merely confirm what you already know or suspect about the land of the vast forests? I'm trying to understand why, over time, so many of you want to leave again, not because you're forced to but because you want to, in fact long to, and reading lines like these helps me understand a little better.

Strangely enough, there's some uncertainty about how many of you ultimately stay on. The Swedish historian Svante Hansson, who in 2004 published the most thorough investigation of the matter so far, concludes that it must be investigated still further, since you're such a difficult group to keep track of. From his own findings, he estimates that in 1951 at least five thousand Jewish survivors still remain in Sweden, although the true total is probably considerably higher because no one knows exactly how many of the survivors marry Swedish citizens and thereby disappear early on from the register of stateless persons. He notes that Jewish survivors continue to leave Sweden for many years. By 1955, only 3,600 of the 1945 survivors are estimated to remain. Between 1945 and 1955, a total of 8,782 persons continue their journey with support from the Jewish community in Sweden. In 1946, there are few countries to which they can go, Palestine and the United States being all but closed to Jewish

195

immigration, South America far away and complicated, Australia far away and expensive, Europe as closed as before the war.

In the beginning nearly all of you want to move on, but as answers fail to arrive and onward journeys have to be postponed, the land of the vast forests and labor-hungry factories takes hold of you, one by one. A temporary stay has to be extended for an indefinite period, and in an indefinite period there are many decisions that must be made and many things that must happen without anyone's really having made a decision about them.

In the end, a decision must be made as to whether Sweden is to be the last stop on the road from Auschwitz and the place to start life anew.

In the early years, it's the labor hunger that decides where a new life can make its beginnings. These are the years when Sweden is transformed from a country convinced it can't tolerate too many "aliens" to a country crying out for them. By 1948, a hundred thousand "aliens" have been granted Swedish residence permits, of whom "almost all are fully employed in the labor market." This last part is carefully recorded on July 31, 1948, on the front page of my newspaper of record throughout this narrative, *Stockholms Läns och Södertälje Tidning*, and immediately clarified with "no one granted a residence permit here has the right just to drift aimlessly." The director of the State Aliens Commission, Nils Hagelin, is also keen to clarify: "Work is the best medicine for those who come from war-torn countries and find it hard to cope with orderly conditions. . . . That is how they will most rapidly become part of society, and there are very few who abuse our hospitality by making trouble."

I don't know what Mr. Hagelin means by making trouble. I only know that in a police report submitted to the Ministry of Justice in Stockholm on March 12, 1954, in connection with your application for Swedish citizenship, personnel manager Stina Fors at Alingsås Bomullsväfveri AB has something to say about making trouble.

Yes, I know, that's much later, and again I'm anticipating events, but this concerns your time in Alingsås—though goodness knows how Miss Fors after so many years can remember this specific thing about you. Anyway, here the word "trouble" appears in connection with your name, which is the reason I mention it, because it might tell you something about what at this time was meant by trouble in reference to people like you.

So that there may be no misunderstanding, let me point out that Miss Fors is the only person in the police report from Alingsås to associate you with trouble, in fact the only one to have anything remotely unfavorable to say about you and the woman who is to be my mother and who is applying for Swedish citizenship together with you. The owner of the Pension Friden, Evald Stenberg, remembers "Mr. and Mrs. Rozenberg" as "very reliable, steady and decent, and he can therefore recommend them for Swedish citizenship." The waitress at Pension Friden, Margareta Åberg, remembers you both as "decent and steady" and recommends the same. Only Miss Stina Fors remembers differently:

Dawid Rozenberg was employed as a weaver at the factory in the period 4/2 1946 – 2/8 1947 and from 19 October 1946 until the time he left, he rented lodgings in the factory-owned property at 29 Lendahlsgatan, where he lived with Hala Staw, who was at that time working at the linen factory.

He did his job satisfactorily and the factory did not have any particular complaints about him, but as a tenant he caused the company some difficulty in that he—or possibly Staw—often made trouble with the other tenants.

Miss Fors is of the view that if Mr. and Mrs. Rozenberg are still behaving as they did during their time in Alingsås, it is questionable whether they should be granted Swedish citizenship.

Thus has the woman who is to be my mother, Hala Staw, or Haluś as you usually address her in your letters, or sometimes Halinka, almost imperceptibly joined the guests at the Pension Friden in Alingsås and taken a job as a seamstress at the linen factory, Sveriges Förenade Linnefabriker, and on October 19, 1946, moved with you into a temporary, factory-owned accommodation for foreign textile workers at 29 Lendahlsgatan, where you and she are now referred to as "Mr. and Mrs. Rozenberg," so perhaps it would be appropriate to explain how this has come about.

The last letter from Alingsås in my hands is dated August 9, 1946, and opens on a despondent note despite the fact that Haluś has finally found her way from Łódź in Poland to Bergen-Belsen in Germany, and the horizon ought reasonably to look brighter:

> I find it hard to begin writing this letter to you as I had so much wanted to have concrete news for you, but everything here has reached deadlock for now. I made a big mistake in my application to the W.J.C. [World Jewish Congress] by referring to you as my fiancée.
>
> If you had signed yourself Staw-Rozenberg in your first letter, I would have known how to go about it. As I wrote to you in my earlier letters, do not think of my exertions, stay watchful and on your guard where you are.

August 22, 1946, brings an icy response from the State Aliens Commission in Stockholm to your application for an entry visa for the woman you unwisely refer to as your fiancée (you already know that's not enough, as only married couples get permission).

On that very same day, a woman going by the name of Hella Cwaighaft arrives in Helsingborg from Bergen-Belsen and is put into three weeks' quarantine at Landskrona Citadel. Description: height five feet two inches, hair black, eyes brown, face shape oval, nose straight, age twenty. When registering, she gives her proper name, Hala Staw, and applies for a residence permit and a foreigner's passport. The reason given for the former is that she wants to join her fiancé in Sweden. The reason given for the latter is that she no longer wishes to be a Polish citizen.

On September 12, 1946, Hala Staw moves in with David Rosenberg at Pension Friden in Alingsås. On September 19, 1946, she's hired as a seamstress at Sveriges Förenade Linnefabriker at a wage of fifty kronor a week. On February 23, 1947, she marries the man who is to be my father at the synagogue in Gothenburg.

The next letter I hold in my hand is dated August 2, 1947, and opens "My dearest Halinka, I got to Södertälje at seven in the evening."

∎

So perhaps it's appropriate to say something about how this has happened, which is to say something about yet another improbable road from Auschwitz. I don't intend to say very much; like you I don't want to bore my readers, and even miracles can get tedious, but something must perhaps be said, nevertheless.

After the selection for the gas chambers on the ramp in Auschwitz-Birkenau in August 1945, there are four members of the Staw family left, four sisters to be precise, among whom

Hala is the youngest and Bluma the eldest. Between them come Bronka and Sima. There are photos preserved of sister Sima in the Łódź ghetto, tiny miniature prints, one centimeter by two, taken to be hidden in the growing archive of documents, jottings, statistics, and photographs that the Jewish ghetto administration is building up in a special room with a special entrance in the house at 4 Kościelny Square, and which after the liquidation of the ghetto is saved for posterity by a man named Nachman Zonabend, who belongs to a small group of a few hundred Jews left behind to clear up the human and inhuman remains of the liquidated ghetto's residents. It's a repulsive job among dead bodies and excrement, and requires special rations of spirits for non-Jews, and special Jews for the most repulsive tasks, but the work allows Nachman Zonabend to survive in the ruins of the ghetto until liberation in January 1945, and the miniature pictures of Sima survive with him. In the summer of 1945, Nachman Zonabend is brought to Sweden by the Red Cross along with two of his brothers, one of whom much later becomes a neighbor of ours on the first floor of a modern block of apartments in a suburb of Stockholm. Through Nachman Zonabend, the pictures of Sima come into the hands of the woman who is to be my mother and are stashed in the back of the frame that holds the only existing photo of my paternal grandfather, Gershon.

The reason the ghetto archive keeps pictures of Sima is that she works in the ghetto administration's orphanage, which is one of the many ghetto activities of which a photographic record is kept for posterity. The photos of her look as if they are all taken on the same day: in all of them she is wearing a dark, short-sleeved, jacketlike blouse over a pale top, and her dark blond hair is combed lightly back into a loose bun at the nape of her neck.

Only the situations and poses change.

Sima assisting at the examination of a naked boy on a chair, in front of a woman in white, the boy looking into the camera.

Sima with a young girl getting treatment in a dentist's chair, flanked by two women in white, the girl's face in profile, gently held still by two hands.

Sima at a desk, against the bright light from a window, reflections from sheets of paper and the desktop softly lighting her face, and through the overexposed windowpane a searching look from a boy whose nose scarcely reaches the windowsill. A photographer with a camera is hardly an everyday sight in the ghetto.

Sima standing behind two children, a boy and a girl, her hands on their shoulders, a cigarette in her right hand. The boy is said to be my cousin Obadja. Also in the picture are two older boys with big Stars of David sewn on the right lapels of their skimpy jackets.

One last photograph of a woman, very blurred, and in fact not of Sima but of the woman who is to be my mother. It's taken in the summer of 1945 in the Jewish cemetery in the city of Słupsk, which until recently was a German city called Stolp, and where the Jewish cemetery was filled mainly with men who had given their lives for *Das Vaterland* in the First World War. In the last week of June 1945, a month and a half after the German surrender, Sima Staw, born August 2, 1920, is buried here. In the blurred photo, the woman who is to be my mother is sitting at her grave.

I'm amazed that the Nazis have left any part of the cemetery untouched (the oldest part is confiscated by the Gestapo in 1942, who turn the chapel of rest into accommodations for civilian forced labor), that they have not taken the opportunity to obliterate the traces of those already dead as well.

In the blurry picture, row upon row of tall gravestones.

When, much later, my sister Lilian tries to find Sima's grave, there's no grave to be found. In the 1970s, the Jewish cemetery in Słupsk is razed to the ground. The gravestones are turned into fragments and building material, the cemetery into something else.

On the ramp in Auschwitz-Birkenau, the Staw sisters are categorized as not fully processed human reserves and a few days later transported onward to Stutthof, a concentration camp near Danzig on the Baltic coast. In August and September 1944, 11,464 not fully processed prisoners are transported from Auschwitz to Stutthof (Polish researchers have unearthed the Germans' lists and counted up the numbers), some 7,000 of them women from the liquidated ghetto in Łódź. The full processing in Stutthof costs most of them their lives. Stutthof too is surrounded by an archipelago of slave camps, but most of the prisoners from Łódź via Auschwitz die of starvation and sickness in the main camp. It also has a primitive gas chamber, about 175 cubic feet in size (still standing), in which a thousand or more people, most of them women, are murdered with Zyklon B between August and November 1944. Others are murdered in a railroad car on a siding leading to the crematorium. Others are murdered by phenol injection or shot in the back of the head in the crematorium building itself. As the Eastern Front draws nearer, the Stutthof slave labor camps are evacuated, and eventually the main camp as well. Of the 15,000 who are evacuated, 3,000 survive. On January 31, 1945, between 3,000 and 4,000 prisoners from Stutthof are herded onto the beach near Palmnicken (today Yantarny in the Russian enclave of Kaliningrad) and driven into the sea. Fifteen survive.

No one is intended to survive the full processing in Stutthof.

Bronka doesn't survive Stutthof. She dies from typhus just a few weeks after her arrival from Auschwitz. Bluma, Sima, and Hala survive until the evacuations in February–March 1945. At the selection of prisoners for evacuation, Hala's sick with typhus and can hardly stand on her feet, still less march on them. In Stutthof, typhus is a method of killing, or a reason for killing by other means.

Yet Hala marches all the same, or rather is carried by her sisters. The prisoners walk in a column, five abreast. Anyone who can't keep up or falls out of the ranks is shot dead. Many can't keep up and fall out of the ranks. Reduced ranks are filled from behind. I picture Bluma and Sima in the middle of a row with Hala between them. None of them remembers how long the march goes on. All of them remember the snow and the cold, and the dread that every night will be their last, but none of them remembers how many days and nights pass before the last night comes. On the last night, the prisoners are herded into a barn. It's rumored that the Germans are going to burn the barn down and them with it. The front is close now, and no one believes the Germans intend to leave anyone alive behind.

On the last night, liberation is as unexpected as it is uneventful. In the morning, the SS guards are gone. Within an hour or two, a Red Army unit arrives and on that day, or maybe on the day after—nobody really remembers—the prisoners are taken from Stutthof to a military camp near Słupsk.

As the war is not yet over, the Staw sisters remain in Słupsk, where they come under the protection of a Soviet major by the name of Klebanov. Women on their own, in a town controlled by young men desensitized by war, are in need of protection, no doubt about that. Why Major Klebanov takes them under his wing, equips them with Soviet uniforms, and has them work for the Red Army isn't clear to me. Though not less clear, really, than why there are people who behave humanely even in the most inhumane of circumstances. The sisters' work consists of sorting and packing drugs from a German pharmaceutical factory in Słupsk for shipment to the Soviet Union. Almost everything of value in Słupsk is to be sorted and packed for shipment to the Soviet Union, so there's plenty to keep them busy until the end of the war in May.

In June 1945, Bluma goes to Łódź to see whether there's anything or anyone to go back to.

A week after Bluma sets off, Sima falls ill. Some kind of poisoning. Her skin turns yellow. It all happens very fast. By the time Bluma receives the telegram from Hala saying Sima's ill, Sima is dead.

Sima dies in a German hospital, which for Hala is a sufficient cause of death.

Hala Staw is not yet twenty when she, alone, buries her sister in the Jewish cemetery in Słupsk.

Though not all alone. Someone takes that blurred photo by the grave. Perhaps someone also takes her arm as she rises to go on. A few weeks later, Bluma takes her to Łódź. There's no longer anything or anyone to go back to, but Bluma's eleven years older and has an enterprising spirit, and soon she has found a way for them both to support themselves, at a firm dealing in surplus textiles. On the firm's letterhead is printed "Textile and fancy goods wholesaler Łódź Drapery, B. Staw, 56 Pietrowska, Łódź— Tel. 122-84."

The business does quite well, and new bonds are being forged, and it's no longer a matter of course for either of them to leave Łódź and continue their journey to somewhere else.

■

On January 15, 1946, David Rosenberg sends a jubilant letter in duplicate from Furudal to Hala at two different addresses. The letter sent to Łódź reaches its recipient in just a few days.

Hala's reply, which takes six weeks to get to Alingsås, is reserved in its tone, with no pet names, no terms of endearment, no promises, no dreams, nothing that emotionally corresponds to the jubilant lines in the letter of January 15. And when the letter from Łódź finally reaches Alingsås, there are so many questions to be asked in return:

> Why do you write so little about yourself, I know absolutely nothing. I do understand how hard it is to put these things down on paper. But I implore you to write it all down. What tragedy have you had to go through? Write to me about it all. Tell me everything, I beg you again.

And in the next letter:

> Why do you write so little, it tells me nothing at all about how you really are. You told me you were going somewhere, but not where, and nothing about how you lost Sima (just that it was tragic). I'm begging you as hard as I can to write me a long letter about everything, about what happened to all of you after we got separated in Auschwitz.

In Hala's next letter from Łódź, sent in March, the reticence is explained:

> My beloved Dawidek!
> Don't be surprised at such a start to my letter. After yours of March 7, 1946, I feel I can safely express myself that way. Please don't think your words aroused any other sort of feeling in me, my feelings were the same as yours.
> The letter of January 18 was the first one I sent to you, before I even knew your address. Dawidek, it was no mistake. I was very careful with my words, in case ... I didn't want to hurt you, but neither did I want to risk my position as a woman.
> Anyway, I wasn't sure until the moment I got your letter, which

reawakened some of my old feelings. And now perhaps you understand me?

So if everything could work out the way we've been thinking it
would be wonderful, Dawidek!

You must now write a very affectionate letter where you sort of
hint that I'm your wife, then perhaps I can take it to the Consulate.

On March 27, Hala receives a letter from Alingsås. It says:

You can't imagine how much I was longing for your letter. I had
reckoned on it coming much sooner, but obviously the postal service isn't working normally yet over there. Every day after work I
hurried home (so to speak), thinking to myself that there might be a
letter from Hala waiting. I didn't know what could have happened,
why there was no word from you. Hadn't my letter got through to
you? Had you moved to a different place?

Hala replies from Łódź on April 8:

I'm ready to risk everything to be with you.

I don't know if I'll be able to come to you. As I told you, it's difficult for a young girl like me to use one of the illegal routes. I've
already explained the reasons. It's not just cowardice.

I have a sister, friends, acquaintances, but still no peace of
mind. I feel dreadfully lonely.

Dawidek! Can you imagine the moment when we meet? The
time seems like a century to me.

Don't worry! Everything will work out. Look on the bright side.

Everything does work out in the end, but not in accordance
with any of their plans. Not the plan for Hala to go to Gdansk or
Gdynia to get smuggled on board a ship to Sweden. Nor the plan
for David to join the crew of a ship to Poland and smuggle Hala

aboard. Nor the plan to find a Swedish citizen who will stand surety of ten thousand kronor for Hala.

Everything works out by dint of two lies.

She gets herself from Poland to Germany as a Polish citizen of German ethnic origins, and she gets herself from Germany to Sweden as Hella Cwaighaft.

Perhaps no more needs to be said about how the woman who is to be my mother comes into the picture.

THE PROJECT

Bertil drags his left leg along after him. It's withered and stunted and a few inches shorter than his other leg and firmly encased in a metal and leather splint. Without the splint, Bertil wouldn't be able to walk, at least not without crutches. As it is, he gets along by twitching his left hip to propel his left leg forward to a point even with his right and then supporting himself on the splint as he throws his right leg forward. His body lurches wildly with each step. Forward and back. Up and down. The cage around his left leg rattles and squeaks.

I've grown used to the way Bertil walks, he walks as fast as I do, anyway, but I haven't grown used to his stunted leg. I try not to stare at it, and not to listen to the thumping and rattling, but Bertil's leg pains me. I never see that it pains him, and we never talk about it, but it pains me because it looks so painful. But then we read more than we talk, Bertil and I. Bertil's two years older and lives on the first floor in the house next to ours along the rowanberry avenue, and he has his own room, full of books and comics. Bertil reads a lot and doesn't go out to play all that much, which suits me fine.

But every now and then we do go out. One day we go to the swings in the playground under the pines, behind the Co-op. Bertil likes swinging on the swings. He swings a bit the way he walks, twitching and lurching, as if the upper part of his body can't adapt to a weightless state.

There's an elderly man sitting on a bench in the park, staring at Bertil's leg. "Go home and have some bilberry soup so you'll grow strong and healthy," the man says.

Bertil doesn't reply, just keeps on swinging, perhaps a bit more jerkily.

"I suppose you've heard that bilberry soup cures polio? It takes a lot of soup, though. At least two bowls a day."

Bertil pretends not to hear but my ears prick up, because I know Bertil's stunted leg is caused by polio. Polio's an incurable disease you can die of. There's nothing to say about polio because there's nothing to be done. We both know that.

Bilberry soup! And no one thought of that before, imagine.

I rush over and grab Bertil's swing.

"Did you hear that?"

Yes, Bertil has heard.

We walk back home.

We say no more about bilberry soup.

Neither of us says anything at all.

The only sound is the thump of his shoe, the creak of the splint, and, I seem to recall, a faint sighing in the pines.

For a long time I remain convinced that bilberry soup must be tried. Could I get a few bowls of bilberry soup into Bertil without him noticing? Could Mom give Bertil some bilberry soup and call it something else? After all, cabbage soup is called *kapusta* in our home, and chicken soup is *rossu*. I fantasize about how one day Bertil, filled with bilberry soup called by another name, gets up from our kitchen table and slowly takes off his splint and looks at me with astonishment and gratitude in his gray-blue eyes.

I still have a child's incapacity to distinguish between what's possible and what's not.

I'm also the child of a time when so much that only recently was said to be impossible is now said to be possible, almost a matter of course, in fact.

So why not bilberry soup?

In that respect, it's a bright time to be a child.

So much darkness that will soon be dispelled

The light shining in polio's darkness is a bright, pinkish-red liquid The syringe for the polio injections is big and terrifying, but the color's inviting and comforting. The polio vaccine won't do anything for Bertil's leg, I realize, but the mystery of polio has been solved, so they say. There are many mysteries that are soon to be solved in the years when I'm making the world my own. Once the polio mystery is solved, the cancer mystery will be, too. "Cancer" is one of those words of darkness, like "polio." The demons of polio thrive in piles of earth and unboiled water. The polio virus is killed by a pinkish-red liquid injected into your body. In the newly built school of pale yellow brick, the school nurse's room is an antiseptic temple of white plastic and shiny stainless steel. We're sent there one class at a time for a resolute jab in the tops of our bared arms, meant to bless us with a future from which darkness has been banished.

It's not only polio and cancer that will soon be eradicated, but malaria and tuberculosis, smallpox, measles, and the common cold.

Perhaps pain, too.

Perhaps even war, but that seems a taller order.

"Exterminate" is a word of light, strangely enough. Until very recently, the extermination of human beings was literally darkening the skies, which should have made the very word a word of darkness, should in fact have rendered it all but unusable, but in the world of polio injections there are still things that can and should be exterminated, like weeds or pests. Poor hygiene also needs eradicating, which is merely a matter of time in the apartment blocks by the rowan avenue, where all the apartments have bathtubs and flushing toilets and the garbage trucks have mechanisms for spill-free emptying and the people are starting to perfume their underarms with something they call deodorant, which goes by the name of Mum. "Mumming," they call it. I don't start mumming until much later, when I realize that the smell of sweaty armpits is a sign of poor hygiene.

Paradoxically, it's the successful combating of poor hygiene that in the twentieth century transforms polio from a benign childhood illness causing a temperature and a headache into a nightmare epidemic that paralyzes the nervous system. The virus is spread through excrement, and better toilet hygiene reduces the incidence of it, but better toilet hygiene also reduces the resistance to the virus and increases the risk that older children and adults with little resistance will fall victim to a life-threatening form of the virus. The advances in hygiene that work so successfully on cholera, typhoid, and diphtheria do not work on polio but actually make it more dangerous.

However, no mystery with no solution. Polio is almost eradicated now, and the battle against lack of hygiene is soon to be won. Not to mention the battle against weeds and pests, waged daily behind the fence in the forest between Havsbadet and the rowanberry avenue. The fence is marked with black-and-yellow skull signs. Inside the fence there's a factory. Between the fence and the factory building, there are barrels with white skulls painted on them. Outside the fence, on the paths through the forest, there are dead rats, sometimes gnawed rat skulls. The factory isn't situated along the footpath to Havsbadet but along a side path leading under a railroad viaduct to the other side of the embankment. Around the factory, a pungent smell of acid and decay. There's a damp, cold draft under the viaduct, and it's always dark, and on the way home I keep running until I get a glimpse of the houses along the rowan avenue.

214

I run as if I'm only playing, so no one will know how petrified I am.

The factory behind the fence with the skulls is called Ewos and manufactures products for the extermination of all kinds of things that get in mankind's way. "Chemistry reclaims farming for the farmers," say the advertisements in the local paper. "Parasites" is a recurring word. Parasites infesting animals and crops are getting in the farmers' way, "microorganisms gobbling up hard currency" are getting in the way of paper and wood manufacturers, and in the barrels with the skulls there are, I assume, things that could kill not only parasites and microorganisms but also playing children from the houses on the other side of the embankment, and the danger needs to be signaled in some visual way. The parasites to be killed have names like cabbage seed weevil, pollen beetle, brassica pod midge, wheat blossom midge, and clover cutworm, and the preparations designed to kill them have names like Arsenol, Pyrenon, Rotoxol, and Ewotox, and they're all rendered more effective by being sprayed from the air. Ewos's handbook for growers and breeders is titled *Death of the Millions*.

I read in the local paper (much later, I admit) that the factory site is somewhat problematic in the sense that drainage for the plot on which the barrels are stored has to be routed through a culvert under the railroad embankment in order to run out where it should, into the sea by Igelstaviken, which is part of the deep, saltwater bay on which Havsbadet lies, with its soft sand and creaky diving tower. That in turn requires "the excavation of an open ditch to a maximum depth of 2.70 meters and a length of 260 meters" because the drainage is so poor. This is in December 1951, and the town finance office applies to the town council for 13,500 kronor to underwrite the project.

215

The factory is completed by the spring of 1952, and the drainage runs as intended.

Havsbadet is the light in the world I'm making into my own. Quite literally so, in fact, since it's toward Havsbadet that the forest thins out, and the sky gleams through the pines, and the white sand reaches out to the sunlit water. Havsbadet's always bathed in light, or perhaps it's just that the memory fragments shine more brightly here. Normally, we walk to Havsbadet, or go by bike, but it's the walks I remember, because what I remember is the warmth of your hand around mine, and the silhouette of your back against the sun when you hurry on, or is it me lagging behind to inspect the cowslips, the lilies of the valley, or the bilberries along the forest path and then having to catch up with the back ahead of me and slotting my hand into the warmth. The road we walk on is warm. The fragrance of the forest is warm. Havsbadet is warm.

The canal's cold but Havsbadet's warm.

When we go by bike, Mom's always with us, with the child seat on her bike, which has a spoke guard. Gun, a girl living next door, got her foot stuck in the spokes, or so they say. Whether that's true or not, she has a built-up shoe and walks with a limp. Maybe they just want me to be wary of the spokes. Maybe Gun has had polio, too.

When we walk we're always on our own, you and me, that's how I remember it, the road warm and the air heavy with the scent of resin, and from the sea a whiff of tarred wood as the sand gleams through the last pines.

The jetty at Havsbadet is as wide as a footpath with railings on both sides and runs out to a wooden castle with two side sections and a tower. From the top of the tower, flags flutter in the wind and brave bodies fly through the air. Reflections from the mirrored surface of the water play restlessly on the wooden planks of the yellow-painted side sections, and behind them naked people are sunbathing around an enclosed pool area. I'm allowed into the naked men's pool, but not into the naked women's. They say you can catch a glimpse of the naked women through the cracks in the plank, but that's only something I hear, not something I remember doing. They also say you can swim under the jetties and see naked women that way. I don't remember who tells me this. We never go to the nude bathing pools. Nor do we rent one of the changing huts on the beach. We always sit on a blanket on the sand, and all around us, on a succession of other blankets, sit new friends in a new world, talking and laughing, burrowing their feet into the sand, and touching each other with their hands, and everything looks so bright.

Södertälje bathing beach is a tourist attraction. There's a wooden pavilion with a dance floor, and a restaurant, and a terrace overlooking the sea, and beneath the pines on the edge of the forest there are tennis courts and miniature golf courses, and along the beach toward the small cape at Näset there are boardinghouses and summer villas with rooms to rent, and every summer weekend caravans of bicycles and cars wind their way along the paved road through the rowanberry avenue, and people come by train from Stockholm and get off at Södertälje Södra and walk the last bit with their blankets and baskets. Is there a bus, perhaps? I don't remember a bus. Before the war, during the summer season, there was apparently a temporary railroad stop as well, situated where the embankment came closest to the beach, but this is something no one any longer remembers.

On July 25, 1949, the local paper reports, "beach crammed with 1,840 paying visitors and 1,200 children." Where do we pay? I can't remember any kind of entrance to Havsbadet, still less a fence. Do we pay to sit on the sand? "Many of the visitors were from Stockholm and clearly there were also a good number of foreigners on the beach, to judge by the confusion of languages, though many of these were perhaps part of the more settled colony of foreigners living among us since the stream of wartime refugees."

The source for the article is Kalle Åbom, the bathing beach superintendent. Did Kalle Åbom walk past our blanket? What does he mean by a confusion of languages? Everybody talks to each other all the time, of course, and the language they usually speak is Swedish. Maybe they don't speak as fluently as Kalle Åbom, but it's Swedish all the same. Janek from Poland speaks Swedish to Ulla from Finland, Birger from Sundsvall speaks Swedish to Ilonka from Sapanta in Romania via Bergen-Belsen, Moses from Poland speaks Swedish to Kato from Hungary,

Karin and Ingvar speak Swedish. You and Mom speak Swedish to me and Yiddish and Polish to each other. The only language I remember myself speaking is Swedish, though I later learn that I speak Polish, too. There are many languages in my world, and their sounds fill it as naturally as the shrieks of the gulls over the flag-topped tower in the glittering water and the faint rasp of naked flesh on warm sand.

One night at the end of May 1954, Havsbadet burns down. I can't imagine the world without Havsbadet, but the building's yellow wings with the separate pools for men and women burn down, and the jetty and its railings burn down, and the scent of tar is overpowered by the smell of burned wood, and nothing remains but the tower, standing alone in the water like a sooty chimney.

The beach and the sand remain too, for now.

What remains for the longest is the light.

On September 25, 1953, assistant vicar Yngve Junel at the parish civil registration office in Södertälje attests "that former Polish citizen Dawid Rosenberg can speak, write and read the Swedish language to a proficient level." I can attest in addition that you're doing all you can to teach your four-year-old son this language, using homemade wooden alphabet blocks laid out on the floor of our living room. I'd assert that you make an excellent job of it, too, or at any rate, that your son is an early and omnivorous reader. He reads the names on the shop signs along the main road, he reads the destination boards hanging from the canopies of the station platforms, he reads the small print on the boxes of washing powder, he reads everything that crosses his path, and you make energetic efforts to ensure that what crosses his

219

path is worth reading, though you don't always succeed. He also reads when you would rather he didn't, with a flashlight under the bed covers, or in the fading evening light that comes through the crack at the side of the blind.

What must be attested to, above all, is that you have ambitions, not only for your son but for yourself too. You journey on to the town with the big truck factory because you're convinced you have a brighter future as a truck builder than as a weaver. At any event, the wage is higher and rises faster. Between 1950 and 1953, it rises from 5,740 kronor to 11,600 kronor per annum. Trucks are in hot demand. South America needs trucks, too. The truck factory's main problem is finding accommodation for all the workers it must recruit to build the ever-increasing number of trucks required to build the world anew. It's a great time for truck builders, and especially for a truck builder who only recently was building trucks in a German slave labor camp, and who instead of sharing a room in a Swedish bachelors' barrack with a "young and quiet snail" is now sharing a modern one-room apartment with the woman who is the mother of the child who is to become me. At the truck factory, they need not only fitters but also designers and engineers, and you have no intention of remaining a pipe fitter all your life. I don't know what a pipe fitter does, or rather what sort of pipes you fit, where they're located on the truck, or how they work, but I know you're a champion at bending and welding pipes.

One day you come home with an eight-branched candlestick made of curved, welded brass pipes. A ninth branch is welded at an angle to the rest, to hold the candle used to light the other candles. You've made the candleholders out of six-sided brass nuts. I remember the candlestick as well as I remember the Christmas tree, a small one for tabletop use, that I nag you into buying at an early stage. A full-length tree is out of the question, even if everybody else has one. I know that we don't celebrate Christmas and that the candlestick is a sort of compromise. It's a Jewish candlestick, a Hanukkah candlestick, and the eight candles are lit from the ninth, one evening at a time, to commemorate an event in the Jewish calendar that coincides well enough with the season of Christmas tree lights and orange advent stars for one set of lights to be equated with the other. And then there are the Lucia candles, which somehow belong to us all. The Lucia Day celebration is a festival everybody at the big truck factory participates in, with hundreds of employees and their families sitting in the huge assembly shop at long tables set with festive ginger biscuits, and the children fishing with long rods over blue fabric screens to pull out bags of presents. The Lucia celebration is my only close contact with the big truck factory, but the sensation of oil, metal, and soot persists in my nostrils and the sparkle of Lucia candles shines in my memory. The intention of the Lucia celebration is to build "bridges between management and employees and between the shop floor and administrative staff," and to strengthen something called the Scania Spirit. To strengthen the Scania Spirit, the employees are also offered subsidized study circles and holiday cottages and loans to build their own homes, and they're given gold pins or gold watches for long and loyal service. There are no two ways about it: the big truck factory is doing all it can to give its employees no cause to dream of a future other than the one already on offer. Benefits for the workers, rewards for the loyal, promotion for the ambitious.

It's a bright time, in short. A time for bright dreams and big projects.

Your Project is to start life anew in the town with the big truck factory. I'd like to see the town as the given place to do it in, since it's the place that's given to me, but one of the reasons you get off the train in Södertälje Södra, apart from your qualifications as an experienced truck builder for Firma Büssing in Braunschweig, is that you're not permitted to get off the train in Stockholm. Nor are you permitted to get off the train in Gothenburg or Malmö. On the series of six-month work and residence permits issued to you from March 1946 to January 1952, those are the stipulated exceptions: not valid for residence in Greater Stockholm, Gothenburg, or Malmö. Once or twice we go to Stockholm on the train that crosses the bridge over the canal and I chant the names of the stations along the line, but for some reason you have no right to live and work there. Nor does Mom.

Perhaps it's just as well. In the forbidden books at Per Olof's, I read nothing but dark things about the morass of the big city, and in the little town with the big truck factory the future looks bright even to foreigners who have just stepped off the train. After work, you stay up late into the evening with your head bowed over the booklets and exercise books of your correspondence courses, since you have no intention of remaining a pipe fitter forever.

Correspondence courses are the Place's dream factory. With the help of correspondence courses, anybody in any small town can become anything. You want to become a mechanical engineer, and on the small round table in the living room lies a thick book with a red binding and the title *Forge and Machine Work*. It begins: "Every individual benefits from being able to do calculations." Hereafter follow calculations galore, thousands of pages filled with detailed, illustrated instructions in the method and technique of handling all the machines of the modern engineer-

222

ing industry: automatic lathe and turret lathe operation, pressure turning, arc welding, spot welding, seam welding, welded pipe bends. The book is recommended by representatives of every interest group and social class in the Swedish dream factory, the trade unions, the employers, the engineers, and the professors, and claims to provide "precisely the modern, practical instructions required for today's accelerated pace of production."

There's a photograph of you at the factory, surrounded by your workmates in the pipe gang. It's taken in 1951. You're standing in the front with your welding goggles flipped up; you've taken off your peaked cap, and you're smiling as if you've just completed a perfect weld and know your own worth as a pipe fitter. The others in the picture are wearing caps or berets and look more impassive. I recognize one of them from the world outside the factory, perhaps from the sand at the beach, but the factory is part of your world, not mine. You vanish in there for forty-eight hours a week, including Saturdays, and exactly where it is that you go once you're inside the factory gate beyond the viaduct, I don't know. The factory's bigger than the rowanberry avenue, in fact bigger than the little town itself. The town has other factories besides, one of which swallows up your Haluš in the mornings, and sometimes in the evenings, to speed-pack tablets in bottles, or sit by a conveyor belt sewing clothes to music, and you're both exhausted when you get home and soon you have two children in a one-room apartment with kitchen, and it can't be taken for granted that you'll have enough money and stamina to sit through late evenings and nights to educate yourself to be something other than a pipe fitter.

Nor that the big truck factory will want you for anything else. Among your papers I find the following letter from the personnel department:

223

With reference to your application to our punch-card department for training as a punch-card operator: As a result of inquiries undertaken by us in response to your application we have learned that punch-card operators are not currently being recruited. Nor is it envisaged that there will be any expansion of staff in that department over the coming year.

It may not be your greatest dream to be a punch-card operator. What does a punch-card operator do? Punch-card machines are early computers, fed with data from punch cards. A punch-card operator ensures that the right card is accessed in the right order, or something like that. I don't see it as any kind of natural progression for a man who can weld perfect pipe joints to become a punch-card operator, but I sense that what you're really seeking here is confirmation that your horizons are open again and that you've started a new life in a new world, in line with the main thrust of the Project.

I call it the Project, as you will have noticed, because that's how I perceive it much later when I want to connect your early concern

for the Child's reading ability and your late-night poring over course books and your restless ambition to move ahead in a life that still surprises you every morning, and which is built on survival and reunion in a configuration too miraculous to be allowed to stagnate or, God forbid, to come apart. Within the parameters of the Project, the letter from the personnel department is no mere trifle, but no disaster either. The Place offers other dreams to be fulfilled. Such as a two-room apartment on the other side of the rowanberry avenue. Or a black 1955 Volkswagen, offered at an employee discount. Or a factory-subsidized house of your own, expected to be built largely by yourself.

Perhaps I'm exaggerating the role of the Place in the Project, I know that you too dream of the road onward, although for various reasons your road doesn't lead onward. And after all, the Place seems to offer a world in which every dream is feasible, since it's a world where no dreams have been shattered, including the dreams that were shattered in the world you come from, which is a world the Project will help put behind you. In that sense, the Place is an ideal one because so few people here remember what you have to put behind you. That is to say, there's no lack of information about what you have to put behind you, the local paper does actually report a thing or two, but it's not something anyone here has experienced or had any direct part in and is therefore easier to forget. There are those who have to forget because they don't want to remember (and therefore remember all too well), and there are those who forget because they have nothing particular to remember. The past doesn't have a very strong position in this place, and oblivion is the foundation of the Project. Oblivion and optimism. As far as optimism is concerned, the Place has a competitive edge against practically the whole world, since optimism has never been challenged here. While the outside world collapses, and with it most people's futures, here nothing's collapsing. Here the best of all worlds is in full swing and needs only to take a short break before beginning again where it left off.

The best of all worlds is called *Folkhemmet*, "the home of the people," otherwise known as the welfare state or the social democracy, and it's an exceptional invention that knits together the individual's need for security and a sense of belonging with her yearning for freedom and self-fulfillment, all of which seems even more feasible after the break than before. In the best of all worlds, no one will ever be without a job and a livelihood and a roof overhead, and all schoolchildren will get a free meal a day, and everybody will be entitled to free medical care and a guaranteed pension at retirement and able to afford the stream of ever-new appliances with which ever-new personal freedoms will be attained. In the best of all worlds, a pipe fitter can become a mechanical engineer or a punch-card operator, or at least a home owner and car owner, and the son of a pipe fitter can become practically anything. By November 25, 1950, the local paper is able to announce that Sweden "is well on the way to being a model of the social state."

The two of you are still categorized as foreigners and have to renew your work and residence permits every six months, and you're not permitted to settle in the big city across the bridge, but conditions for beginning a new life in a new world must nevertheless seem favorable, since a new world is in fact being realized here. "From cradle to grave we will provide care for our citizens to an extent that the pioneers of the labor movement surely could never have dreamed of," writes the local paper, and much later I envision people pinching themselves in the arm as they read on:

At the foundation is maternal care: free medical support for mothers during pregnancy and childbirth, supplemented with maternity benefits in cash. For families with children up to the age of 16, the load of providing for them will be alleviated by annual cash allowances. In addition, there will be free care for infants. A higher living standard for families with children will be achieved through housing subsidies for large sections of the population. This will continue at school with free school meals, free dental care, and, during vacations, with free outings and country sojourns. At the appropriate age, talented students with limited financial means will be eligible for financial support. And when the next generations enter the labor market, they will be secured against loss of earnings resulting from illness, accidents, or unemployment.... On top of all this comes social assistance for times of particular need, doing away with the old poor relief.

I don't think the two of you can yet imagine such a world, still less dream about it, but before long the Child is planted in one of the newly established kindergartens of the model social state. State-supported kindergartens are a newfangled addition to social welfare, and the official term for them is daycare centers, but kindergartens live on in the language. Kindergartens and crèches. A linguistic affirmation that daycare centers too are expected to provide both care and love.

The Child instantly takes root, he has no problems with being left in the morning and no longing to be picked up, and one evening when the picking up is taking a long time and he's left alone with Miss Naima and it's getting dark outside, it still takes a while for him to get anxious. Miss Naima lives in Vagnhärad, which is one railroad stop to the south, and if Mom's too late the Child will go to Vagnhärad with Miss Naima on the train. Mom's late, and it's dark outside, and anxiety has grown into fear, and all that remains of being picked up so late is the sensation of a soft fur collar against a cold coat in the doorway.

The Child's two years old when he starts being left and picked up at the new daycare center on the bottom floor of one of the apartment blocks below the railroad station. Before the center opens, the local paper informs its readers that "those wishing to avail themselves of the option of having their children cared for during the day should register their interest at the Child Welfare Office in the old town hall." The daycare center comprises two rooms and an office, which is to be used as an isolation room "in the event of a child falling ill during the day and it not being possible to contact the parents." It's a small daycare center, taking fifteen children at most, which according to child welfare assistant Kerstin Malmkvist is a drop in the ocean because there are all too many children in the apartment blocks along the rowan-berry avenue, and there are bound to be far more applications than there is capacity, so means-testing will be needed, and it will be "primarily single mothers who can count on getting a place for their children here." Anyone interested in a place at the daycare center is however encouraged to apply, "even by telephone if necessary," and by one means or another you apply to the Child Welfare Office in the old town hall, and one of the fifteen places is given to me, which means that your Haluś can again cycle off in the mornings to sew clothes at piecework rates to the accompaniment of music in Tornvall's garment factory.

Otherwise, most mothers stay at home with their children during the day and are referred to as housewives or homemak-ers, and for them ever-new machines or products are invented to make housework easier and more enjoyable. "A brighter living for Mother," notes the local paper, which is nevertheless somewhat concerned that housewives "are weighed down by the bad habits of previous generations" and therefore don't yet fully understand how to use the new machines. In the advertisements in the local paper, a housewife is always a well-dressed woman, smiling as the machines do her work.

The new machines are also supposed to make life easier for the increasing number of women who nevertheless must go off to a factory in the mornings, and who may sometimes be late picking up their children in the afternoons, but who are still expected to fit all the housework into what's left of the day. "Many have a working day of up to 16 hours, sometimes even more," declares the head of the Domestic Research Institute in the local paper. She doesn't see machines in the home as the solution to the problem. The solution to the problem is to shift housework out of the home and allow the model social state to supply not only daycare centers but also the tidying, cleaning, sewing, baking, and cooking. A few machines at home may still be a good idea, a pressure cooker and a vacuum cleaner, for instance. The vacuum cleaner can encourage children to help with the housework because they like pressing buttons and changing the nozzles, so they feel like "proper mechanics."

In the small one-room apartment overlooking the railroad platform, there's no room for machines. In the two-room apartment on the other side of the rowanberry avenue, there's room for a round, sausagelike Volta vacuum cleaner, but it fails to make me a button-happy vacuum mechanic. I fear my mother is one of those weighed down by the bad habits of previous generations. To make my favorite dish, she sets sheets of newspaper alight in the sink and singes the last feathers off a chicken. Chicken soup is food for weekends and special days, as is gefilte fish, which she makes with fresh bream that she buys from the lift-netters on inner Maren, the small sea inlet in the middle of town. The big lift nets are wound up and down from little boats moored to the quayside. The bream have big scales that glitter as they flap in the lift nets. On the draining board in the kitchen, they're still flapping. By the time Mom has scaled and stuffed them, they're not flapping anymore.

I think the only semiprocessed product she ever uses is frozen cod fillet. She breads and fries the fillets until they're an appetizing golden brown, but frozen cod fillet isn't my favorite semiprocessed product. Frozen food is seen as a major step along the road to easier and more enjoyable housework, but I can't fathom why, because there's not a single kitchen in the apartment blocks along the rowanberry avenue with a freezer to keep the frozen food in, only a refrigerator at most, where you can't even keep ice cream for more than an hour or two. For a while the new Co-op below the railroad station boasts the biggest freezer cabinet in town (10.8 shelf meters of cold, as the local paper puts it), and it's precisely here that so many housewives and so many children and so many big plans for the future can be found.

Big plans for the future are the hallmark of the Place. It's believed to have a great future, although the plans haven't yet been finalized. Since the railroad drew a line through the plans for a meandering garden city with a church on a hilltop and a square with a covered market and a tram running to the sea, there are now plans for a modern cityscape housing six thousand people. A new tunnel will be dug through the high embankment, and around the growing cityscape land will be set aside for new homes, industries, and workplaces.

Including the land where the rowanberry avenue ends and the forest toward Havsbadet begins.

Beneath the sparse pines behind the Co-op, town planning architect Fritz Voigt is planning a playground, and in the forest toward Havsbadet he's planning industrial units.

The forest is larger in my memory than in real life. In my memory the forest is both dark and light, and the houses on the rowanberry avenue are both visible and invisible from it, and the trampled paths through it are both familiar and secret.

A forest doesn't need to be any larger than that to compete with architect Voigt's playground.

Architect Voigt has plans for the town center, too. One plan is to make more space for the growing numbers of cars that have to pass through the center on their way between Stockholm and the world. This plan presupposes that large parts of the existing center will be pulled down and rebuilt, and that the low wooden buildings along narrow pedestrian streets will be replaced by tall concrete buildings along wide thoroughfares. In America, architect Voigt has learned that cars can be parked on third and fourth "decks" above shops at ground level. For the fifth floor he proposes "a green deck" with playgrounds for children. That way, the cars that have to pass through the town center anyway will have an opportunity and a reason to stop for a while.

On Sunday afternoons, the growing numbers of cars that have to pass through the center of town are congested into traffic lines several kilometers long. Most of the car models are bulbous in shape: Saabs, Volvos, Morrises, DKWs, and Volkswagens, all shimmering like beetles in the sun. From a rise just above the southern approach to the town, I can see the line stretching to the horizon and unmoving for long periods of time. The air must be blue-hazed from all the exhaust fumes and heavy with the noise of engines, but I'm deaf and blind to such things. I keep a note of unusual makes of car and unfamiliar license plate numbers in a school exercise book. In Sweden, cars are registered by county. The local ones all have a B, the cars from Stockholm an A. It's much less common to see a Z, Y, AC, or BD. I can't imagine that the recording of car makes and plate numbers is my idea; I never learn to recognize car makes, yet there I am, sitting on the rise with someone I can't remember, taking an interest in car makes and plate numbers. The traffic jams are an intrusive Sunday sight and we have to come up with something to make it more fun. The best thing of all is to stand by the bridge over the canal, see the drawbridge rising, and watch the motorists reluctantly getting out of their cars to catch a glimpse of the ship interrupting their passage, and listen to them complain about the "drawbridge misery."

The bridge across the canal splits the little town into its two historically incompatible interests. The interests of those who just want to pass through demand the quickest possible thoroughfare, while the interests of those who want people to make a stop demand that they be able to slow down, park, and get out of their cars. The years when I'm noting down the exotic plate numbers of cars in stationary traffic lines are the years when the big plans for the town center are finalized. One plan proposes pulling down the old wooden buildings and widening the shopping street to provide more space for the cars and the thoroughfare while also making room for cars to stop for a while. The other plan proposes that a new road and a new bridge over the canal bypass the heart of the town, taking a route near the railroad bridge, leaving Södertälje on a turning off the main highway, just as it was left at the end of a spur off the main railroad line.

232

For a time the plans exist side by side, unresolved.

All futures still seem compatible and possible.

Everything that's new heralds brighter times, including the traffic lines and the drawbridge misery.

If a forest or a town or a bathing beach happens to stand in the future's way, the future has precedence.

I prefer traveling by train rather than by car. The train that runs on the single-track spur between Södertälje Södra and Södertälje Central is powered by a shunting engine and has coaches with open platforms and wooden benches. The journey takes five minutes. From fourth grade on, I take the train to school. The train to Stockholm has bigger engines and bigger coaches with corridors and compartments with upholstered seats. On the express trains making their brief stop at Platform 1, closest to the rowanberry avenue, there are coaches going to Copenhagen and Hamburg, and clattering dining cars, and sleeping cars from foreign railroad companies marked Schlafwagen or Wagon-Lit, their curtains drawn. One day I find myself peddling the Södertälje specialty, twisted buns, on Platform 1. Or perhaps someone else is in charge of the peddling and is just letting me have a try. The memory fragment will not shine forth. The passengers reach out from the windows. Where are they going? Where have they come from? With trains, you always know that sort of thing. It's written on the signs hanging down from the platform roofs and on the signs attached to the sides of the coaches, and it's announced from the loudspeakers fixed to the platform pillars. On Platform 1 I stay in close and frequent contact with the towns of Katrineholm, Hallsberg, Nässjö, and Alvesta, and by extension with the world as far as I can imagine it. I can't imagine the world any farther than the town of Borås, with a change of train in Herrljunga. In Borås there are black steam trains, hissing and belching out smoke. Borås is where my uncle Natek and my two cousins live. Trains are for traveling from one place to another. Trains don't run or stop just anywhere. Taking the train is always a bit of a ceremony, and people buy special platform tickets so they can meet and wave good-bye, and laugh and cry as the trains pull in and out of Platform 1 and the rowanberry avenue comes into and out of view.

So I don't really understand why we need a car. To get to Havsbadet, we walk or cycle. To get to work, the two of you take your bicycles or the branch line. Going to Stockholm or Borås we take the train, as I've explained. Cars aren't very common on the rowanberry avenue. Anders's dad has a car that's usually parked in the yard outside the house and sometimes needs to be cranked up with a large handle, but then Anders's dad has a store in the main square selling spare parts and maybe that's why he needs a car.

Our car's a 1955 black Volkswagen, registration number B 40011, and it's the latest model, with a small back window and semaphore arms for directional signaling. Anders keeps going on about the Beetle's having its engine at the back and being cooled by air, whereas his dad's car and all other cars have the engine in the front and are water-cooled. It's safer to have the engine at the front and the petrol tank at the back, Anders says, but I'm not interested in the difference. Nor am I particularly interested in the car as such. One hot summer day, it just happens to be there. I remember that whole summer as very hot and very nice, and we use the car for day trips on holidays and Sundays. A car isn't for going from one place to another, but for going nowhere in particular to unpack a picnic basket or a deck chair, or just see the world through the car window. A car ad in the local paper reads "Everything's so much easier now. On Sundays and work-free days we can get out into the countryside, go for a dip, pick berries and mushrooms — or just take a spin. Try a Volkswagen for that wonderful feeling of independence."

We take the car to Lake Malmsjön instead of walking or biking to Havsbadet. We take the car in the summer when Aunt Bluma and my cousins from Tel Aviv stay with us in the small two-room apartment on the other side of the rowanberry avenue. We take the car to Karin and Ingvar's self-built little country cottage. We take the car to Stockholm now and then, even though the train is quicker. We never take the car to Borås. When the car's full of people, I squeeze into the little space between the back seat and the engine compartment. The roads are narrow and winding, and the wind rushes noisily through the open windows, and the engine whines through the compartment wall, and it's tiring to travel by car. Lots of people on the rowanberry avenue spend their Sundays and work-free days washing and waxing their cars until they shine like new.

The simple truth is that a car is a luxury, just yesterday unthinkable for a pipe fitter at Scania-Vabis and a seamstress at Tornvall's, but in the new life in the new world, so many things that were unthinkable only yesterday are not anymore.

The car becomes a part of the Project in the same way as the plans for a self-built house in Vibergen and citizenship.

On May 7, 1954, the two of you become Swedish citizens.

■

The clearest indication that I overestimate the Place's importance to the Project is that for quite some time, you continue to consider leaving it and moving on. Many of the people who contribute to the confusion of languages around our blanket on the sands of Havsbadet in the first years do what the express trains do, they make only a brief stop and then move on. Some cross the bridge to Stockholm once that route is opened to them, but most move on to begin their lives anew in another world. The other worlds are called Israel and America, *Jisroel unt Amejrika*. The Wyszogrodzki family, who live in the apartment block opposite ours on the rowanberry avenue, move on to Israel, where one no longer has to travel illegally by freighter. Moniek Wyszogrodzki is a pastry cook and a racing cyclist and my godfather. In Jewish tradition, the duty of the godfather or *sandak* is to hold the child's head at the circumcision ceremony, which takes place when I am eight days old. My image of Moniek Wyszogrodzki is formed much later, when he's a pastry cook and a racing cyclist in Israel, living with Mania and four daughters in a lovely house on the slopes of Mount Carmel, looking out over Haifa Bay and the gold-glittering Bahá'i Shrine. Moniek, now Moshe, Wyszogrodzki has red hair, a freckled face, and gray-blue eyes that radiate the energy and will of a competitive personality. Mania bears the physical marks of the road to and from Auschwitz, a lined face and gaps in her teeth, but not Moshe. Moshe lives by the cycling theorem: if you don't keep pedaling, you fall off. In Södertälje, he's a member of the Amateur Cycling Club.

Much later I realize that some of his energy and will also benefits you. Besides holding my head steady during circumcision, he also has a hand in the housing miracle, the little one-room apartment with the window facing the railroad tracks in the house across from the bakery.

It doesn't surprise me that the Wyszogrodzki family's departure from Södertälje prompts an article in the local paper. It's December 17, 1949, and the article makes the front page, and it's the result of Moniek Wyszogrodzki energetically and on his own initiative striding into the newspaper office and requesting to express, through the paper, "his gratitude to Södertälje for the hospitality he and members of his family have enjoyed." In particular he wants to thank his friends in the Amateur Cycling Club. The article reveals that the Wyszogrodzki family has already departed by train for Malmö, from where they will fly to Marseille and continue to Haifa by boat, and that they have left Södertälje together with "the tailor Adam Glusman [sic] and his wife Polla." It's obvious from the article that the writer has difficulties in fully comprehending Moniek Wyszogrodzki's story about his road to Södertälje, and I don't think it's due to a confusion of languages. I rather think it's a certain rigidity inherent in the journalistic language of the day that manifests itself here. In any event, it's a contemporary historical document, and I'll let it speak for itself:

> We both came from Germany in 1945 after having spent a rather long time in concentration camps. We didn't arrive here together, but by sheer chance happened across each other in Karlstad in December 1945. We hadn't seen each other for five years. It goes without saying that we were happy to see each other.
>
> Sadly, my wife had contracted TB in the difficult years in Germany and had to spend two and a half years in various sanatoriums. Fortunately enough, she has made a complete recovery.

This is the only article I can find in the local paper about the temporary community of survivors in Södertälje, apart from the one about the confusion of languages on the sands of

237

Havsbadet. Within a few years, virtually the whole community has moved on. The majority are women from Bergen-Belsen or Ravensbrück, who have come to Södertälje to make clothes at the Tornvall garment factory, where the yearly staff turnover is 100 percent. Many of them live at Pension Fridhem, which is a large, privately owned, red-painted wooden house at a walking distance from the factory. There are pensions where people stay to rest, and there are pensions, such as Friden in Alingsås and Fridhem in Södertälje, where people stay to work.

One of the residents at Pension Fridhem is Auntie Ilonka, who comes from Bergen-Belsen via the aliens' camp at Kummelnäs, outside Stockholm, where on September 20, 1945, she's declared fit and "ready to be sent to work." A year later she marries Uncle Birger from Sundsvall and changes her surname from Hellman to Sundberg and moves from Pension Fridhem to a cold-water apartment with a dry privy in the yard, not far from the big pharmaceutical factory, and some years after that to a fully modern flat in the newly built, eight-story apartment house at the other end of the rowanberry avenue. Uncle Birger works at the truck factory and earns money on the side as an insurance salesman, and Auntie Ilonka soon stops sewing for Tornvall's and opens a tobacconist's shop in a red-brick apartment building, and as far as I can tell they're an ill-matched and happy couple. Their marriage is childless, but in their home I'm their child. It's a fragile home, full of glittering china and glass figurines, crystal chandeliers hanging from the ceiling, embroidered lace cloths on the tables, and sets of hardback novels in matching bindings on the bookshelves. The tables are laid with thin, gold-edged china cups and saucers with elegant floral patterns, lemonade glasses with drinking straws, and serving plates in nickel silver filled with homemade cakes, buns, and Swiss

238

rolls. Auntie Ilonka's deep love of children often expresses itself in highly calorific forms. Their home is also one of the first to boast a radio gramophone of dark mahogany, and at the earliest possible instant, a piece of furniture combining the radio gramophone with a television. When the television broadcasts live matches from the Stockholm World Cup in 1958, we put the radio commentary on. No one can stand the silence on TV. There has to be that constant radio blare, otherwise nothing can really be happening, can it? Auntie Ilonka has glittering black eyes and a gold tooth that glints when she laughs, and her Swedish sings with a different lilt from yours. There's a Polish lilt and a Hungarian lilt, and I grow up to the sound of them both. Uncle Birger speaks a northern Swedish dialect, and the dishes served in their kitchen are somehow northern as well, often lingonberries. If Auntie Ilonka has brought any dishes from her home in the previous world, I don't remember them. What I remember is meatballs with cream sauce and lingonberries. And the cakes. And Uncle Birger's northern lilt as he says my name. There's no need for you to say good-bye to Auntie Ilonka, or to Auntie Ethel who marries Uncle Sven, Birger's brother, or to Uncle Miklós and Auntie Elisabeth, who live across the railroad bridge and are staying on here for roughly the same reasons as you are.

And that's about the size it remains, the refugee colony of Jewish survivors in Södertälje; most people move on. From America come shiny photographs of flourishing babies in bulbous baby carriages, from Israel thin blue aerograms with tightly written sentences on every folded flap of the single sheet. When I tear off the stamps, they leave holes in the sentences.

On second thought, Södertälje isn't the most obvious place to start life anew. At least not for those who want that life to have anything Jewish about it. The prerequisites for Jewish life don't exist in Södertälje. Jewish life demands a basic, minimum number of Jews, and in Södertälje that number is never to be reached. During the brief period when it might have been reached, the Jews in Södertälje have other things to think about than Jewish life, assuming they want to think about Jewish life at all. I sense that being Jewish is not something to make a big show of. Not in a place like this. When I tell the two of you that Mr. Winqvist always calls out *"Herein!"* in German when anybody knocks at the classroom door, you worry that I'll think I know a bit of German and try it out on Mr. Winqvist, when what I possibly might know is a few words of Yiddish. I never let Mr. Winqvist find out that I know a few words of Yiddish. The Jewish elements of our life are toned down. On Friday evenings, Mom blesses the Sabbath candles with a gentle movement of her hand, and on the big Jewish holidays we go to Stockholm. At school I'm excused from Scripture lessons, but when I resist having to be the only exception in the school, there's little opposition. On summer vacations I'm sent to a camp for Jewish children in the archipelago north of Stockholm that no doubt fulfills its educational purposes, but it's far from clear what role Jewish life plays in the Project.

I don't think it's missing Jewish life that for so long makes you consider moving on. I think it's the horizons of the Place that refuse to open up to you, in spite of the miracle apartment, and the truck factory, and the mapped-out future, and the day-care center, and Havsbadet, and the Child who's supposed to make his world yours.

And in spite of Karin and Ingvar.

Ingvar's the team leader in the pipe gang at the truck factory and a few years older than you; I'm not sure by what words and gestures you soon become friends, but very early on, hanging in the one-room apartment below the railroad station, there's an oil painting by Ingvar—a vase of flowers. Karin and Ingvar are there before the Child. It's Karin and Ingvar who suggest giving the Child a name that doesn't stand out. Karin and Ingvar are there at the Child's circumcision. "All those people who would soon spread around the world," Karin writes, much later. "Nobody could speak Swedish. All the men wore hats."

In what language do Karin and Ingvar become your friends? Not only your sole friends outside the refugee colony, but your best friends at that. You celebrate your first New Year's Eve in Södertälje in their home. They're the first to see your first curtains in your first apartment on Villagatan. You raise your first glasses in a toast to Karin and Ingvar's firstborn child. You also serve coffee in your first glasses, since Ingvar doesn't drink tea. Ten months later, when your firstborn is due to arrive, Ingvar comes along to the hospital, so that there will be no confusion of languages. After all, Ingvar has some experience by now, and he's from the Place.

Confusion of languages is my term for the invisible wall rising up between you and the Place, not a wall between languages so much as a wall between worlds, between the world you carry with you and the world you hope to make your own; a wall that no language whatsoever can penetrate. After all, the words are there already—ghetto, death camp, gas chamber, annihilation, extermination—but nobody understands what they mean.

Insofar as they care what they mean.

It must be lonely to live in a place where nobody understands what the words mean, even though you take such pains with them.

Karin writes that you search among the books on their shelves and ask for Strindberg. She writes that you learn Swedish by reading Strindberg and that before long you can write "without spelling mistakes and completely grammatically."

It's certainly in the language of Strindberg that you study for your correspondence courses late into the night, in the hope that the horizon will open and the confusion of languages cease.

It's also certain that as soon as the Child can add one letter to another on the living room floor, you come home carrying a briefcase heavy with library books. The Child's early reading includes classics like *Children of the Forest*, *Hat Cottage*, *Cat Goes on a Journey*, and *Spotty*, about a rabbit who's different from all the other rabbits; but also—and far too early—*Conqueror of the Seas: The Story of Magellan*, by Stefan Zweig.

Karin and Ingvar understand you better than most people, not because they understand more of your words but because they like you and want to understand you and want you to stay on so that your children can grow up together and you can all cycle out together to the little wooden summerhouse Ingvar has built out of spare packing cases from the truck factory.

The fact that you two hesitate for so long over whether to move on or not, I believe, has something to do with Karin and Ingvar.

On July 9, 1953, carrying two heavy suitcases, you board the train to Marseille via Copenhagen and Paris. You spend a few days in Paris, lugging the cases around. Your French is not on a par with your Swedish, so when you happen to knock into some one on the sidewalk you say *S'il vous plaît* instead of *Excusez-moi*, which doesn't go down very well. You immediately learn to say "sorry" and not "please." Another sort of confusion of languages, for sure, and easier to sort out.

In Paris you also carry lists with names and addresses of people who might have known people who might have survived the world you come from.

That's what's left of the world you come from: lists of names and addresses.

In Paris, one of the names at one of the addresses takes you along to Jo Goldenberg's newly opened Jewish restaurant on rue des Rosiers, where they serve food that smells and tastes of the world you come from.

That too is left of the world you come from: smells and tastes.

In Marseille, if not before, it comes home to you that the Place is a paradise after all. In Marseille there's destruction and poverty as far as the eye can see. Walking that last bit through the district around the docks, you keep a tight hold on your suitcases, which are loaded with necessities from Paradise for the Promised Land: clothes, fabrics, canned goods, batteries, light-bulbs. On the ship, a photograph of you in profile. You're standing by the rail on the top deck, gazing toward the horizon. You're wearing white shorts and white sandals and are stripped to the waist, your ribs just about visible beneath the tanned skin, no scars visible anywhere. The wind's blowing your hair back from your high forehead. I'd like to read yearnings for another world into your gaze, but I don't know whether the picture was taken on the way to Israel or on the way back, so it could just be that what I see is homesickness for the one-room apartment on the rowanberry avenue.

In Israel you'll find most of the names and addresses on your list of persons who might know persons from the world you come from. Israel is largely populated by people from the world you come from. Israel is a world you don't have to make your own since it already belongs to you, a world where you don't have to be afraid of being foreigners, still less of being Jews, since this is a world of Jews.

At any rate, that's how it looks on paper.

On paper, it's a very attractive world, and it will take a lot to make you turn your back on it.

Six weeks later, you turn your back on it. The photos of your trip reveal nothing of what makes you do that. You have a very nice reflex camera that makes a resolute click as it takes sharp pictures of trimly dressed people in bright sunshine. There you are on the promenade in Tel Aviv with a warm breeze ruffling your hair, and Bluma has her hands on Jacob and Isaac, who are standing there in white shoes, white shirts, and white shorts with white suspenders, while in the background men in white shirts and women in flowery dresses stroll along; it must be a

Saturday afternoon. There you are on the slopes of Mount Carmel with Bluma and Moniek Wyszogrodzki, who has opened a cake shop and cafe in Haifa and has just been handed spare parts for a bread-making machine out of one of the suitcases you've brought along, and you're all looking out over Haifa Bay, where the cargo ships lie at anchor in the humid summer haze.

What the pictures fail to reveal is the economic crisis. You come to Israel at a time when everybody asks if you're out of your mind, thinking of leaving Paradise for Hell. Yes, this is how they describe the situation in the country. I don't find any letters from your trip to Israel, but the question is clearly stored among the fragments of my memory: are you out of your mind? The country is on the brink of ruin and all consumer goods are strictly rationed: meat, bread, vegetables, clothes, shoes. In the shops, the rations run out and leave people still standing in line, the factories have been brought to a standstill by a lack of raw materials and electric power, the newspapers have halved in size because of the paper shortage. It's not even certain that you'll be allowed to emigrate here. The Israeli government is toying with the idea of rationing Jewish immigration, too, so that there can be sufficient food and necessities to go around for those who are here already. The idea is that only Jews in acute physical danger will be allowed in. The idea never has to be put to the test, because there are so few Jews knocking on the door in these days of distress. The years of mass immigration from Europe are over, and the years of mass immigration from North Africa are yet to come, and for a few lean years in between, people shake their heads despairingly over anyone crazy enough to want to leave Sweden for Israel.

In the summer of 1953 the Israeli economy is turning around, but you probably don't notice it, and people probably don't dare to believe it, and besides, there's an ominous clamor about the main reason for the upturn: the Reparations Agreement with West Germany. On July 30,1953, in the middle of your trip to Israel, the first delivery of German iron under the Reparations Agreement is loaded onto the freighter *Haifa* in the port of Bremen. Some people use the term "damages," but the German word is, *Wiedergutmachung*, "reparations." The Hebrew word is simply *shilumim*, "payments." The summer you turn your back on Israel, West Germany starts to compensate for the annihilation of your world by means of cash payments and deliveries of iron and steel for the construction of the state of Israel, thus allowing the economy to turn around. In the 1950s, reparations from West Germany cover 29 percent of the deficit in the Israeli balance of payments. Soon the Israeli economy is growing by 8–9 percent, and within ten years the per capita income rises by 74 percent. If your trip had been a year or two later, no one would have shaken their heads despairingly at you. Two years later, your brother Natek is divorced and moves from Borås to Tel Aviv, while we move from one side of the rowanberry avenue to the other. That's all.

No, not really all, there's the citizenship too, and the house in Vibergen, and the second child.

After your journey to Israel, only one future seems to be left, the one already mapped out.

■

You travel to Israel on a Swedish alien's passport valid for one year. In your passport application of September 17, 1952, your description is certified by Acting Deputy Sergeant Sture

Blomgren: height five feet three inches, hair brown, eyes dark brown, face shape oval, nose straight. "To the approval of the alien's application, I have no objections," reads the annotation by Ola Olsson at the office of the public prosecutor in Södertälje.

The alien's passport is a sort of recognition, after all. You're still an alien, but now you're a Swedish alien. Sweden keeps a careful watch over its aliens. In the passport application, a thorough account of your background and conduct, the confusion of languages, the onerous kind, is still apparent. The report from the local police in Södertälje notes that up to August 1944, the applicant

> held assorted positions in Lodz, the most recent of which was as a postman in the Ghetto where he lived with other Jewish families. In August 1944 he was deported and taken to the Auschwitz concentration camp, where he stayed for about a month. He was then transferred to a similar camp in Braunschweig, where he was made to stay until 3/21/1945, during which time he worked for the Germans in a truck factory.

As regards your fellow applicant, my mother, the report notes that after war broke out she "was employed in a clothing factory, where she worked in the office for about a year and then became a seamstress in the factory," after which she was deported to a concentration camp in Germany.

That's all.

How much of this is a product of what you actually say, and how much is a product of what Acting Deputy Sergeant Sture Blomgren is able to understand from what you say?

But maybe this is about as much as either of you wishes to say. Maybe your only wish is to qualify for Swedish alien status, and therefore you emphasize what you believe will be seen as qualifying, such as your conscientiousness and your willingness to work.

The two of you have no trouble qualifying for Swedish alien status, and a scant two years later for Swedish citizenship too, although the eye of the needle appears narrower here. At any event, the pile of documents in the archives of the State Aliens Commission is bigger, mainly thanks to the interviews with all the people who have observed you on your road through Sweden, and who are now sought out by the police to pronounce on your suitability for Swedish citizenship. Among them is, as I've previously mentioned, personnel officer Stina Fors at Alingsås Bomullsväfveri, who considers you unsuitable on the grounds of something she remembers having observed seven years earlier. As said, she's the only one to take that view. Caretaker Rolf Larsson at 22 Villagatan in Södertälje certifies that the applicants "were reliable people." Caretaker G. Carlsson at 42A Hertig Carls väg in Södertälje certifies that the applicants "fulfilled their obligations as tenants and there is nothing to complain of as regards their conduct." Engineer Rune Fridholm at Scania-Vabis AB considers "the applicant to be professional in his work and generally liked at his place of employment." As for you, you state that you have permanently settled in Sweden, which you view as your second native country. I think you mean to say that you now have a second native country replacing the first, which no longer exists. This you solemnly declare on October 12, 1953.

On the subject of your fellow applicant Hala Rozenberg, engineer G. Bogler at Tornvalls Konfektion AB states that she is a capable seamstress and that there are no complaints about her conduct. In a handwritten note on the application is added: "By phone Mrs. R. has specifically requested that her surname be spelt with an *s* (not *z*)."

The citizenship certificate is dated May 7, 1954.
From now on, Rosenberg with an *s*.

A few months later, the local paper reports from Israel that bakery worker Israel Sinai has hanged himself as a protest against the high taxes, and that tradesmen and shopkeepers in the country have gone out on a four-hour sympathy strike in his memory, but I don't think you need to have your choice confirmed any longer. In the autumn of 1954, there's another child in the one-room apartment below the railroad station, and on the round table in the living room lies the prospectus for Vibergen.

There's an allotment somewhere too. Just a patch of soil, no hut or toolshed, long uncultivated and overgrown with weeds. We cycle to the allotment along the road to Havsbadet and past Näset to the edge of a forest, where the checkerboard of allotments stretches as far as the eye can see. There are lots of mosquitoes that summer and we have no hut or shed to escape to, only an oily repellent to make a mess with. I don't see why we need the allotment. In the parts we've weeded and dug, we plant strawberry plants. No, we don't plant the strawberries, you do. I do nothing. The mosquitoes don't seem to trouble you in the slightest, but between me and the allotment they build a wall. I don't think you've realized how much work there is with strawberry plants, how weeds love strawberry plants. And besides, they send out runners all over the place. I don't remember the strawberries themselves, only the runners. The following summer we don't have the allotment anymore. The following summer we have a stony plot of land in Vibergen instead, with spruce trees growing on it. In the telephone directory you already appear at the new address, David Rosenberg, 22 Vibergsvägen.

It's nothing but a plot of land that you must clear before a house, built at least partly by you, can go up there. There's still snow on the ground when we drag the branches and twigs and uprooted stumps of felled spruce into a big pile, which will still be there when the mosquitoes come.

Vibergen is a special offer from the truck factory. Employees who want to build their own house in Vibergen are offered all sorts of assistance. They're also offered an interest-free loan of three thousand kronor, with no amortization needed. A hundred people attend the first Vibergen information meeting, and thirty-six of those decide to accept the offer.

One of them is you.

It causes a bit of a stir that one of them is you.

In the house magazine of the truck factory, *Kilometern* (The Kilometer), there's a photo of you. You're standing at a workbench, bending pipes. "David Rosenberg is an able and industrious pipe fitter," it says under the picture. "His calm eye as he goes about his work would certainly strike anyone who saw him a few years ago, when the horrors of war were still very much alive for him, and all dreams were nightmares. Now he's thriving."

Yes, you do look very calm in the picture, your hands firmly gripping the pipe for bending, and your eyes fixed on the vise it's clamped in.

Another photo: the Rosenberg family at the round table in the living room. On the table, a white lace cloth and the Vibergen prospectus. Your right hand's holding up the prospectus, and your left is on my shoulder. I'm wearing a checked shirt and leather suspenders and looking down at the prospectus. Lilian's eight months old, sitting on Mom's knee and looking up into the camera. "Within the next year, the Rosenbergs hope to be living under their own roof," runs the caption. The piece that accompanies the pictures is headlined "HOME AT LAST," and it relates

the story of David Rosenberg from Poland…, who shared his destiny as a refugee with millions of others in wartime and postwar Europe, a story that starts in the Polish city of Lodz one October afternoon in 1939 and leads, via starvation, assault, privation, general misery, and horror, to the spring of 1955, when it ends at Scania-Vabis in Södertälje.

Well, that's undeniably the way it may look; as if Södertälje were the last stop on your journey, and as if your future beneath the factory-subsidized roof were all mapped out already. It is, after all, an extremely favorable offer, practically a gift, from the truck factory, since it's not only interest-free but also written off at an annual rate of 10 percent, which means that after ten years you owe nothing without having repaid anything. Assuming, of course, that you stay on at the factory for another ten years. If you want to leave before that, you'll have to pay back the outstanding amount of the loan. If you want to leave after five years, you'll have to pay back half. You say nothing in the magazine piece about your ambitions to be something other than a pipe fitter. Getting the loan requires no ambition. Getting the loan requires that you continue to be an able and industrious assembler at Scania-Vabis in Södertälje for another ten years. The house in Vibergen is, in short, the happy ending to the story of David Rosenberg from Poland and his family. Home at last.

"Our old home no longer exists, we have no relatives. In reality we have already died once, it is just that we were granted a rebirth. And here in Sweden we have tried to start all over again. It has gone quite well, the years have slipped by, and we no longer have

251

those nightmares," says David Rosenberg. "I have a job I like, and good friends. And now I am going to try building my own house."

It seems to me that the writer of the article in *Kilometern* does what he can to overcome the confusion of languages, the onerous kind. He writes of "the chimneys of the extermination camps," of your brothers and sisters, fathers and mothers going up in smoke before your eyes in Auschwitz, of the dead and frozen bodies in the open freight cars on the railroad track en route to Ravensbrück, of the nineteen-year-old American soldier who on seeing you and Natek in Wöbbelin "bursts into floods of tears."

Yet nowhere does he say that you're Jews. The word "Jews" doesn't occur in the text, nor the word "ghetto." Is it because you don't mention them? Is it because the writer doesn't want to complicate the story?

A few weeks later, you receive a letter from the writer:

Mr. Rosenberg!

I don't know if you're a reader of *Dagens Nyheter*, the newspaper where I'm on the permanent staff, but if you happen not to be, I'd like to tell you that starting on Thursday, *Dagens Nyheter* is going to publish a series of articles in which we recapitulate what happened and what came to light during these days, ten years ago.

Please don't think I'm writing in order to recruit a new subscriber. I just think that these articles will be of great interest to you. And you will presumably be pleased that this newspaper is thinking along exactly the same lines as you—the concentration camps absolutely must not be forgotten.

Please give my regards to your sweet wife and your lovely children!

I see this letter as a sign that after ten years, the two of you give the impression of being at home. At any rate, you give the impression of being potential subscribers to *Dagens Nyheter*. A subscription to *Dagens Nyheter* is scarcely an issue one would raise with people who give the impression that they're on their way somewhere else. Among the memory fragments from the two-room apartment on the other side of the rowanberry avenue, there's definitely the glint of a morning paper. I'd like to say it's *Dagens Nyheter*, but it might just as well have been the local paper. The brightest glint comes from the glossy weekly *Folket i Bild*, which means "The People in Pictures." *Folket i Bild* has large pictures on its covers. On one cover there's a naked woman cooking food in a kitchen. On the inside there's an illustrated story about nudists, which is a word I learn from *Folket i Bild*.

No newspapers ever get delivered to Vibergen. The following year, the address is gone from the telephone directory. The following year, we're not under our own roof in Vibergen but in the small two-room apartment on the other side of the rowanberry avenue. Nothing comes of Vibergen but a painstakingly cleared forest slope. This has something to do with the loan and the factory. With the fact that the conditions of the loan have tightened and the costs have risen, so that the ties to the factory have stiffened. With the fact that the factory doesn't want you as anything other than an able and industrious pipe fitter. You don't want to tie yourself to the factory for another ten years on those terms. The snow has long since melted and the air has become warm and humid and the mosquitoes are dancing in the evening sunshine above the whitewood stakes marking our plot at Vibergen when you close the prospectus for the last time and decline the loan and the house and the future mapped out by the factory.

I like to think the car has something to do with it. At any rate, the car comes into the picture the same summer as Vibergen disappears from it. It's a hot summer, as I said, and the wind is blowing through the open side windows, and the freedom of the road tickles the nostrils, but a new Volkswagen, the 1955 model, costs 6,375 kronor (almost half your annual salary), "including delivery to Hälsingborg," and even if you can purchase it with a staff discount from the truck factory and perhaps a small personal loan as well, it's still hard to understand why you say no to the house but yes to the car—unless the car is part of a plan for another future than the one already mapped out.

Be that as it may, this is the point at which you invent and construct a luggage rack for VW Beetles. It's made of "top-quality tubular steel" painted a matte silver shade "to go with any automobile color" and simply slots into two holders screwed to the back bumper mounts. Thus fixed, a bit outside the rear hatch and just above the license plate, this platform can accommodate two stacked suitcases or a bicycle or everything one needs for a picnic. It's an ingenious construction that admittedly has the slight disadvantage of needing to be removed if one has to check the oil or change the fan belt or do anything else that requires opening the rear hatch, but on the other hand the rack can be neatly folded and stowed away in that little space under the front hood and above the gas tank that's not much use for anything else. You name your invention the Piccolo, weld together a couple of prototypes all by yourself, and market it with a spartan leaflet, slipped under the windshield wipers of every VW in sight. On a few Sundays I come along to help out and keep you company, and I don't know too much what it's all about, but a Beetle I can recognize, and the windshield wipers I can reach, and I manage to place a few leaflets. "Volkswagen owners! Novelty!" it says at the top of the leaflet, and below are two pictures of our black and still shiny VW with the Piccolo mounted on the back and the Piccolo folded in the front, and a presentation text written by yourself, concluding with "Yours faithfully" and a signature. It's a well-written and informative text, telling the reader that "Piccolo doesn't come into direct contact with the bodywork, obscure the license plate or brake light, or obstruct the air-cooling system." At the bottom of the leaflet there's an order form that can be cut off along the black line and sent directly to D. Rosenberg, 42A Hertig Carls väg, Södertälje, to place an order for a Piccolo "at 55 kronor plus shipping, with full right of return within eight days."

I have to admit to a certain partiality here, but the Piccolo's a splendid invention that efficiently and elegantly solves a luggage problem inherent in all VW Beetles. It's a splendid leaflet, too, personal and persuasive, even providing our telephone number—0755/38157—which can be called anytime before 8 p.m. You assure the reader that the Piccolo has been subjected to strenuous testing and has proved itself "the sturdy, convenient, and reliable luggage carrier with which all VW owners should be equipped."

I don't know what strenuous testing you subject the Piccolo to, but Anders and I subject it to two children swinging up and down on it, which makes the Beetle rock violently while the Piccolo stays firmly in place. The matte silver color gives the Piccolo's tubular steel a silky surface that feels warm to naked skin, a detail that the leaflet neglects to mention.

255

Much later, I'm holding the yellowing leaflet in my hand, astonished by your energy and initiative. Where do you find the time to do all this? I don't remember anybody helping you. Yours is the only name on the leaflet. It is to you that customers are told to phone or write. You're the inventor, manufacturer, and salesman, all in one. You're working forty-eight hours a week at the truck factory and you're clearing a forest plot in Vibergen and you're the father of two children in a tiny one-room apartment below the railroad station and you design, make, and sell the Piccolo.

I don't know how many Piccolos you make and sell. All I know is that the Piccolo disappears from our lives as abruptly as Vibergen.

Or maybe the Piccolo disappears first.

Or maybe the two disappearances are connected.

The memory fragments refuse to piece themselves together.

Much later, I can see how alone you are with your invention. There's no evidence of a partner or financial backer.

Much later, I'm surprised at how far you get with it, alone.

I don't know what causes the project to founder in the end, but I suspect it's lack of capital and contacts and possibly, when

I think about it, a lack of that kind of boldness that borders on foolhardiness. You're bold enough to invest, but not foolhardy enough to keep on once you realize the risks you're running. Or rather, once the fear of risking the life you have gets its claws into your ambitions to start a new life. At any event, this is how I, much later, feel impelled to interpret the momentary explosion of energy and activity and confidence in those first years after the Israel crossroads, and the equally swift retreat to your starting point as an able and industrious fitter, bending pipes at the truck factory. You simply cannot be allowed to fail, and when the demons of failure get their claws into you anyway, you lack the required boldness (or foolhardiness) to take up the fight. The Piccolo fades away, leaving behind an unembellished black Volkswagen Beetle, and Vibergen becomes a small two-room apartment on the other side of the rowanberry avenue, where the kitchen window looks down on the outer harbor and some small villa gardens, their apples ripe for swiping as the hot summer of 1955 turns into fall.

In the year 1955, 25,452 VW Beetles are sold in Sweden. One in every five cars sold is a Beetle. The Beetle's the best-selling make of car in the country. A Piccolo on one out of every hundred, at least to start with, and you would have owned your own business and lived in a house of your own. Now I see only one Piccolo in the Södertälje area, and I don't recall us ever using it for anything but tests.

Do you ever have doubts?

I mean, not just about the invention, but about the Beetle itself, which after all was Hitler's contribution to motoring. Much later, I come to understand that there were people who wouldn't even consider driving a VW, let alone buying one, but when the import ban on foreign cars is lifted in 1954 and the Beetle becomes the best-selling car in Sweden, few people associate it with Hitler.

I associate the Beetle with you.

With your tanned elbow leaning out of the open side window and the warm breeze blowing through your hair as the car zooms along, and the silvery Piccolo visible through the back window, following us on its sturdy bumper mounts.

I associate the uniform with the Beetle too. It's a greenish sort of gray and has big breast pockets with deep pleats and bulging buttons, and a folded cap tucked under the shoulder strap, and really seems too heavy to wear in summer, but it's early summer or late spring and you're behind the wheel and we drive down an avenue of tall trees to a big, grand house and I see men in uniforms through the side window and gray-green military trucks through the windshield. I don't know where we are, or why, but it has something to do with the uniform.

What I do know is that on May 15, 1956, you're called up to the Royal Svea Logistic Regiment in Linköping, and between August 3 and November 12 you're taught how to maintain and repair military vehicles. Not exactly a new horizon, but you shoot well. With the army-issue Mauser M-38 you shoot your way to the army's Silver Medal for shooting, scoring 86 out of a possible 100. The only picture of you in uniform is in a weapons store with straight rows of Mausers lined up in racks behind you, and you're holding an army-issue submachine gun, the M-45. It's November and you're in the army's white winter camouflage coat with the fur collar, and on your head you have the army's lined leather cap. You look small in the winter uniform. The summer uniform suits you better. You do most of your military service in the summer and autumn of 1956. Having completed 180 days, you're excused from the remaining 180 days and the compulsory refresher course.

You're thirty-three years old, and you have a family with two children to provide for.

And a horizon that doesn't quite want to open up.

■

There's something indistinct about the horizon, not just the small one, beyond the rowanberry avenue, the railroad bridge, and Havsbadet, but also the big one, beyond the radio set that stares at me with its blue-green Cyclops eye and over which you bend your head in the evenings. Sometimes you press your ear closer to the loudspeaker fabric and gently turn the right-hand dial and move the indicator through the radio stations, and the blue-green eye pulsates with the wavelengths of the world and the sounds of the world burst in from the big horizon. Much later, I realize that what comes bursting in are the sounds of war, the sounds of Israeli tanks charging toward the Suez Canal, and Soviet tanks charging toward Budapest, and in the small two-room apartment on the other side of the rowanberry avenue you hang your uniform in the hall and bend your concerned head toward the world.

Are you concerned about Caryl Chessman, too? A Caryl Chessman fragment glints brightly in the darkness around the uniform and the radio set. Caryl Chessman is waiting for his death sentence to be carried out. Year after year, he waits for his death sentence to be carried out. Chessman is also a brand of cigarettes, sold in a yellow packet with black and white checks. Auntie Elisabeth on the other side of the railroad bridge chain-smokes Chessmans, and Chessman is reprieved, time and time again, until he's taken into the gas chamber to die. There's always a last-minute reprieve for Chessman. A film about Caryl Chessman, based on a book by Caryl Chessman, is showing at the Castro cinema, and I can't stop thinking about death in the gas chamber when Auntie Elisabeth lights a new Chessman with the glowing end of the previous one.

No, I don't think you're bowing your head for Caryl Chessman, not even when the last minute comes, and not for Tumba-Tarzan either, I assume. Tumba-Tarzan is the Caryl Chessman of the rowanberry avenue. Tumba-Tarzan is hiding out in the woods around Tumba and Rönninge but has also been sighted in the forest around Havsbadet and in the woods near the riding school on the other side of the railroad bridge, and some people say they've seen his abandoned lair in the woods around the Ewos skull factory. Tumba-Tarzan's lairs are always abandoned when the police find them. The hunt for Tumba-Tarzan never ends, and in the school playground we replace the hunt for Robin Hood with the hunt for Tumba-Tarzan. In the local paper he's referred to alternatively as a desperado and a pathfinder, reflecting pretty well the atmosphere of combined terror and admiration that the hunt for Tumba-Tarzan arouses in the rowanberry avenue and surrounding area. When no one has sighted Tumba-Tarzan for a while, the local paper wonders anxiously if he's left the vicinity, and when someone immediately thereafter spots a tent or a couple of bikes hidden under some spruce branches in the woods on the other side of the truck factory, the local paper hopes that they're Tumba-Tarzan's and he's come back. When he's finally caught, we're all convinced he'll soon find a way to escape. Tumba-Tarzan has broken out of a penal colony to go and find his Jane, whose name is Alice, and take her away, over the water on a raft, to live as an outlaw in the vast forests around the rowanberry avenue. They live on pheasants' eggs they find on the ground and canned food they steal from empty villas and summer cottages, and they let the police find the still-warm campfires they've just abandoned on their freedom flight through the Swedish summer. Tumba-Tarzan is the first rebel of the rowanberry avenue, and we keep on seeing him in the forest on the way to Havsbadet and in the woods around the skull factory long after he's been caught.

Much later, I read the report of the proceedings at Södertörn District Court against Rolf Johansson and understand once again why he was a rebel and not just a common thief:

> Tumba-Tarzan admitted all the charges against him and clearly had a good memory for his actions. He occasionally stated that the chronological order of some of the break-ins was wrong, and he made one objection in the course of his hearing. This concerned the theft of some bottles of beer, which he absolutely denied. The prosecutor accepted this and removed that particular charge.

The mapped-out future generates its rebels. After Tumba-Tarzan there are Tommy and Elvis, who split the school playground into two camps and fill the local paper with ominous warnings about young people going astray. Then Tumba-Tarzan again, in the form of two young brothers who quickly bring the brand into disrepute by behaving more like thieves than rebels.

The local paper is also full of debates about whether people were happier in the old agrarian society than in the new industrial one. Much space is given to a survey of Swedish factory workers, who answer the question with "an unqualified yes." Much space, also, is given to a front-page article about a public meeting to protest against "the widespread vandalizing of parks in Södertälje." Park vandals are held to include people creating their own paths across the grassy areas. Young children are said to vandalize out of ignorance ("training is needed here"), older children out of a desire for opposition ("they need to be guided toward other activities in which they can vent their feelings").

I certainly know who vents their feelings by twisting the swings several times over the top of the frame in the playground behind the Co-op. I certainly know who eventually ends up in the young offenders' prison at Hall. I certainly know there are things we do because they're forbidden.

I'm no rebel, far from it, but I'm tempted by forbidden things, too.

In the light of later understanding, I think it has something to do with that mapped-out future, the one staring at us all and not blinking, not flinching, not paying any heed to the shadows behind us and the confusion around us and the fear inside us, the one we therefore want to see through and give the finger to, which is what the rebels are doing for us. Against the mapped-out future, the rebels hold out the forbidden dangers and freedoms of untrodden forest.

You're no rebel either, far from it, but when the horizon of the truck factory refuses to open and the mapped-out future threatens to suffocate you, untrodden forest starts to attract you, too. "I've made a huge mistake in staying at the factory for so many years, I would have been better off doing a variety of jobs," you write to Natek on October 11, 1957, my ninth birthday. The factory has started to measure the time each stage of your job takes, using a method called MTM, demanding that you do the same amount of work in a shorter time, and you're beginning to suffer from persistent headaches that you suspect have something to do with your "unhappiness" at the factory.

You write the word in Swedish, *vantrivsel*, in a letter otherwise in Polish. Natek has made the leap from Borås to Tel

Aviv, and you're ready to make the leap from the truck factory to almost anywhere else. The more the horizon closes in, the more important the leap becomes, and the longer the leap is postponed, the more the horizon closes in. You tell Natek that you recently replied to an advertisement "for a job as a service engineer for the Toledo automatic car," and the company called you back and everything looked very promising—until you told them you were thirty-five.

I know nothing about the Toledo automatic car (*automatvagnen*). You're writing in Polish, so the problem could have something to do with the translation, or with your Polish, which quite often has some Swedish mixed in, making it hard to understand what you mean, particularly when the Swedish and Polish words are similar. You may possibly mean a service engineer for the Toledo automatic scales (*våg* rather than *vagn*), but I'm not familiar with those either. What I do know is that you speak the language of Strindberg with the accent of Mickiewicz, and what I suspect, much later, is that the obstacle to your becoming a service technician for Toledo wagons or scales is not your age but the confusion of languages.

In a letter to Natek on February 17, 1959:

PS. If you have any good contacts with firms in the textile trade who are interested in exporting to Sweden (Scandinavia) and have still not been introduced into these countries, do try to get hold of some samples. It could be ladies' blouses, thin cotton and wool sweaters, but only the latest fashion, original designs, and the right sort of price.

Time and again you raise your head to see if the horizon is opening, but instead you see time running out and the Project stalling.

Let me say something about the big horizon as I see it, much later. There's something about the light. It's too bright. It eats away the shadows and burns off the gray shades. The world becomes too light and too dark. The brightest of horizons shines over the darkest of experiences and the most menacing of times.

"The residents of Södertälje can protect themselves against a dreaded nuclear death by throwing themselves to the ground and ensuring that no part of the body is left uncovered," pronounces Captain Curt Holmfrid at a public meeting of the Södertälje Civil Defense Association on April 29, 1957.

"The atom bomb can shorten wars and reduce casualties," asserts Colonel Erik Graab at the meeting of the Rotary Club on August 20, 1957.

"More than half of New York's eight million inhabitants are estimated to have died in a mock attack in which five hydrogen bombs were dropped," reports the local paper on July 21, 1956.

"The USA has hydrogen bombs that can displace the earth's axis by sixteen degrees," says the local paper on October 27, 1956.

"The mystery of life will soon be solved and religion abolished," pronounces the director of studies at the Workers' Education Association, Torvald Karlbom, in the assembly hall of my local school on August 18, 1956.

"Ours is an age characterized by lack of moral and spiritual direction," warns study ombudsman Thorsten Eliasson of the Workers' Education Association in the music room of my local school on August 21, 1957.

Light in the assembly hall, darkness in the music room.

Light on the big horizon, darkness on the small.

■

Darkness descends only gradually, almost imperceptibly, over Havsbadet. On July 11, 1956, the local paper reports a water temperature of 19 degrees C (66 degrees F) and two thousand bathers. On July 18, 1956, the Chemical Analysis Agency reports 7,000 E. coli bacteria per liter of seawater. On August 6, 1956, the local paper reports sunshine and a party spirit at a packed bathing beach for the 38th swimming gala, "the loveliest element unquestionably the formation floating, which a bouquet of pretty girls had mastered to perfection."

The darkness is falling and nobody notices.

Nobody wants to notice.

Havsbadet is too indispensable to be unfit for use.

The unfitness follows from the toilets. Year after year, human waste is flushed from toilets straight out into the bays of Igelstaviken and Hallfjärden and can sometimes be seen washing up on rocks and beaches in semisolid form. Over the course of twenty years, the number of toilets in Södertälje increases twentyfold. Toilets— called water closets or WCs—are to be found in all the apartments in the blocks along the rowanberry avenue. It's only the tenements in Baltic that still have dry privies in the yard, or dry closets as the local paper calls them. The dry privies are rows of dark stalls, separated by thin walls of rough planking. I can hang on for days to avoid going to the dry privies. I'm scared to death of something crawling up out of the dark holes or of falling into them. The WC is a blessing for humankind in general, and for me in particular.

The price of having a WC, however, is Havsbadet, even if nobody wants to accept the fact and the payment keeps being postponed. Summer after summer, the question is raised of

whether Havsbadet should be closed or cordoned off so people who should know better will keep away, but summer after
summer, thousands of people who don't know better burrow
their feet into the white sand of Havsbadet and take a dip in
the tainted waters and reluctantly use the new beach showers to
rinse off the E. coli bacteria afterward. The showers are installed
after the fire and are intended to replace dips in the sea, but dips
in the sea are not easily replaced. Particularly not as long as the
Chemical Analysis Agency is vacillating about the water quality
and the Public Health Board is vacillating about the closure and
there are experts claiming they can purify the water at Havsbadet within two weeks. A Dr. Pettersson from Stockholm is given
the opportunity to test his method, which employs compressed
air to force the water from the bottom up to the surface and a
propeller to push it toward the shore, which presupposes that
the water at the lower level is cleaner than the water at the surface, a fact that even the local newspaper calls into question.
"There's doubtless a large volume of polluted water even at the
deeper level, extending a good way out to sea."

In the record-breaking hot summer of 1959, health inspector
Torsten Lysell issues a warning in the local paper, saying that the
water quality is steadily deteriorating and when last measured
was found to contain 90,000 E. coli bacteria per liter, which is
potentially life-threatening. He's also worried by the fact that
the public seems entirely unconcerned. A few weeks later, he
proposes that Havsbadet be closed down, because people are
tearing down the notices prohibiting its use and continuing to
bathe there.

I don't remember when we swap Havsbadet for the lake of
Malmsjön. The transition is gradual and almost imperceptible.
The summer I'm learning to swim, we go by car to Malmsjön. I

associate the swap more with the car than with the water. Malm-sjön has no sandy beach, and no restaurant with evening dances and no horizon to hold your gaze, but there are no swimming lessons at Havsbadet anymore.

Yet I don't remember that we stop going to Havsbadet.

That we ever stop going to Havsbadet.

Havsbadet continues to be a place we go, I remember, for the sand and the light, and the scent of resin and pine needles along the path through the trees.

■

What makes you go back to Łódź? I have no memory of your doing so and for a long time I live with the certainty that you would never have done so, but on April 24, 1958, you unquestionably write a letter to Natek from Łódź. It's clear from the letter that you have a cousin, Jerzyk, still alive in Łódź and that he meets you at Kaliska station, although you have trouble recognizing him because you haven't met for twenty years, but he recognizes you from the photo you've sent in advance. You write of how glad you are to see each other again, and how common memories have brought you close, and how cordially his "little family" welcomes you, but I find it hard to believe that you return to Łódź to meet a cousin, even if he's the only cousin you have who's still alive. I suspect you return to Łódź to confirm with your own eyes that the world you once made into your own no longer exists. I suspect, too, that it has something to do with the horizon, the one that's not really opening, and with the Project, the one threatening to stall.

Your search for confirmation is soon over. "As for Łódź, the town made the most terrible impression on me, and I had a heavy heart those first days. All I wanted was to fly away, back home again. I haven't felt so forsaken since the war. Like a child."

No, there's nothing left in Łódź of the world you once made into your own.

Not even the graves. You go with Jerzyk to the Jewish cemetery to look for your father Gershon and your brother Salek. You're quite sure that Gershon's grave, at least, must be there somewhere, since it's registered in a document. In a small box, on the thin airmail paper the letter's written on, you've made a note of the date of death given in the register, July 25, 1943.

So you stay in Łódź for three weeks instead of the planned two, to continue the search, but you don't find the graves. Nor do you find much else from the world that was once yours. "There are so few Jews left here. Even in Stockholm, you're more likely to bump into a *Jid*."

You discuss the next leg of the journey with Jerzyk. His journey, not yours. As soon as the opportunity arises he wants to move on, ideally to America but more likely to Israel. There's nothing to stay in Łódź for.

And your journey? Do you consider it over?

One day we take the train to Stockholm, you and I. I don't know why it's just the two of us or why we're not at school and work, respectively. It must be fall: you're wearing your herringbone-patterned coat and black hat, and the station platforms, wet with rain, are glistening yellow, and I rush to the compartment window to catch sight of the black canal running vertiginously far below the railroad bridge before the train almost immediately stops in Östertälje. The station names along the way are reassuringly familiar, whereas Stockholm remains a thoroughly strange and scary city. I hold your hand from the instant we get off the train until we've gone through a tall front doorway and into a big entrance hall with a red carpet on a marble floor and solid walls of dark wood, and into the first-ever elevator of my life. I let go of your hand only when you tell me I can press the elevator button. It's a big moment, the first press of my first elevator button, and I get a faint sinking feeling in my stomach as the elevator silently carries us up past floor after floor of dark wood doors and shiny brass plates. On the floor where we get out of the elevator and go through a door, a long corridor with yet more doors is revealed, and from the corridor with all the doors a short man with a bent back comes toward us, greets you, and addresses me by name, asking me to wait in a room smelling of cigars while he talks to you on your own.

I remember the trip mainly for the watch. After meeting the man in the building with the elevator, we go to a fancy shop and you buy me a watch, an Atlantic. I haven't asked for a watch, nor is it my birthday, but perhaps you have something else to celebrate. You seem happy.

We celebrate the new watch together by counting the minutes and seconds between the stations on the way home.

On November 5, 1959, I too write a letter to Natek. I write that I'm sorry for not writing sooner. Why am I sorry? Why do I write the letter at all? I've just had my eleventh birthday and I write a letter to my uncle in Tel Aviv with a pen I have just been given by my Auntie Kerstin and my cousin Assa, who have come to visit us that day. They're divorced, Natek and Kerstin, and by this time they've also divided up my two cousins Assa and Anders, both about my age, Assa to Borås and Anders to Tel Aviv. I see them increasingly rarely, and before long hardly at all, but I don't miss them. Not in the way I realize, much later on, that you must miss your brother and Mom must miss her sister, making your letters to each other loaded with longing, admonitions, and guilt.

Why haven't you written? Why this silence? Is there anything wrong? Please, don't wait to answer!

As for me, I pen a very dutiful and self-absorbed letter, prompted by the fuss of my cousin's rare visit, which serves as a reminder of how small our family is, how scattered and fragile, and how important, therefore, it is for me to take up my new pen and write a letter to Uncle Natek and cousin Anders in Tel Aviv, and how I really ought to apologize in some way for not having written earlier. So I make my excuses and complete the correspondence duties imposed on me in a rapid, careless hand:

We have already had a bit of snow but it melted right away. We have bought a TV too. I am still playing the violin and getting on very well. Lilian is getting big now and goes to preschool. I have my model train out at the moment, it is a Märklin train and really good. It is quite rainy and there are big puddles in the roads and sometimes it literally pours, so I mainly stay at home and play with my train or read a book. On my birthday (Oct. 11) I got a game which I play sometimes. Tomorrow I will start going to school by train. I used to go by bike. At school we are going to learn about Iceland in Geography.

We often watch TV because there are lots of interesting programs full of information. And we are mostly at home so it is useful to have that (the TV, I mean, not the information). I played the violin for Assa and Auntie Kerstin, and they thought I played well, but it takes more than that before you can be called good. I mostly play

270

classical music, e.g. Pleyel, Bela Bartok, Mozart, Bach and Handel. My teacher, who is from Borås, is very keen on modern music. I am going to perform at Christmas. I will be playing a Pleyel duet with my teacher.

With my letter to Natek, starting on the same sheet, comes a letter from Mom in which she apologizes for my "chaotic" account, giving as an excuse the fact that I have been exposed to "too many impressions all at once." She's also keen to supplement my uncritical image of television:

> It has revolutionized social life here. People largely stay at home, because TV has something for everyone, just like the radio. The programs are mainly broadcast in the evenings, and even if one has guests, everything and everyone is focused on the TV.
>
> How are you both? Why don't you write more often? We know you are very busy with your work but you must have a little time to set aside for your brother.

You're not at home when Auntie Kerstin and cousin Assa come to see us and the two letters to Natek are being written.

Nor are you at the factory.

You've handed in your notice, and you're on the road.

It's not clear from Mom's letter where you are or where you're going, only that it has all happened very fast and things are still rather vague, and that you will explain more yourself, in your next letter.

Nor is it clear from the letter that only a day has passed since you left the factory.

"Left on 4 Nov. 1959 at his own request," says the official testimonial from the personnel department at the factory where you worked for twelve years.

271

"Final hourly wage rate: 294 öre. Conduct: Creditable. Working capability: Excellent."

For a day now, you've been in untrodden forest.

The local paper on December 16, 1959, runs a picture on the front page with the caption: "Göran Rosenberg and Paul Överström played Campra's 'Minuet' in fine accord."

I can't remember your being there.

What became of the duet by Pleyel?

THE SHADOWS

In the local paper on January 24, 1959, a thought for the day as usual. On this particular day, a thought about the Jews. In the story of the Good Samaritan in St. Luke's Gospel, Jesus wanted to show "how wrong the Jews were in their hatred" and how "unprecedented it must have been for a Jew to listen to Jesus" and how Jesus "does what no other Jew would have done," namely follow the commandment of love and not that of self-love.

Much later, I find out that you're involved in a violent argument at the factory. It happens in the changing room, where you try to throw a punch at someone and this someone slams you against a locker so hard you end up with a concussion. This someone had wondered out loud what a person like you was doing among the ordinary workers. Why someone like you was not busy lending money or living off other people. Said he'd never seen a Jew working.

After the argument in the changing room, your headaches come more often. The headaches and the nightmares. Early one morning in May, I hear you calling unfamiliar names in your sleep. I don't remember the names, but your voice frightens me. It's not your usual voice. It's a child's voice, wailing helplessly through the wall between the living room and the bedroom where you both sleep. It's already light outside and I lie awake waiting for the day to begin, because it's the day the king's coming to visit the truck factory and all the children of Södertälje have been given time off school to wave flags along the motorcade route, and I associate the sound of your voice calling out with the day I didn't get to see the king.

On Thursday May 23, 1957, the king of Sweden and the queen of the Netherlands visit Södertälje. It's a glorious late spring day, and just in the driveway down to the truck factory's main offices the local paper counts thousands of children, all waving flags presented to them by Scania-Vabis as the king and queen drive past in a black Daimler and get out onto a red carpet to sit on a royal blue platform, and the reception committee bows and curtseys, and the entire program runs "immaculately."

You stay at home that day.

I also stay at home that day.

Are we both ill?

I can't reconcile the voice in the night with your lighthearted playfulness. You're generally cheerful and jolly, pulling faces to make me laugh, yodeling with your hands cupped around your mouth, tapping out rhythms on your teeth with a pencil, giving silly names to things that have no name. *Kigelmigel* is your name for a fruit salad of oranges, apples, and bananas, topped with whipped cream. *Kigelmigel* sounds the way it tastes: soft, smooth, and sweet. Your invented names are all soft and rounded, with an *-l* or a *-le* at the end. Maybe it's the affectionate Yiddish diminutives stepping in to soften the harsh language of Strindberg. I can hear them in the voice calling in the night, too. *Mamale. Tattale.*

Nor can I reconcile your restless activities and irrepressible ambitions with your frailty and fatigue, and with the recurring visits to the doctor. As I attempt, much later, to piece together all the activities you set in motion and all the projects you're planning, they can't all be fitted into the calendar; they trip over each other, overlap, squeeze each other out, as if not even the smallest chink of idle time is allowed to open up. Yet by 1947 you're already consulting Dr. Paul Lindner at 26 Jungfrugatan in

Stockholm about your headaches, anxiety, insomnia, and paranoid thoughts. From then on you go to see Dr Lindner twice a year for a checkup and prescriptions for vitamins and sleeping pills. In 1950 your anxiety worsens for a time, and Dr. Lindner prescribes a powerful tranquilizer, Oxicon. The anxiety deepens into "particularly severe depression" over the course of 1959, and in a report dated March 3, 1960, Dr. Lindner proposes referring you for special psychiatric care.

Ambition and anxiety competing fiercely with each other, year after year, and I don't see it. You don't let me see it. You don't let anyone see it.

You're always so cheerful, Karin writes.

It's only much later that I see the shadows dogging your every step, threatening to plunge you into darkness if you drop the pace even slightly.

It's only much later that I'm able to reconcile the voice in the night with the voice that so lightheartedly and playfully gives softly resonant names to components of my world.

Time to say something about the term "survivor" as applied to people in your situation, the term that slowly crystalizes out as all others are tested and found inadequate, making the central element of your situation the fact that you're still alive. People survive things all the time, of course, war, persecution, accidents, epidemics, without necessarily being termed survivors except with specific reference to the event they've survived, and mainly as a mere statement of fact. People who survive go on living, they don't go on surviving. Surviving is normally not a continuous state but a momentary one. I think the term "survivor" initially has the same significance—a statement of fact—

for people in your situation too. You've survived against all odds and must now go on living in one of the categories available to you: refugees, transit migrants, *repatriandi*, displaced persons, Polish Jews, stateless individuals. Initially it's also clear to the world what exactly it is that you've survived and how implausible it is that you're still alive. At least there's no shortage of evidence. Or of pictures, for those who can bear to look at them. The words are still unfamiliar and unreal, and are sometimes prey to the confusion of languages—gas chambers, death factories, extermination policy, final solution, annihilation—but those of you who have survived have no reason to doubt that the world knows what you've survived, and that the world is shaken to its very foundations by the knowledge, and that the world afterward is no longer the same as the world before. It's impossible to think anything else. It's impossible to think you've all survived in order for the world to forget what it's just been through and to go on as if nothing has happened. There must be some point to the fact that you've survived, since the main point of the event you've survived was that none of you were supposed to survive, that you were all supposed to be annihilated without a trace, without leaving even a splinter of bone behind, still less a name on a death list or a death certificate. So initially you all survive with the assurance that you are the traces that weren't supposed to exist, and that this is your survival's particular point. It may seem superfluous to attribute a particular point to your survival, as there is generally more point in being alive than in being dead, but how else to justify the fact that you're alive whereas so many others are not? You all know, if anybody does, that your survival is a result of the most unlikely of circumstances and the most arbitrary of chances, and that by every realistic calculation of probability you should be as utterly annihilated as all

278

those whose faces and voices continue to follow and haunt all of you. You may actually feel that you need to atone for being alive when they aren't, particularly as I suspect that none of you can free yourselves from the thought that some of them deserved to survive more than you did. It's a crazy thought, of course, since death and survival in Auschwitz depended not on merit but on the annihilation capacity of the gas chambers and crematoriums; however, I can appreciate that survival in such circumstances might seem unfair, or at any rate undeserved. Why me and not the others? Naturally it's also an unbearable thought, which has to be pushed aside sooner or later if surviving is to turn into living. So I think it's initially pushed aside by the assurance that you haven't survived for yourselves only but for the others, too; that you're the traces that must not be eradicated, and that you therefore owe a particular duty to the life you've been granted, against all the odds and beyond any notion of fairness, and that through this life you must justify the fact that you're alive while the others are dead.

At any rate that's how I like to explain, much later, the restlessness and the ambitions, and perhaps also the lightheartedness and the playfulness. Like Lot's wife, people in your situation can go on living only if they don't turn around and look back, because like Lot's wife, you risk being turned to stone by the sight. Nor, however, can you go on living if nobody sees and understands what it is you've survived and why it is you're still alive, in spite of everything. I think the step from surviving to living demands this apparently paradoxical combination of individual repression and collective remembrance. You can look forward only if the world looks backward and remembers where you come from, and sees the paths you pursue, and understands why you're still living.

It's not that you're crying out for the world's attention and demanding its collective remembrance and recognition. On the contrary, your reticence about what you've been through is a matter of record. I think the world you survive into is populated by two categories of people, those who know and those who don't. Faced with people who know, there's not much that needs to be said, and faced with people who don't know, it's hard to say anything that doesn't risk being perceived as unreal or exaggerated or pathetic. Before long you also discover that what you have to say risks being perceived as frightening and repugnant. In any case, the world soon stops listening, because it can't bear looking back either. Within a few years the newsreels disappear from the cinemas, the testimonies from the newspapers, and the confusion of languages, the onerous kind, is spreading. The world looks forward without looking back, and you try to do the same, as best you can. I see the lightheartedness and playfulness as a response to the silence that spreads around and the loneliness that encircles you. Being alone with your thoughts, as you point out in your letter to Haluś, is terrible for people in your situation. I don't know what you joke and laugh about in the shrinking circle of survivors who gather late in the evenings in the haze of cigarette smoke under the lamp above the round table in our living room, the languages merge and I'm too young for humor, still more so for black humor, but whatever it is I think it helps you keep your focus on the way forward, even when the world lapses into silence and the loneliness closes in.

The fact that the lightheartedness and playfulness are just a mask is quite easy to spot with the naked eye, particularly in the case of your brother Natek, who's nearly always joking and fooling around, but with a kind of compulsive restlessness far more marked than yours. Natek's in perpetual motion, flying up from seats and down into them, pacing floors, and riding his black Husqvarna motorbike (he lets me test-drive it with him, sitting on the gas tank) with a jerky impatience as if he were permanently on his way to somewhere else, and before long he really is on his way to somewhere else and you no longer have your brother on hand to help keep the silence and loneliness at bay. I imagine that Natek's presence compensates for the mounting confusion of languages and that his departure from Sweden exacerbates it. The tightly written aerograms can hardly fill the vacuum left by perhaps the only person who, with an impatient glance, a restless gesture, or a timely joke, can confirm where you come from, and what it is that you've survived, and that it's not you who are mad, but the world.

Did you know that long ago, survivors of war and disaster were sacrificed to the gods as scapegoats or were declared insane because no one wanted to hear what they had to say?

Not being able to take the step from surviving to living, always having to live with your survival as the central element of your existence, is a kind of insanity, I suppose, even if it's not necessarily the survivors who are insane.

It seems to me that your situation deteriorates when you no longer have Natek at your side, and when someone in the changing room at the truck factory wonders what people like you are doing there, and when the world starts viewing people like you with distaste and would rather have you sacrificed to Oblivion and Progress. At any rate, the world seems increasingly disinclined to be shaken to its very foundations, which is what I think people like you ultimately ask of the world you're to continue living in.

So you quicken your step to prevent the shadows from catching up with you, and you make sure your projects restlessly succeed one another so that not even the tiniest of voids can arise when one of them stalls. Only a few years have passed since you rejected the move to Israel in favor of the mapped-out future in Södertälje, but the mapped-out future appears more and more like a dead end, and the truck factory more and more like a prison.

The winter of 1956 is very cold, "the harshest of all our time in Sweden," you write to Natek on February 17. We've just moved into the small two-room apartment on the other side of the rowanberry avenue, which has been substituted on short notice for the canceled house-building project in Vibergen, but we almost lose the apartment as well, as "there was a risk until the very last minute that someone else would get there first." You describe it as "nice" but grumble that unlike the upper-floor apartments, it has no balcony, though goodness knows what you want with a balcony when the temperature outside the kitchen window drops to nearly twenty-five below, week after week, and you're restlessly awaiting your call-up papers so you can get your military service out of the way before the end of the year, because you can't *röra på dig* ("move on") until then.

As usual, you sprinkle your Polish letters with Swedish words and phrases.

You must be able to move as soon as possible.

■

A survivor named Hans Mayer, confronted with the world where people like you are expected to forget and move on, changes his name to Jean Améry because he most definitely does not want to forget and move on. There are survivors who change their names in the hope of being able to move on, or to protect themselves against the next Hitler, or to hide from the subsequent world, but Hans Mayer changes his name because he doesn't want to be reconciled with the world where his name so recently belonged, which is the world that has taken his name and his home from him forever and then has the gall to view people like him with distaste and move on as if nothing has happened. The world is shaken for a few years and then is shaken no more, but Jean Améry cannot and will not reconcile himself to such a world. Nor can the survivors in such a world stop being survivors, because they can't stop reminding the world by their unforgivingness—yes, even bitterness—that nothing has been forgotten. In his book *Jenseits von Schuld und Sühne* (translated into English as *At the Mind's Limits: Contemplations by a Survivor on Auschwitz and Its Realities*), Améry describes traveling in southern Germany in 1958 and meeting a businessman who on realizing Améry has an "Israelite" background assures him that the German people do not bear the slightest grudge against the Jewish people and that the West German government has proved this by its magnanimous payments of damages, making Améry feel like Shylock, doggedly declining to forfeit his pound of flesh.

Refusing to be reconciled to a world that wants to forget and move on becomes, for Améry, a way of resuming moral control over his life: "In two decades of contemplating what happened to me, I believe to have recognized that a forgiving and forgetting induced by social pressure is immoral [*daß ein durch sozialen Druck bewirktes Vergeben und Vergessen unmoralisch ist*]."

Améry thus mistrusts the attempt of "objective science" to pathologize the refusal to be reconciled. It may well be, writes Améry, that the survivors are marked by what has happened, and that this causes some to exhibit symptoms in common that can thus be grouped into a syndrome of some kind, Concentration Camp Survivor Syndrome, for example, which at a purely clinical level turns survival into an illness, but in that case it's an illness that renders the survivors' state morally and historically superior to the state of normality. At any event, there are no moral or historical reasons for the survivor to accept what has happened just because it has happened. The only world the survivor can be reconciled to is a world shaken to its very foundations by what has happened. Time may heal all wounds in social and biological terms, but morally it heals nothing. Morally, a human being has the right, and even the privilege, to revolt against what has happened and demand that the clock be turned back so that the perpetrator can be firmly nailed to his deed and "join his victim as a fellow human being [*als Mitmensch dem Opfer zugesellt sein*]."

Améry is naturally aware of the quixotic nature of his battle, aware that time is his enemy, and that what has happened, "such murder of millions as this, carried out by a highly civilized people, with organizational dependability and almost scientific precision," will soon go down in history as one among many other acts of violence in "the Century of Barbarism," and that "*We*, the victims, will appear as the truly incorrigible, irreconcilable ones, as the antihistorical reactionaries in the exact sense of the word, and in the end it will seem like a technical mishap that some of us still survived."

The irreconcilability is not there from the beginning, of course. Initially Améry, like you I believe, is convinced that the world afterward also belongs to you, and to those like you, that it can't move on without you, that you are the traces it can't lose sight of without losing itself.

The irreconcilability comes with the silence and the confusion of languages.

The irreconcilability, and the restlessness, and the fatigue, and the impulse to halt your steps and turn your heads and allow the shadows to catch up.

Morally to "annul time" so that the world is never allowed to forget what you've survived is Jean Améry's condition for moving from surviving to living, and the longer I travel at your side along the road from Auschwitz, the more clearly do I see that this is your condition too.

■

The confusion of languages is exacerbated by the German reparations. In 1953, Germany (West Germany, to be more precise) decides to compensate the survivors with money. The financial reparations are provided as the result not primarily of German benevolence but of the victorious powers' insistence that Germany provide them. To be considered for German reparations, the survivors have to prove that their time in Auschwitz, Stutthof, Wöbbelin, or their equivalents has inflicted permanent damage, rendering them wholly or partially unable to work. Those who can't prove they've lost at least 25 percent of their capacity for work will not receive reparations. Those who have survived without suffering physical harm will not receive reparations. Psychological harm doesn't count for much with the *Vertrauensärzte*, the medical examiners appointed and paid by the German state for the task of deciding which survivors are to receive reparations and which are not. To claim German reparations, the survivors have to fill out an extensive form on which they're required to show, in German and in minute detail, that they have suffered more than 25 percent damage as a result of the annihilation policy of Hitler's Germany. Along with the form, claimants are to submit certified copies of all relevant documents, certified transcripts of sworn witness statements, and certified copies of medical records, on receipt of which the authorities will allow themselves a year, or maybe two, to verify the details provided, call for supplementary information, and, above all, await the report of their *Vertrauensarzt*. Germany demands that a *Vertrauensarzt* have a license to practice medicine in the survivor's country of residence and be able to submit his or her report in German, which turns out to mean that in practice, the physicians for whom the survivors must bare themselves, literally and figuratively, are generally German-born or of German origin.

Among the most frequent grounds for rejection of reparation claims are contradictions in the survivor's account. Even minimal contradictions, even irrelevant contradictions in largely correct accounts can be grounds for rejecting a claim. One survivor is refused reparations because a witness claims to have seen him in 1943 when he could have seen him only in 1942. One survivor is refused reparations because he has given contradictory information about his date of birth. Paragraph 7 of the law regulating German reparations, the *Bundesentschädigungsgesetz* (later *Bundesergänzungsgesetz*), makes it possible to refuse reparation to anyone making inexact statements with the intention of simplifying his or her account, or making inexact statements unintentionally and unconsciously, or making inexact statements as a result of the confusion of languages, between German and Polish, say, or Yiddish. In applying for reparations, the claimant must submit to being treated as a suspected liar and fraud until he or she can prove the contrary. The German reparations authority is not required to prove anything or to let itself be troubled by contradictions concerning who was murdered by the German state when and where, but it can deem the slightest contradiction or inaccuracy on the claimant's part to be grounds for throwing out the claim. In some cases, trivial inaccuracies identified at a subsequent stage trigger demands for repayment of reparations already granted. Having demonstrably survived Auschwitz carries less weight in the eyes of the reparators than a demonstrable inaccuracy in the account of an event and its consequences. Before the reparators' court, the survivors must constantly turn and look back, recalling in detail every step along the road to and from Auschwitz and ensuring that every step along that road is substantiated by sworn witness statements and certified copies of original documents, and the slightest error can turn the survivor into a liar and a fraud.

In short, the reparations do as much harm as good and, much later, I'm better able to understand those who refuse to take up the offer. At the same time, I can't help noticing how the reparations impose themselves on the survivors, tempting them with attention and confirmation during those very years when the silence and the confusion of languages is spreading, and the world is busy forgiving and forgetting, and the survivors are becoming more and more alone with their survival and therefore clutching at any straw liable to confirm that what happened really did happen, and that the world is a little shaken by it, after all.

Dr. Herbert Lindenbaum is the German Federal Republic's *Vertrauensarzt* in Stockholm. He examines you on September 6,

1956, between 11:30 a.m. and 1 p.m., and his report of October 15, 1956, is written in impeccable German. I slowly read through the questions and answers on the eight-page form that precedes the verdict because I want to be on my guard against unintentional inaccuracies. How, for example, will you deal with the conflicting information about your date of birth? Somewhere along the road, your date of birth has been changed from May 14, 1923, to April 14, 1922, or it might be the other way around. We celebrate May 14 as your birthday, but in the sworn affirmation in German that you enclose with your application for reparations, you explain that April 14 is in fact correct and that the discrepancy is the result of a misunderstanding. At some juncture, someone has entered the date incorrectly. On your work permit, alien's passport, and citizenship certificate, your date of birth is April 14.

So why do we celebrate your birthday on May 14? In a letter I write you on May 14, 1960, I've drawn a special garland around the date. "Since today is your birthday, we would like to send you our warmest congratulations," I write in capital letters slanting boldly to the left. I'm evidently writing on behalf of the whole family. "We miss you very much. It's so empty without you, in fact it feels worse than when you were off traveling."

Presumably, then, May 14 is your actual birthday, but April 14 is the date reproduced on all your Swedish documents and is thus the one that runs the least risk of being contradicted by other sources. Do I detect a slight hesitation as you, under oath, forswear your actual birthday? May 14 doesn't seem to be correct, you write.

Es scheint nicht richtig zu sein.

That doesn't sound entirely convincing.

The reparations impose themselves on you as early as the autumn of 1953, demanding that you prove what it is that you have survived and what the consequences thereof are. On November 24, 1953, Josef Leib Goldstein and Feliks Zeligman affirm in a sworn declaration, an *Eidesstattliche Erklärung*, that they were in your company when you survived Łódź, Auschwitz, Vechelde bei Draunschweig, and Wöbbelin. On April 13, 1954, E. Öberg at the State Aliens Commission issues, for a stamp duty fee of 4 kronor, a certificate, *Bescheinigung*, to confirm that you came to Sweden from Germany on July 18, 1945, through the agency of the UN and the Red Cross and that you have been in possession of a Swedish alien's passport since September 24, 1952.

Your first sworn affirmation, the *Eidesstattliche Versicherung*, is dated November 13, 1954, with the signature certified by notary public Gunnar Nordin in Södertälje, and bears the 2-kronor stamp fee as well as another official stamp for 1 krona. I can find only one inaccuracy in the sworn account of your road to and from Auschwitz. You write that you're liberated from Vebelin on May 2, 1945. It ought to say "Wöbbelin." It's a brief, terse document. A single typewritten page. Clearly a case of better too little than too much. Under oath, you tell the Germans very little. Very little in which to find any inaccuracies. Nothing about damage or suffering or reduced capacity for work. Nothing at all, in fact.

Perhaps you thought Auschwitz, Wöbbelin, and the liquidation of your world would be enough?

Toward the end, an intimation that life has not turned out as you imagined. "When war broke out I was a student at a textile college. I have not been able to resume this activity in Sweden. I have slowly worked my way up to the job of pipe fitter." But you write in German, of course: *Als der Krieg ausbrach, war ich Student in einer Textilschule. Diese Tätigkeit habe ich in Schweden nicht fortsetzen können. Jetzt habe ich mich langsam zum Monteur heraufgearbeitet.*

Evidently supplementary information has been requested by the German authorities, such as an authorized German translation of your marriage certificate, but above all yet another sworn affirmation in which you put words to the physical injuries and suffering inflicted on you by the German state, and for which you are now claiming reparation. That's what matters, after all, nothing else. I understand very well why as long as possible you postpone putting words to your injuries and suffering, but reparation demands words for everything, even for things for which there are no words, or at any rate, no words that can break through the confusion of languages.

So on August 27, 1956, you put German words to your injuries and suffering.

Kurze Schilderung des Verfolgstatbestandes unter Darlegung der gelten gemachten Körperschäden.

I can find no adequate words in my own language for such a sentence.

Your affidavit is short, at any event, a bare page in length. In the ghetto you were forced to work far beyond what you had the strength for, you write. In the ghetto you were severely assaulted by an SS man, you write. In Vechelde bei Braunschweig you were forced to work very hard and were very hungry and weak, you write. When you were unable to get up one morning, you were called a malingerer, beaten repeatedly about the head, and dragged to work by force, you write. As for Auschwitz, you write only that you were delivered there and sent on from there. And of Wöbbelin (Vebelin again, but nobody corrects you, the camp's on its way to being erased from the annals), nothing more than that you were sick when you were liberated.

Near the end, nevertheless, an attempt to demonstrate lasting damage inflicted by the German persecution: "Since my arrival in Sweden I've been receiving medical treatment. I still suffer from headaches, insomnia, and such bad nerves that I often find it difficult to go to work. My capacity for work is reduced because I am often weak and tired, *weil ich oft schwach und müde bin.*"

Your words seem equally weak and tired to me. Not much to go hunting for inaccuracies in. Not much else, either. What is there to say? You're alive, while all the rest are dead. From the outside you look healthy, in good shape even, with no physical damage as far as the eye can discern, so what is there to say that doesn't risk being branded inaccurate and internally contradictory and making you appear like a liar and a fraud?

I think you yourself realize how little you're actually saying, or perhaps someone else points it out to you, so you bring with you to the examination by Dr. Lindenbaum a certified report by Dr. J. Lando in Stockholm, who confirms that you've been consulting him for several years about severe headaches and serious depressions, attributable to your experiences in the concentration camps. "I have signed the patient off sick for considerable periods and judge his capacity to work to be reduced by at least 50 percent," attests Dr. Lando.

So a figure is finally put on the damage and suffering inflicted on you.

Dr. Lindenbaum takes little notice. Or rather, the impression you make on Dr. Lindenbaum is one of health. He attributes the headaches to the concussion you sustained at the factory, and he attributes the insomnia and restlessness to nothing at all. At any rate, there are no "physical defects" to be seen that would reduce the patient's functional capability.

"Without a doubt, the patient is exaggerating his difficulties [*Es steht ausser Zweifel, dass Pat. seine Beschwerden übertreibt*]," writes Dr. Lindenbaum.

"He also gives the impression of doing all he can to prevent any investigation into his past [*dass er alles versucht Nachforschungen in seinen Antezedentia zu verhüten*]."

Dr. Lindenbaum doesn't trouble himself to substantiate this impression. Nor indeed his overall impression (*Gesamteindruck*), which is that

> the patient, unlike most of his comrades in misfortune, seems to have survived his internment in the concentration camps without suffering any persistent consequences harmful to health [*Pat. scheint im Gegensatz zu den weitaus meisten seiner Leidensgenossen die Internierung im KZ ohne nachhaltige Folgen für seine Gesundheit überstanden zu haben*]. The symptoms of psychoneurosis [*Psycho-Neurose*] that the patient alleges he has can no longer necessarily be linked to possible harm inflicted in the concentration camps [*steht heute nicht mehr einwandfrei in irgendwie ursächlichen Zusammenhang mit einem Schaden, in KZ erworben*].

Dr. Lindenbaum doesn't write explicitly that you're a malingerer, nor that you're a liar and a fraud. He writes that your illness has been triggered by your desire for reparations. There's a special name for this illness in Dr. Lindenbaum's German vocabulary, *Renten-Neurose*, which in English might be called "pension neurosis" or "pension hysteria."

"In this respect, the illness is to be regarded as a pension neurosis."

Die Krankheit ist in dieser Hinsicht als Renten-Neurose aufzufassen.

As I understand it, Dr. Lindenbaum writes that you're ill because you want reparations, not because you've survived Auschwitz. In other words, if it weren't for your craving for reparations, you'd be entirely well. The reduction in your working capacity as a result of Auschwitz is thus, in his judgment, 0 percent after January 1, 1948. How Dr. Lindenbaum arrives at this date isn't clear. Nor how he can determine that your working capacity is reduced by 100 percent in 1945, by 60 percent in 1946, and by 30 percent in 1947.

Your post-Auschwitz reduction in working capacity from 1948 onward is assessed at 0 percent.

On the basis of Dr. Lindenbaum's report, your claim for reparations for lasting damage resulting from your persecution by National Socialism is rejected.

■

I'm not a small child any longer. In the summer of 1957, I'm sent to a summer camp for Jewish children on the island of Väddö, north of Stockholm, and I grow accustomed to being away from home. And to the fact that you, too, are away from home. After the unsold Piccolo, and the unbuilt house in Vibergen, and the ungranted German reparations, and the completion of your military service, you tend to come home late in the evening and sometimes not at all. One evening when you're at home, we go out to watch for *Sputnik* but fail to find it. *Sputnik* is supposed to look like a star moving quickly across the sky, and you've checked precisely when and where to watch, but no matter how intensely we watch, we can't see it. While we're watching, you explain to me how it's possible for *Sputnik* to leave the earth without falling back down again. It has to do with the speed of the launch. *Sputnik* has to reach a launch velocity of 11 kilometers per second, otherwise it will fall back down again.

The VW Beetle's speedometer goes up to 120 kilometers per hour, but the indicator never gets that far around the dial.

When I finally do see *Sputnik* moving up there, I'm not with you. I think I'm with Bertil, and there's snow on the ground, and we've gone out specifically to see it.

With you, I watch the 1954 solar eclipse through a developed but unexposed strip of film—but that's an entirely different memory fragment.

In 1957, *Sputnik* breaks free of the earth's gravitational pull, and you make repeated attempts to break free of the factory's. Or at least that's how, much later, I'm inclined to interpret the late evenings, and the appointment in the building with the elevator, and the names in the night, and the handwritten draft of a business contract that I find among your papers. Under its terms you are to work full time as a traveling salesman for a company that imports a Japanese camera called Taron and are prohibited under penalty of a 50,000-kronor fine from revealing company secrets to outsiders. Japanese cameras are cheap and have a poor reputation, and the draft contract has been annulled. You can't sell your own, hand-welded Piccolo for fifty-five kronor including postage and the right of return, so how can you sell cheap Japanese cameras with dubious reputations?

Are there other annulled contracts? Other buildings with elevators in Stockholm?

What I realize, much later, is that time after time you make a run-up toward the horizon, and time after time you fall back to earth again.

Maybe I ought to realize it even now, or at least to be concerned—I'm no longer a small child, after all—but this is when horizon after horizon is opening up to me with no effort at all and my world is inexorably breaking loose from yours, and it's only with difficulty that I can recall the sensation of that day when you get home earlier than usual and we go down to the port to see if there are any Polish or Russian ships in, so you can find someone to chat with and maybe buy a surreptitious bottle of vodka from, but you don't chat with anyone, not even me. We walk in silence along the quay and do not stop by the Polish ship unloading its cargo of coal, or it might be coke, nor do we stop by the gantry crane as it screeches past us along the rails on its broad, rickety legs, its soot-blackened grab bucket dangling in the air above our heads, first gaping wide like a crocodile's jaws, then firmly clamped around its prey. I try to say something, perhaps I'm scared, but I have a powerful sense of your being somewhere else. I can feel it through your hand as it holds mine, and the sensation penetrates my body and hides there, waiting to be summoned again by a closely written aerogram in Polish, by a letter in Swedish with bold, leftward-slanting capitals, by a medical report in German, by an annulled draft contract, or simply by the lively imagination of someone determined at any cost to unearth a memory fragment or two and piece together a narrative.

It's so much easier to recall the sensation, or in fact more than that, of Ester's damp hand in mine at the Last Night Party down by the steamer landing stage, and of Inger's hot cheek against mine during the last dance in the dining hall, and of Anita's tongue touching mine when we're playing Postman's Knock in the hideaways of the coastal defense bunkers on Secret Mountain. Inger is a year or two older, and one evening she lets me put my hand on her breast. Well, not directly on her breast, but on the jumper with the stiff, pointy brassiere beneath it. It must be one of the last summers at the camp, and the bright evenings are fraught with throbbing expectations, furtive looks, and the bulging rumps of the draft horses in the pasture below the cowshed, and my body speaks a language I don't understand, one that draws me inexorably toward yet another world to discover and make into my own.

Anita must be the last summer, when I stop and think about it.

Otherwise, I don't have to stop and think very much to remember the last summer.

■

Much later, I read in a Swedish medical journal (*Läkartidningen*, no. 40, 2005) "that there is not a single scientific study to support the hypothesis of so-called pension neuroses." On the contrary, studies show that "symptoms persist even after the pension has been settled."

Your symptoms persist. That, at any rate, is the opinion of doctor after doctor even after the pension has been "settled" and you should therefore, according to Dr. Lindenbaum's diagnosis, be restored to health and fit for work again. Instead there are signs of deterioration as the reparations you've been denied eat their way into your life and poison it. You may not have suffered from "pension neurosis" before Dr. Lindenbaum, but you certainly do afterward. After Dr. Lindenbaum, the question of reparations grows into something much bigger than a pension question, ultimately becoming a matter of life and death. I know that sounds dramatic, and I don't mean it literally, but it's indisputable that Dr. Lindenbaum's verdict launches a heavy German torpedo right into the fragile foundations of your survival. Now you have to live not only with Auschwitz and the liquidation of your world, but also with Dr. Lindenbaum's verdict.

Es steht ausser Zweifel, dass Pat. seine Beschwerden übertreibt.

So you apply again, in the hope of erasing Dr. Lindenbaum's verdict from your life. This time you know that Auschwitz and Wöbbelin are not enough. This time you know that a German *Vertrauensarzt* is an enemy who must be defeated by all the means at your disposal. So you arm yourself with new testimonies, new documents, and new medical certificates, and the stamp duties mount up at the office of the notary public. You're even prepared to counter numbers with numbers. In a sworn statement on February 9, 1957, you affirm that your father had a cotton mill at 78 Sienkiewski Street with warehouse space in the building at 36 Piłsudskiego, where you all lived "in a large, attractive apartment." You also affirm that you were in your third year at a textile college in Łódź and were preparing for further study to become a textile engineer when your world was destroyed, and you now want the financial means to complete your training and escape the assembly-line work at the factory that you find mentally and physically draining.

And you have no more illusions. There's a calculating, almost cynical tone to the letter you write on February 8, 1958, to Natek in Israel, explaining what it takes to outwit the enemy:

> You must not make light of the issue. I've talked to a private lawyer here who's in contact with the swindlers in Germany. He takes a 15% cut, but in return they undertake to press one's case. Make

sure the medical certificates go into sufficient detail. In your case you must claim damages for your left hand. You need to get a certificate signed by two witnesses and the *notarius publicus*. You must make sure the certificate says that you used to play the violin and were very good at it, and that you had a great future ahead of you in that area, you still had your musical studies to complete, etc.

You must also go to a doctor, or two doctors. They must describe the injuries to your hand and state the level of your incapacity for work as a result of these, in percentage terms, and try to get it up to 75%. From the second doctor you need a certificate that says you're suffering from deep neuroses after your wartime experiences.

I'm sure I've bored you with this business, but it's in your own interest and it would be a pity to miss out on it and let them get away with it.

I don't want to bore anyone with this business either, so I won't reproduce what Dr. Paul Lindner says about your condition in his certificate, Ärztliches Zeugnis, of May 21, 1959, except for the last sentence: "Since liberation, his working capacity has been permanently reduced by 60%." *Er ist dauernd, seit der Befreiung, 60% arbeistsunfähig.*

I have no idea how Dr. Lindner arrives at the figure of 60%, but it's undeniably not the same as 0%. Dr. Lindner refers you to Dr. E. Goldkuhl, who's the senior consultant at the Långbro mental hospital in Stockholm, and who arrives at the same conclusion in a certificate dated June 13, 1959: "In my opinion, Mr. Rosenberg's working capacity is to be considered reduced by 60% as a result of chronic psychoneurosis."

On February 5, 1960, a consultant and specialist in mental health, Dr. Harald Rabe, certifies that since December 11, 1959, you've been on sick leave, "being entirely unfit for work as a result of mental depression." Dr. Rabe also identifies a clear causal link between "the experiences in the years 1939–45 and the nervous illness."

On March 3, 1960, another certificate from Dr. Lindner, an Ärztlicher Bericht.

On March 9, 1960, another certificate from Dr. E. Goldkuhl

They all assert the same thing, time after time. You're ill as a result of the persecution, and as a result of the illness your capacity for work has been reduced by at least 60%.

On February 10, 1960, your reparations claim is examined by another German-appointed *Vertrauensarzt*, Dr. Herbert Lebram, who makes yet another decision on your case:

> In the processing of this case, there is a complete divergence of opinions between the previous medical examiner and the psychiatric specialists consulted, showing how difficult it is to judge afflictions largely manifesting themselves subjectively [*wie schwer eine gerechte Stellung bei derartigen hauptsächlich subjektiv manifestierte Leiden einzunehmen ist*]. From the information provided by the claimant, it is not possible to prove anything with certainty, particularly as the claimant—possibly because of mistrust—proved unwilling or unable to establish closer contact with my examining colleague. Since no damage resulting from persecution—lasting deterioration as a result of constitutionally determined psychoneurosis—can be proved with certainty, I judge the claimant's working capacity to be reduced by 25% up to 1955, and subsequently by 20%.

It's not clear how Dr. Lebram, in February 1960, can judge that your condition improves by five percentage points from 1955 to 1956. From the start of 1956, at any event, he judges you to be precisely as well as is required to absolve Germany from its obligation to compensate you for lasting damage and injury as a result of Auschwitz, etc.

∎

On November 4, 1959, you break free of the factory's gravitational pull and find yourself traveling in untrodden forest. You're not going to sell Japanese cameras under the brand name of Taron but imported costume jewelry from somewhere or other, I'm hazy on the exact details. I hear the phrase "costume jewelry" mentioned a few times but take little notice and only much later understand what it means. Costume jewelry is a fancy name for cheap baubles or trinkets. You, who can't sell a hand-soldered luggage rack of the finest quality, who actually can't sell anything particularly well when I come to think of it, are to travel around Sweden in your black Volkswagen Beetle selling costume jewelry to local jewelers' shops, or to whatever sort of shops it is that stock costume jewelry.

It's not your idea, of course, any more than the Japanese cameras are.

Your increasingly fixed idea is to get away from the factory at pretty much any cost.

The costume jewelry is the Rosenblum brothers' idea.

You know the Rosenblum brothers from the aliens' camp in Öreryd.

It strikes me that you go back to Öreryd in order to go forward.

It strikes me that nowhere in the little town with the big truck factory is there anyone with the sense to harness your burning ambitions and give them the extra thrust they need to reach a proper launch speed, one that will make the horizon open and turn surviving into living.

I don't know much about Mordka and Zalman Rosenblum's road to Sweden. What I do know is that they're transferred together with you and Natek from the quarantine camp in Lund to the aliens' camp in Öreryd and from there to the aliens' camp in Tappudden-Furudal, and that from there your roads separate. I don't know when the Rosenblum brothers break free from their factories and start their wholesale business in costume jewelry.

Because that's how it is, most survivors have a factory to adapt to or break free from, since factory work is what the survivors are largely considered suitable for. The factories undoubtedly also need punch-card operators and machine engineers and people who can construct ingenious luggage racks or whatever, but those aren't horizons that open up so readily to people like you. The horizon that most readily opens is an enterprise of some kind, a tobacconist's, a tailor's, a cake shop and cafe, an import company, a wholesale business, or even a factory of one's own. You undeniably try to go that road yourself, and setting your aims very high, as I see it, going for a factory of your own, just like Grandfather, and a house of your own as well, just as in Łódź, but for some reason you lose heart and momentum. Some might say that you aim too high, that a factory and a house of your own aren't for people like you, but I'd say that you're simply too alone in a too-small town with a too-big truck factory.

Too alone by far to move on by yourself.

The only Rosenblum brother I remember is Zalman. Zalman is the name I find on the Öreryd and Tappudden transport lists, but Zygmunt is the name I remember. Uncle Zygmunt. In the world after Öreryd, it's spelled Sigmund or Sigismund, just as Rosenblum is spelled with an *s* instead of a *z*. Uncle Zygmunt is almost fifteen years older than you, wears thin-rimmed glasses, and looks more like a schoolteacher than a traveling salesman in costume jewelry, and I remember him not only for what happens next but also for the fact that he actually looks at me and talks to me. I don't think it's primarily for your talents as a salesman that you're offered the opportunity to take over Uncle Zygmunt's sales district in southern and western Sweden. I think it's because Uncle Zygmunt sees and understands more than most people.

What happens next is that Uncle Zygmunt is killed in a car accident.

This happens during your first week as a traveling salesman in costume jewelry. You get home late Friday night, and I can't get to sleep until you're back, and by Saturday morning Uncle Zygmunt is dead. The telephone rings and you answer and I realize something terrible has happened.

Much later, I realize that this is the morning you give up. You've left the factory for untrodden forest and you're all too alone again and darkness is falling. Sheer momentum keeps you traveling for a few more weeks, and I find it hard to get to sleep in the evenings and dream of your little Beetle being crushed beneath a huge semitrailer truck, just like Uncle Zygmunt's Volvo in the glossy photo in the brown envelope on the chest of drawers in the hall.

On December 15, 1959, you're unquestionably home again, writing a letter to Natek about what has happened. You wait four weeks before you tell him, and when you finally do your tone is neutral, almost unconcerned, and has an obviously false ring to it. "Everything will sort itself out, health permitting," you write in Swedish, and continuing in Polish, you say that "all is fine at home." About me you write that I'm "still a comfort and delight, thank heavens." About Lilian you write that she's "coming on wonderfully, thank heavens." About yourself you say almost nothing. You merely write that you're back home and will consider your future once the weekend is over.

On January 13, 1960, another letter to Natek. You're still considering what to do next: "I'm at home for now, and haven't looked for any other work but am taking a little rest.... Göran and Lilian are hale and hearty, thank heavens."

Doesn't anybody notice how ill you are?

I don't.

■

The international news roundup in the local paper, January 9, 1960: "Several ugly instances of anti-Semitism have been reported in recent weeks, not only in West Germany but also in England and Holland."

The front page of the local paper the same day:

> In protest against anti-Semitic and neo-Nazi incidents, a torchlight procession held in West Berlin on Friday evening attracted tens of thousands of young people.... Large white banners carried at the head of the procession bore slogans such as "Against Racial Hatred," "Against anti-Semitism," and "No Nazis at our University."

The first page of the local paper on January 27, 1960:

> A more thorough education about the true nature of Nazism and the methods of anti-Semitism have been demanded by young people at Sweden's schools, represented by eight pupil organizations due to present their demands on Thursday to the Minister of Education and Ecclesiastical Affairs.... [A working group from these

303

organizations] has carried out a survey of modern school textbooks and found coverage of the political history of the 1930s and 40s to be totally inadequate.

The front page of the local paper on March 2, 1960: "The well-oiled training machine at Scania Vabis. Every employee will get an opportunity to improve at his trade."

The local paper's cinema advertisements on April 25, 1960: "Eagerly anticipated Paramount premiere. Danny Kaye and Louis Armstrong in *The Five Pennies*. Captivating tunes. Inspiring rhythms. Laughter galore."

Patient record no. 200/60, opened on April 26, 1960: "[The patient] has been in a progressively depressed state. Adm. [admitted] 4/20 u.d. [under the diagnosis of] Neurosis to Ulvsunda nursing home. Scarcely admitted before attempting to drown himself. Taken to the general hospital and revived following tracheotomy and respirator treatm."

Letter from Mom to Uncle Natek on April 29, 1960:

I've thought of writing to you many times, but felt I had no right to worry you. But now David has written to you himself about his mental breakdown after so many failed attempts to tear himself away from the factory. After Rosenblum's accident his nerves went to pieces and he fell into a depression. He stopped sleeping at night, the pills didn't work any longer, and he was *signed off sick* [in Swedish] for a while. To get over his anxiety he wanted to start work again at any cost, even if it was only temporary because of his other plans. So he went back to Scania-Vabis even though it was like facing his own death sentence and the whole experience triggered a reaction in him that I could never in my life have foreseen. He completely lost all his self-confidence and the usual medical care could do nothing for him anymore. God knows that it is with a heavy heart I share this with you, and perhaps I ought not to, but you are his only brother. So David was admitted to hospital for treatment on 4/19, and on 4/20 when I went over to visit him (David's alive and will get better) I couldn't find him, because he was in a serious condition after an unsuccessful suicide attempt. He had thrown himself in the water. The staff realized and got him out after 15 minutes. But he'd swallowed an awful lot of dirty water. It took him 12 hours to come around and he was in critical condition. They kept him on a respirator for 3 days, which was one of the things that saved his life. His physical condition soon started improving, but the anxiety stayed for a long time. David's now in the general hospital but as soon as his physical health is restored they'll move him to a psychiatric hospital. He's probably going to have what they call electric shock treatment, which we hope will have positive results. The children know nothing about this and neither do any of our close acquaintances. This is for David's sake. This is harder for me than anything in my life before, but with the way things are, I have to stay strong if I'm not to break down.

Whom do I see *The Five Pennies* with, if not you? I remember it was with you, even if, much later, I realize it can't have been.

No, the children are told nothing. The children are wrapped up in their own affairs. The memory fragments are few, far between, and firmly trampled into the darkness and silence. Your mute back one cold winter's day on the way to Havsbadet. The gray herringbone coat flapping around your legs and hanging heavily on your shoulders. You want to go on your own but I've asked to come too. Why are we going to Havsbadet in winter? An early morning at the start of summer in Auntie Ilonka and Uncle

305

Birger's summer cottage by a seawater inlet south of Södertälje. The day before, we rowed out together, you and I, and jigged for herring in the sound. We jigged bucket after bucket of herring, and you promise we'll row out and jig for more the next day, but the following morning you get up very early and row out on your own and come home with a zander, which you put in a bucket outside the door. The zander, unable to stretch out straight, is curled into a circle as it moves gently in the bucket. An hour or two later, it's floating belly up. We go back to the rowanberry avenue that same afternoon. At the annual music school concert, I play the second part in Vivaldi's Concerto in A Minor for Two Violins and Piano.

You're there, aren't you?

■

Jean Améry doesn't want to pathologize the Auschwitz survivors' irreconcilability, or their mistrust, or their restlessness, or their fear of losing a foothold. Jean Améry thinks it's the world, which moves forward without looking back, that ought to be pathologized, not the survivors.

Easy to say for those who have the ability to write a world of their own.

Harder for those who find that the world is against them.

Not that easy for Améry either, when I think about it, since he sees all too well how lonely he is, with his irreconcilability and his bitterness and his inability to move on as if nothing has happened, and at the end of the day he draws the logical conclusions from his predicament and kills himself. Before that he writes a book about suicide, or as he prefers to call it, voluntary death, *Freitod,* in which he maintains that a life of humiliation and helplessness might be worth bringing to an end, that suicide might be an act of dignity and not an act of resignation.

He doesn't say that in so many words, but that's what he means.

Parts of the text make for uncomfortable reading, as Améry is so clearly obsessed with his subject, attempting rather desperately in places to make poetry and philosophy out of it, but I read the book to try to understand why so many survivors kill themselves. The suicide rate of survivors is three times that of people in general. It's as if a latent virus has fastened onto people like you and suddenly, without warning, manifests itself in a resolute wish to take one's own life. Améry doesn't deal with the issue of survival, not even his own, in this context, but it's impossible not to read this book, too, in the light of his inability or disinclination to be reconciled to the world after Auschwitz. What Améry refuses to admit is that this inability or disinclination, like the accompanying feelings of humiliation and helplessness, can also develop into pathological states, and that this in many cases may lead to suicide. I can feel respect for Améry's refusal to let himself be diagnosed as diseased because of Auschwitz, and for his attempt to give suicide some moral dignity, but that doesn't prevent him from appearing, in my eyes, as diseased and damaged as all of you are.

You who have survived Auschwitz are all damaged, whether it shows or not, and whether you care to admit it or not. Some of you deal with the damage better than others and are able to build a new world on the ruins of the old one and see all kinds of horizons opening up, and after a time no one can see or even suspect where you come from and what you're carrying with you—but no one is safe from the shadows.

For many, the shadows come later in life than they do for you. Sometimes right at the end, as momentum is inexorably lost and it gets harder not to stop and look back.

I try to understand why your shadows come so early, but I don't find very much to understand.

You just happen to get off at the wrong station on your road from Auschwitz.

Yes, I think, in the end, that the Place has a part to play in this.

It's too small a place for someone like you, with too few people who appreciate where you come from and what you carry with you, with a factory too large and too dominant to free oneself from, with too few exits to a future other than the one already mapped out, and with a horizon that never really wants to open up.

The place where I make the world into my own is also the place where the world turns its back on you. And the place where you finally turn your back on the world.

It never becomes a home to you. Not the way it does to me.

Homelessness is an underrated hell for people like you, I think. Homelessness and the confusion of languages. The one has something to do with the other. To be at home is to be understood without having to say all that much.

I don't think any place can replace the place where we put our first words to the world, and share it with other people, and make it our own. I know there are those who think such a place can be re-created anywhere, at any time, but I don't believe that. I believe the place that has shaped us will keep shaping us even after we've left it and made our home elsewhere. Or rather, we can only make our home elsewhere if some kind of link lives on with the place, the people, and the language that shaped us.

But for people like you, there's no such link. The place that shaped you is no longer there, nor the people, nor the language, nor even the memory. Between you and the world that you once made your own towers a wall of pain that memory cannot penetrate.

So you must make a home in a place where you aren't understood, no matter what you say, and where you're deprived of every link with the place where you first put words to the world and didn't have to say all that much to be understood, which is my definition of being at home, and just about Améry's definition too. "Home [*die Heimat*] is the land of one's childhood and youth," writes Améry. "Whoever has lost it becomes a loser himself, even if he has learned not to stumble about in the foreign country as if he were drunk, but rather to tread the ground with some fearlessness [*einiger Furchtlosigkeit*]."

Améry makes much of his homelessness, of the fact that not only has he seen his home desecrated and liquidated by the Germans, but the Germans have forever turned that home into a hostile, alien place and by so doing transformed the whole world into a place of loneliness and lost bearings. Perhaps Améry's homelessness is made worse by the fact that his language is also that of the perpetrators, but I don't think there's too much difference between you and him. The confusion of languages doesn't reside in the language.

"How much *Heimat* does a person need?" asks Améry.

"The less of it he can carry with him, all the more," he replies.

A home can certainly, to some extent, be replaced by other things—memories, objects, smells, tastes, dreams, hopes, promises—but it presupposes that somewhere, sometime, there was a place that was a home.

If no such place has existed, or if the links to it have forever been ripped up and broken and you haven't been able to carry with you anything at all, I imagine that in the end homelessness can become unbearable.

■

Sundby hospital, like Ulvsunda nursing home, lies by a lake. It's not literally an old castle like Ulvsunda, but there's undeniably something of a castle about it. For a time it was more or less taken for granted in the land of vast forests and innumerable lakes that castlelike buildings would be erected or acquired to house the slow-witted or deranged or mentally ill, or whatever name was chosen for those people who were to be kept apart, possibly for good, from society as a whole. Sundby hospital, opened in 1922, nestles like most mental hospitals of the time in a large area of parkland with peaceful strolling paths lined with shady maples and linden trees. The therapeutic conviction of the era is that external peace fosters internal harmony, and that proximity to open water can be particularly soothing. At any rate, one doesn't have to walk very far from the main building at Sundby hospital, along one of the paths through the park, to reach the shore of Lake Mälaren and there look out over the soothing water and see on the other side of a narrow sound the idyllic cathedral town of Strängnäs, bowing down to the soaring spire at its heart.

For many years the hospital and the town were linked only by a ferry, and the risk of any lost soul straying among the normal citizens of the town by mistake was therefore minimal. Besides, the lost souls were rarely left unsupervised. That the ambitions of mental care were high, one might even say impressive, is clear from the account of the ceremonial opening of the Strängnäs asylum, as it was originally called. The account is published in the magazine *Humanitet* (Humanity), the house journal of the Swedish Association of Asylum Staff, and from reading it you realize that the opening of an asylum is a big event at the time, and that the hopes invested in its future are of almost epic proportions:

> The local press describes the institution as a beautiful monument to some of the *brightest and most hopeful* sides of our culture. This is evident not only in the building itself, but also in any comparison of past methods of treatment in this area and those used today, clearly highlighting the humane spirit in modern care of the mentally ill. It is in phenomena of this kind that man must firmly invest his hopes, even while so much else in our age makes him doubt how far progress, so often invoked, has actually improved the lot of humanity.

This is yet another postwar period, it strikes me, and the memories of unimaginable destruction are still fresh, and its human aftereffects still profound, and the bishop of Strängnäs, Uddo Lechard Ullman, finds reason to say something in his inaugural speech about the impact of the age on the human mind. As I understand it, he wonders whether it is in fact the age that is mad. He doesn't say so directly, and my understanding is based on a magazine account only, but according to an article in the February 1922 issue of *Humanitet*, Bishop Ullman is saying

> that in the present age it may seem as if the whole human race were an immense hospital, in which all the hellish powers of destruction have conspired to imbue our race with misery. One glaringly conspicuous manifestation of the world's current state of distress is the kind of suffering for which this magnificent nursing institution ...

311

is intended to be a place of refuge, or if possible salvation, or at least relief.

On April 26, 1960, you are taken by ambulance from Mörby general hospital to Sundby mental hospital, to be afforded salvation, or at least relief.

Your case notes for that day: "On waking exhibited motor disturbance and extreme anxiety, intermittently wandering in corridor. In conversation exhibits signs of classic depression. Feels generally useless, as if does not deserve to live. Persistence of serious suicidal thoughts."

No more confusion of languages. For conditions like yours, modern mental health care has a growing arsenal of highly specific and unambiguous words at its disposal. Lergigan, for example, and Heminevrin, Truxal, Diminal Duplex, and Catran, and electric shock treatment.

The first electric shock is administered on May 4.

After the second electric shock, on May 6: "Appears calmer but will not admit he feels better."

After the fourth electric shock, on May 13: "Thinks he is in a lighter mood and that the treatment is having the desired effect."

After the fifth and final electric shock on May 17, a session with the chief physician at Sundby, Dr. Segnestam: "The patient lucid and controlled, happy and content, feels he is completely recovered.... What he wants is to be allowed home for May 28, as his son who is a scout [?] will be playing the violin, which the patient would like to see and hear."

You express your gratitude to the Swedish healthcare system. "Happy and grateful."

312

On May 21, you're moved from the closed ward for disturbed patients to the open ward for calm patients. "Happy and grateful."

On May 23, another session with Dr. Segnestam. "Patient's behavior nicely calm and controlled. Happy and grateful that he has become so much better."

May 27: "Allowed leave of absence to go home to Södertälje."

May 30: "Has returned from leave of absence with no incidents reported."

There I have it, in black and white, that you're at the concert! You're sitting on one of the tightly packed rows of chairs in the tall hall with yellow brick walls, no doubt with Mom and Lilian, too. The municipal music school in Södertälje holds its annual pupils' concert on May 28, 1960, and the hall is full of relatives, and you have been granted leave of absence from the Swedish mental health service to hear me play Vivaldi's Double Violin Concerto in A Minor.

Only, I have no idea why that memory fragment refuses to reveal itself.

I dig and dig, but I can't see you.

I can see only your back, not your face.

After your leave of absence, more sessions with doctors, all recorded in exhaustive detail. The Swedish mental health service is investing time and effort in you. You're also making an effort with the mental health service, maybe because someone seems to be listening at last. Listening is, after all, what the doctors of the mental health service are there to do. So you make an

313

effort to tell them how worried you are about the new swas-tikas daubed all over the world, which make you feel insecure even though you know you have nothing to fear in Sweden. You also make an effort to tell them about the freezing sensa-tion in your knees that "seems to come down from the spine," and that it's the same sensation as the one you had just before you were admitted to Ulvsunda, and this makes you wonder, and that some things have dropped out of your memory, and that on the way to Ulvsunda you were considering throwing yourself in front of an underground train before you decided to throw yourself in the lake, and that you spent your first days in the closed ward for the disturbed at Sundby hospital looking for a live electric cable and a radiator to grab hold of, and that now you don't understand how you could have done so, and that the sleeping tablets sometimes make you itch and it's hard to get to sleep at night.

But above all you tell them about the horizon that will not open up. About the intensified working pace at the big truck factory, and the time and motion studies, and the fatigue and the unhappiness. About the little town that's turning its back on you. About the onward journey that's still unfinished. About the necessity of moving on, if only over the bridge.

Case notes, May 31, 1960: "The patient says everything went well during his leave of absence and he was happy to be allowed home."

Aerogram from Strängnäs, May 31, 1960:

Dearest Natek! As soon as you get this letter you must drink a toast of whatever you feel like and *stop thinking of me as a sick person once and for all*. The dreadful black nightmares are behind us now. I look wonderful now (tanned and fattened up) and the most important thing of all—I feel like I did in the old days, and simply can't get enough of enjoying life. My last treatment was 1½ weeks ago and I am now in the convalescence ward, where I spend my time resting, walking in the lovely grounds, reading, and doing various sports. Most of all I enjoy reading, because I didn't think I'd ever be able to read again. The chief physician—a wonderful person— is very pleased with me. When I was first here at the hospital he told me I would feel like a human being again in a few weeks, and that made me want it and I managed to believe it. When I spoke to him recently I told him how guilty I feel in front of him and the other doctors and nurses, because their advice to me had gone in one ear and out the other.... Now I find it hard to understand any of it. I told myself—you have everything a person could wish for, a wife to soothe your pain, children who love you and are so well behaved, who all worship you, and everyone worships you so much. A son who brings you nothing but joy, longing to talk to his father, a dear brother. No, you needn't worry about a thing. Shrug it all off!!!... I won't write any more about this nightmarish time, perhaps when we meet I'll tell you.... I only feel very sorry for having given you such cause for concern. On May 28 Göran performed in the music school concert—for this the chief physician allowed me 3 days' leave of absence. You can imagine what it was like when I got home. We had never had such a festival day. To say we were celebrating would be putting it mildly. Göran almost suffocated me and Lilian kissed and *hugged* me, which in her case does not happen every day. In that respect she's a lot like Assa—hugs and kisses on the lips are very hard to get. Hala was astonished at my appearance—my tanned, healthy look. And the mood was just like old times. Göran was glad I could come to the performance. He'd practiced for this performance like never before and told me it wouldn't be anything like as nice without Dad.... I'll stay here at the hospital a few more days, and I'm sure they'll let me go home for good next week.

Thanks so much for the birthday present, I'm very pleased with the tie and already wearing it.

Warmest regards and lots of kisses.

David

Case notes, June 3: "A little nervous but mentally balanced, feels 'fine.' Still occasionally has the sensation of cold air blowing around him, but this, too, is considerably reduced. In good spirits, very much wants to live, enjoying life. Thinking clearly. Feels calm. Discharged provisionally."

Case notes, June 10: "The patient returned to the hospital of his own volition. Says he has started feeling uneasy and anxious again over the past few days. Calm and controlled on readmission but later becomes increasingly anxious."

Case notes, June 11: "Wanted to take a walk this afternoon. Although the conversation revealed no suicidal tendencies, the patient is until further notice to leave the ward only when accompanied by a member of staff."

Somewhere here, the Swedish mental health service stops having an effect on you. Doses of all kinds of medicines are stepped up, but to no avail.

The entries in the case notes are increasingly disconnected and sketchy.

Case notes, July 10: "Visited by wife. V. happy and grateful for visit."

Case notes, July 14:

Abt. 4 hrs. restless sleep last night acc. to night nurse. Nervous and in low spirits, asking constantly about the drugs and their effects. Appetite poor. The patient found to be greatly influenced by the weather. In view of his current condition the patient very dubious about leave of absence around July 20 (when his son goes to a summer camp). Complains he has lost interest in everything.

Case notes, July 19: "Still in low spirits and brooding, poor sleep." Increased doses of Truxal, Catran, Diminal Duplex, Pentymal.

Case notes, July 22 a.m.: "Around 2 hours' sleep last night on the prescribed drugs. Feels uneasy and restless. Asks for electric shock treatment to get past this difficult period."

Case notes, July 22 p.m.:

This a.m. patients report that the patient is in the lake. Alarm sounded at once. Dr. Sandelin and Supervisor Uddén are first on the scene and commence artificial respiration as soon as the patient is on shore. The patient, who is lifeless, is transported by car to the pharmacy where attempts to resuscitate continue for 1½ hrs. The death has been reported to the police. Report in accordance with §34 to the Board of Medicine. Deceased.

■

That's how the shadows catch up with you and kill you. That's how I see it. The shadows don't kill all the people they stalk, but they kill you in the end. The Swedish mental health service doesn't see it and writes, "Cause of illness: endogenous," which means the shadows that kill you come from inside.

But the shadows that kill you don't come from inside. They come from outside and catch up with you and surround you with darkness.

"Cause of illness: exogenous," I would have written if I had been a doctor in the Swedish mental health service. Or a *Vertrauensarzt* in the German reparations bureaucracy.

Cause of death: Auschwitz etc., is what I would have written.

You yourself write on an unstamped borrower's card from the hospital library. You write in pencil on both sides, the lines crammed closer and closer together toward the end, and when you run out of space you write sideways down the edges, just as in the aerograms.

No, it's not you writing, it's the shadows writing.

I can tell from the handwriting. It's so tiny, so weak, and so unlike the hand in the letters from Furudal, Alingsås, and Södertälje.

These are your words of farewell. You have enough presence of mind to say good-bye and ask for forgiveness, or perhaps understanding, before you take a walk down to the soothing lake beneath the summery lindens and maples in the therapeutically beneficial hospital park. Enough presence of mind, too, I realize, to avoid the supervision of the Swedish mental health service.

You're very energetic now, and very singleminded, and beyond all salvation.

Dearest Halinka, forgive me for being forced to take this action. I cannot fight and live with such torment that no one can stand. Everything feels hopeless to me now. Do not reproach me for this step. I know I'm doing you a great wrong and it will be a severe blow

318

to the whole family. If I didn't do it, the misfortune that has struck us would still be a fact, the difference being that I would not have freed myself from the terrible torment. It's an awful illness and there is no salvation from it. Halinka, you have done everything in your power to help me. I felt you putting your soul into your conversations with me. But it cannot go on like this, I feel the torment in my whole body. I know I'm leaving the children in good hands. Forgive me, Halinka. Dearest Natek. Forgive me. Believe me when I say I could not have acted in any other way, and that I would still not have been able to enjoy things with you. What pleasure could you have taken in a living brother in such a condition. I suffer the agonies of hell and I can't go on. I can't live with normal people. I can't even talk to those who are very ill but have calm in their bodies.

On November 1, 1960, Dr. Segnestam, the chief physician at Sundby hospital, affirms that the shadows that kill you come from outside, not inside. His affidavit is translated into German and intended for the German reparations authorities, and the accuracy of the German translation is certified on November 24, 1960, by Dr. W. Michaeli, head of the URO office in Stockholm. URO stands for United Restitution Organization and is a body set up to help people like you plead their case against the German state. It's my mother who asks them to plead your case even though it's too late to plead your case, maybe because it may then be put on record somewhere that the German state was wrong and you were right; that it was not you who were exaggerating the problems you had as a result of persecution by the German state, but the German state that was exaggerating the problems it had as a result of people like you; that it was Auschwitz etc. that damaged you and ultimately killed you; that Dr.

Lindenbaum and Dr. Lebram and the German state were wrong about the degree of your incapacity for work as a result of the National Socialist persecution; and that this at least should be put on record.

Dr. Segnestam, chief physician at Sundby hospital, puts the following on record:

> In summary, it should be stated that David Rosenberg carried with him his extremely bad experiences from the war years and concentration camps, and that in his years in Sweden, though appearing to adapt, he was simultaneously suffering from recurrent depressive episodes, and that toward the end of 1959 these episodes developed into a permanent depressive state with suicidal thoughts. It appears very likely to me that his experiences in the concentration camps were responsible for the worsening progress of his illness in 1959–60 and made it more difficult to treat him (fear of incarceration), and consequently were among the contributory causes of the disastrous outcome.

I remember that last summer very well.

The air quivering in the afternoon heat above the dirt road up to the cowshed, the car park and the entrance.

The little procession emerging from the green foliage.

How infinitely slowly it advances.

As if dragging out not only its steps but time itself.

Dragging out the time between before and after.

Three people advancing slowly through the last summer.

Mom, Natek, Kerstin.

I understand already, before there's time to.

A year later, we leave the place where I first put words to the world and take the train north, over the bridge.

For me, a place with all horizons open.

For you, a place with all horizons closed.

For you, a brief stop on the road from Auschwitz.

MUCH LATER: AN AFTERWORD

In the mid-1960s Havsbadet in Södertälje was land-filled. Where once there was a sandy beach and a glittering sea inlet, there is now a concrete floor used as a depot for containers and imported cars.

Beginning in January 1995, trains between Stockholm and the world do not make a brief stop at Södertälje Södra. They don't even pass through Södertälje Södra, still less cross the bridge over the canal. The railroad now runs even farther from the center of Södertälje, along an even shorter route between Stockholm and the world, and Södertälje Södra is now called Södertälje Hamn (Harbor).

At Södertälje Hamn, the rowanberries still glow in the autumn.

In the summer of 2010, the old railroad bridge over Södertälje canal was pulled down. The new bridge can't be crossed on foot.

■

"Much later" in this book is a recurring expression for the hopeless impotence felt by a writer who has made up his mind not to let the events of the future burden his story, still less the individuals in it. In reality, of course, this book could not have been written without knowing what can only be known much later. Or without the people who much later helped me excavate the fragments of memory. First and foremost my mother, Hala Rosenberg, whom I have plagued over the years with all manner of questions, reasonable and unreasonable, and who has without reservation placed at my disposal the letters and documents she has preserved. Thanks also to my sister Lilian Rosenberg-Roth for help with crucial documentation, and to my cousins Assa and Anders Rosenberg, who have dug assiduously into their own memories. I have Lena Einhorn to thank for documentation on the food parcels sent to Ravensbrück, and I'm grateful to Anders Bodegård for the translation of letters and documents from Polish to Swedish. Without Dr. Karl Liedke, one important chapter in this book could never have been written.

I have chosen not to burden my text with footnotes, but will list below some of the sources that have been with me throughout my writing.

For the sections dealing with Södertälje and its history, and the view of the world from there, I had access (via the Royal Library of Sweden) to an invaluable time machine: the daily editions of *Stockholms Läns & Södertälje Tidning* from 1938 to 1960. The Södertälje Municipal Archive helped with all kinds of local authority plans and decisions. Södertälje historian Göran Gelotte shared with me his memory fragments, pictures, and knowledge. Without Karin Sterner's stories and letters, many fragments would have remained buried in darkness.

For the sections on the Łódź ghetto, I relied on the detailed and comprehensive documentation that miraculously survived the ghetto's liquidation, primarily the "official" ghetto chronicle referred to in the book and published in an edited version (Lucjan Dobroszycki) in English in 1984, under the title *The Chronicle of the Łódź Ghetto 1941–44*. Some of the German documents from the ghetto, among them the one concerning the extra spirit rations needed for the "dejudification of the Warthegau," I have taken from a yellowing Polish collection, *Dokumenty i Materiały,*

Tom III, Getto Łódzkie, ed. A. Eisenbach (1946). The notebooks of Josef Zelkowicz are published in English under the title *In Those Terrible Days: Notes from the Lodz Ghetto* (Jerusalem: Yad Vashem, 2002). Another indispensable document from the Łódź ghetto is the diary kept by David Sierakowiak, published in English under the title *The Diary of David Sierakowiak: Five Notebooks from the Łódź Ghetto*, ed. Alan Adelson (New York: Oxford University Press, 1996).

The lines of Czesław Miłosz in the introduction to the chapter "The Carousel" are from his poem "Campo dei Fiori," published in English in his *Collected Poems*, trans. Louis Iribarne and David Brooks (New York: Eco Press, 1973).

For documents and facts about the deportations from the Łódź ghetto to Auschwitz and from Auschwitz to the German slave camp archipelago, I have made extensive use of Andrej Strzelecki's *The Deportation of Jews from the Łódź Ghetto to KL Auschwitz and Their Extermination* (Oświęcim, Poland: Auschwitz-Birkenau State Museum, 2006). Dr. Karl Liedke's study of the route taken by some thousand Polish Jews from Auschwitz to the Büssing slave camps in Braunschweig is published in *Yad Vashem Studies* 30 (Jerusalem, 2002), under the title *Destruction Through Work: Łódź Jews in the Büssing Truck Factory in Braunschweig, 1944–45*. Karl Liedke also ensured that a copy of the handwritten SS list from Ravensbrück found its way into my hands. In addition, Dr. Liedke was my tireless guide through the camp archipelago in the surroundings of Braunschweig. Information about the conditions in the SS camps at Firma Büssing in Braunschweig is largely taken from the vivid eyewitness account of the doctor and fellow inmate Geoges Salan in his book *Prisons de France et bagnes allemandes* (Nîmes, France: Imprimerie L'Ouvrière, 1946), one of those many contemporary testimonies that were printed only once and then vanished into oblivion.

The sparse documents from the aliens' camps at Tappudden-Furudal and Öreryd are kept at the National Archives in Stockholm, as are the personal case files opened on aliens resident in Sweden, which also include the police investigations undertaken in connection with applications for aliens' passports and citizenship.

For newspaper comment of the period on the reception of Jewish survivors in the Swedish camp archipelago, I primarily have to thank the cuttings archive at the Sigtuna Foundation, which also gave me a writer's grant allowing me an untroubled month's stay in a restful setting. For further material on Sweden's encounter with the survivors, I have consulted the consecutive volumes of *Judisk Krönika* (The Jewish Chronicle) and *Judisk Tidskrift* (The Jewish Journal), beautifully bound and put at my disposal by Peter Freudenthal.

The following are a few more works that in various ways have played a part in the preparation of this book.

Améry, Jean. *At the Mind's Limits: Contemplations by a Survivor on Auschwitz and Its Realities*. Translated by Sidney and Stella P. Rosenfeld. New York: Schocken, 1986.

Benjamin, Walter. *Berlin Childhood around 1900*. Translated by Howard Eiland. Cambridge, MA: Harvard University Press, 2006. First English edition 1950.

———. "A Berlin Chronicle." In *Reflections*, translated by Edmund Jephcott. New York: Schocken, 1986. (For the image of the fragments in the darkness.)

Berggren, Lena. *Nationell upplysning. Drag i den svenska anti-semitismens idéhistoria* [National enlightenment: Traits in the history of Swedish anti-Semitism]. Carlsson Bokförlag, 1999. This work set me on the trail of Elof Eriksson, the newspaper editor who wanted to free the world, and Södertälje, from the Jews.

Bergmann, Martin S., and Milton E. Jucovy, eds. *Generations of the Holocaust*. New York: Columbia University Press, 1982. On the Janus-faced nature of German reparations.

Borkin, Joseph. *The Crime and Punishment of I.G. Farben*. New York: Free Press, 1978. A groundbreaking early study of how the ramifications of the Nazi slave system extended deep into German industry.

Browning, Christopher R. *Nazi Policy, Jewish Workers, German Killers*. New York: Cambridge University Press, 2000.

Charny, Israel W., ed. *Holding on to Humanity: The Message of Holocaust Survivors*. From the Shamai Davidson Papers. New York: New York University Press, 1995. All I needed to know (and more) about the psychology and pathology of survival.

Diner, Dan. *Beyond the Conceivable: Studies on Germany, Nazism and the Holocaust*. Berkeley: University of California Press, 2000. A collection of essays about the inconceivable nature of the experience I have nonetheless tried to put into words.

Einhorn, Lena. Handelsresande i liv [Traveling salesman in life]. Stockholm: Prisma, 1999. A painstaking study of the surreal game of life and death played out in the negotiations about, among other things, the food parcels to Ravensbrück.

Friedländer, Saul. *Memory, History and Extermination of the Jews of Europe*. Bloomington: Indiana University Press, 1993.

————. *Nazi Germany and the Jews*. 2 vols. New York: Harper-Collins, 1998 and 2008.

Gavin, James M. *On to Berlin: Battles of an Airborne Commander 1943–1946*. New York: Viking, 1978. For its account of the liberation of Wöbbelin.

Giertz, Eric. *Människor i Scania under 100 år*, Norstedts ekonomi. English-language version: *Saab-Scania Celebrates Scania 100 years*. Saab-Scania, 1991. A glossy official history that yielded important information about life at the big truck factory over the years.

Gottfarb, Inga. *Den livsfarliga glömskan. Överlevande berättar om vägen tillbaka* [The fatal amnesia: Survivors' stories of the way back]. An important piece of Swedish oral history, first published in 1986.

Hansson, Svante. *Flykt och överlevnad. Flyktingverksamhet i Mosaiska Församlingen i Stockholm 1933–1950* [Escape and survival: Refugee activities in the Jewish community in Stockholm 1933–1950]. Hillelförlaget, 2004. Another scholar who made my task easier.

Hilberg, Raul. *The Destruction of the European Jews*. 3 vols. New Haven, CT: Yale University Press, 2003. Three substantial and invaluable volumes on the rise and implementation of the policy of annihilation.

Johansson, Sven. *Kyrkbyn som togs i beslag. Dokumentär berättelse om lägren i Öreryd under andra världskriget* [The requisitioned church village: A documentary account of the camps at Öreryd during the Second World War]. Self-published, 2002.

Judt, Tony. *Postwar: A History of Europe Since 1945*. New York: Penguin, 2005.

———. "The 'Problem of Evil' in Postwar Europe." *New York Review of Books*, February 14, 2008.

Langer, Lawrence L. *Holocaust Testimonies: The Ruins of Memory*. New Haven, CT: Yale University Press, 1991.

Levi, Primo. *The Drowned and the Saved*. Translated by Raymond Rosenthal. London: Michael Joseph, 1988. Levi's last book includes a chapter entitled "The Grey Zone," about Chaim Rumkowski and the Łódź ghetto

——. *The Periodic Table* (especially the chapter "Argon"). Translated by Raymond Rosenthal. New York: Schocken and Penguin, 1984.

Mazower, Mark. *Dark Continent: Europe's Twentieth Century*. New York: Vintage, 2000.

Ricœur, Paul. *Memory, History, Forgetting*. Translated by Kathleen Blamey and David Pellauer. Chicago: University of Chicago Press, 2004.

Svanberg, Ingvar, and Mattias Tydén. *Sverige och Förintelsen* [Sweden and the Holocaust]. Stockholm: Dialogos, 2005.

Keep in touch with
Granta Books:

Visit grantabooks.com to discover more.

GRANTA